First Encounters

Ripley P. Bullen Monographs in Anthropology and History, Number 9
Florida Museum of Natural History

First

Spanish Explorations in the Caribbean

University of Florida Press / Gainesville

Florida Museum of Natural History

Encounters

and the United States, 1492–1570

edited by Jerald T. Milanich
and Susan Milbrath

Chapter 2 is adapted from "The Columbus Chronicles" by William F. Keegan, *The Sciences* (January–February 1989), a publication of the New York Academy of Sciences.

Chapter 11 is adapted from "Pedro Menéndez's Strategic Plan for the Florida Peninsula," by Eugene Lyon, published in the *Florida Historical Quarterly* (July 1988), a publication of the Florida Historical Society.

Charles Hudson gratefully acknowledges a faculty research grant from the University of Georgia Research Foundation which supported the final revision of chapters 6 and 9.

University Presses of Florida is the central agency for scholarly publishing of the State of Florida's university system, producing books selected for publication by the faculty editorial committees of Florida's nine public universities: Florida A&M Universtity (Tallahassee), Florida Atlantic University (Boca Raton), Florida International University (Miami), Florida State University (Tallahassee), University of Central Florida (Orlando), University of Florida (Gainesville), University of North Florida (Jacksonville), University of South Florida (Tampa), University of West Florida (Pensacola.

Orders for books published by all member presses should be addressed to University Presses of Florida, 15 NW 15th Street, Gainesville, FL 32603.

Ripley P. Bullen Monographs in Anthropology and History, Jerald T. Milanich, general editor

NUMBER 1. *Tacachale: Essays on the Indians of Florida and Southeastern Georgia during the Historic Period*, edited by Jerald T. Milanich and Samuel Proctor (1978).

NUMBER 2. *Aboriginal Subsistence Technology on the Southeastern Coastal Plain during the Late Prehistoric Period*, by Lewis H. Larson (1980).

NUMBER 3. *Cemochechobee: Archaeology of a Mississippian Ceremonial Center on the Chattahoochee River*, by Frank T. Schnell, Vernon J. Knight, Jr., and Gail S. Schnell (1981).

NUMBER 4. *Fort Center: An Archaeological Site in the Lake Okeechobee Basin*, by William H. Sears, with contributions by Elsie O'R. Sears and Karl T. Steinen (1982).

NUMBER 5. *Perspectives on Gulf Coast Prehistory*, edited by Dave D. Davis (1984).

NUMBER 6. *Archaeology of Aboriginal Culture Change in the Interior Southeast: Depopulation during the Early Historic Period*, by Marvin T. Smith (1987).

NUMBER 7. *Apalachee: The Land between the Rivers*, by John H. Hann (1988).

NUMBER 8. *Key Marco's Buried Treasure: Archaeology and Adventure in the Nineteenth Century*, by Marion Spjut Gilliland (1989).

NUMBER 9. *First Encounters: Spanish Explorations in the Caribbean and the United States, 1492–1570*, edited by Jerald T. Milanich and Susan Milbrath (1989).

Contributors

Edward Chaney, Department of Anthropology, Florida Museum of Natural History, Gainesville, FL 32611

Kathleen Deagan, Department of Anthropology, Florida Museum of Natural History, Gainesville, FL 32611

Chester B. DePratter, South Carolina Institute of Archaeology and Anthropology, University of South Carolina, Columbia, SC 29208

Charles R. Ewen, Arkansas Archaeological Survey, P.O. Box 1249, Fayetteville, AR 72702

Charles Hudson, Department of Linguistics and Anthropology, University of Georgia, Athens, GA 30602

William F. Keegan, Department of Anthropology, Florida Museum of Natural History, Gainesville, FL 32611

Emilia Kelley, 2009 Powhatan Road, Hyattsville, MD 20782

Eugene Lyon, Center for Historical Research, St. Augustine Restoration Foundation, P.O. Box 1027, St. Augustine, FL 32085

Jerald T. Milanich, Department of Anthropology, Florida Museum of Natural History, Gainesville, FL 32611

Susan Milbrath, Department of Interpretation, Florida Museum of Natural History, Gainesville, FL 32611

Jeffrey M. Mitchem, Department of Geography and Anthropology, Louisiana State University, Baton Rouge, LA 70803

Marvin T. Smith, Department of Linguistics and Anthropology, University of Georgia, Athens, GA 30602

Maurice W. Williams, Department of Anthropology, Florida Museum of Natural History, Gainesville, FL 32611

Acknowledgments

First Encounters is published as an accompaniment to the Florida Museum of Natural History's traveling exhibit of the same name. That exhibit is funded by grants from the National Endowment for the Humanities and by fees provided by the host institutions. Venues for the exhibit are the Florida Museum of Natural History (Gainesville), the Museum of Science and Industry (Tampa), the South Carolina State Museum (Columbia), the Witte Museum (San Antonio), the Albuquerque Museum, the South Street Seaport Museum (New York City), the Houston Museum of Natural Sciences, the Southwest Museum of Science and Industry (Dallas), the Cincinnati Museum of Natural History, the Science Museum of Minnesota (St. Paul), and the Historical Museum of South Florida (Miami).

The editors thank the volume contributors for their interest in this project and their willingness to help bring the story of the first New World encounters between Spaniards and native peoples to the public. We would like to thank also the staff of the Department of Interpretation of the Florida Museum of Natural History, epecially photographer Stan Blomeley, for their efforts in manuscript preparation. The staff of the University Presses of Florida's Central Publishing Unit, especially managing editor Judy Goffman, production manager Lynn Werts, and designer Larry Leshan, did their usual excellent job and are responsible for the timely publication of the book. We are grateful to them.

We are also grateful to the many individuals and institutions that cooperated in providing the artwork to illustrate *First Encounters*. They are listed in the illustration credits at the end of the book. This entire project (exhibit and book) owes its genesis to U.S. Senator Bob Graham and Ney C. Landrum, former director of the Florida Division of Recreation and Parks, and their interest in the Florida route of Hernando de Soto. We thank them both.

Contents

Jerald T. Milanich

Susan Milbrath

1 / **Another World**

Scholars continue to argue whether Columbus was the first European to reach the Caribbean islands or other New World shores and whether we can even say he *discovered* anything because the lands he visited were already inhabited by millions of people. But what is certain is that Columbus's voyages, beginning in 1492, opened the way for a major exchange of people, resources, and ideas.

It is unfortunate that the exchange was largely stimulated by European desires to possess the wealth of the Caribbean and the Americas, wealth that was laid open by the European voyages of exploration. Spain and other countries hastened to extract riches and to conquer the native Americans and colonize their lands. Their success spelled disaster for the people of the New World. It is estimated that today only one native American exists for every one hundred who lived in the New World in 1492. The major languages used throughout the Western Hemisphere are English, Portuguese, Spanish, Dutch, and various Creole dialects, while native American cultures and languages are increasingly endangered.

A major reason for the success of Spain and the other European monarchies was that European diseases introduced by the earliest expeditions and African diseases transmitted by the African slave trade

It is hard to imagine that in the sixteenth century, when it was painted by John White, this pineapple was a novelty from the New World, one of many plants that crossed the Atlantic to Europe following Christopher Columbus's initial voyage. Other plants taken back to the Old World were potatoes, tomatoes, and corn. Wheat, barley, oranges, and sugarcane were introduced to the New World, as were cows, pigs, horses, and chickens as the Columbian exchange shaped the modern world.

as early as the second decade of the sixteenth century often led to population reduction, cultural changes, and genocide.

"Sailing the ocean blue in fourteen hundred and ninety-two," Columbus changed the course of history in both the Old and New Worlds. The knowledge that another world with its array of plants, animals, and human populations and cultures existed apart from Europe, Asia, and Africa profoundly affected the Old World, influencing habits and cultural factors as different as diet and art. The Columbian exchange was just that: an exchange that altered both hemispheres (see chapter 13).

Historians and archaeologists, working with other scientists, are studying Christopher Columbus's voyages and his attempts to establish settlements in the Caribbean. In the process they are bringing forth new information to solve old questions. Archaeologists have recently located some of the earliest Spanish settlements on the island of Hispaniola, now the site of Haiti and the Dominican Republic.

In the early sixteenth century Spain's New World empire began to flourish, fueled by silver and gold and slaves. Exploration and settlement spread from Hispaniola to other Caribbean islands and the mainlands of Central and South America. As early as 1513, Spain began to explore to the north of the Caribbean, touching the coasts of what is today the United States. By the late 1520s the coastal geography of the eastern United States had been identified.

Voyages were followed by attempts to explore and settle the interior of the land Juan Ponce de León called La Florida, so named because it was discovered at Easter time (Pascua Florida). Soon La Florida came to refer to all the known land north and east of Mexico. Expeditions led by Pánfilo de Narváez (1528) and Hernando de Soto (1539) traveled to the southeastern United States, and Francisco Vásquez de Coronado (1540) and his army marched into the Southwest. All of these men sought wealth, but none was successful. Attempts to found colonies on the Atlantic coast (1526 and 1561) and at Pensacola Bay (1559) also failed.

Historical and archaeological research is also under way to further our understanding of these Spanish expeditions that were sent into the United States in the sixteenth century. For the first time there is a concentrated effort to trace the actual routes and find archaeological evidence in the form of Spanish artifacts.

In 1562 the French Crown initiated explorations along the Atlantic coasts of the southeastern United States with an eye to establishing its own colony and wresting La Florida from Spain. When the Spanish crown learned of the French activities, which included building a fortified settlement at the mouth of the St. Johns River in northeast Florida, plans for another Spanish colony were hastened.

Pedro Menéndez de Avilés sailed to La Florida; in 1565 he defeated the French at Fort Caroline and established St. Augustine as the headquarters of a Spanish colony. By 1570 he had also placed garrisons and, in some cases, Jesuit missions along the Atlantic coast, from Miami to Chesapeake Bay, and along the Gulf coast of peninsular Florida, but only St. Augustine managed to survive.

The story of Spain's attempts to explore and settle the Caribbean and the United States is largely an unknown part of our history. Few textbooks make the point, for instance, that Florida was a part of Spain for nearly 300 years, much longer than it has been a part of the United States. And although the Spanish heritage of the Caribbean and the Southwest is widely recognized, the earliest colonization efforts in La Florida have been poorly understood.

First Encounters seeks to remedy this oversight. It is the story of the period of early Spanish contact, focusing on the Caribbean explorations and settlements that were a prelude to the exploration and settlement of the United States. Spain's Caribbean endeavors marked the beginnings of her New World empire, and the events that took place in the United States were a part of her colonial expansion.

To understand this Hispanic heritage and its impact on native New World peoples, we must place the exploits of Columbus, de Soto, and other early explorers in a historical and cultural context. Because their story begins in the Iberian peninsula, it is there we must first travel.

Spain at the Time of Columbus

In the land we know as Spain, the last few decades of the fifteenth century were a time of change and reform, of unification, and of expansion of political and military might. Seven centuries before, in 711, the Moors had invaded the Iberian peninsula, conquering it in only seven years. The next seven centuries were spent in the *reconquista*, the expulsion of the Moors from Iberia, Spain's attempt to purify its Catholicism by removing those who adhered to other religions. Only in 1492 was the final Moorish stronghold of Granada defeated, completing the reconquest.

In the early fifteenth century the portion of Iberia that was wrested from Islamic control was divided into a number of small political units or provinces with independent governments. Over time, through military and diplomatic means, especially marriages among royal families, the provinces became federated into larger units ruled by monarchs. Two of the most powerful were Castile (controlling about two-thirds of the land area) and Aragon. Diversity in life-styles and even language existed within and among provinces.

Arches in Grenada's Alhambra reflect the influence of the Moors on Iberian culture at the time of Columbus.

King Ferdinand and Queen Isabella are portrayed in a 1522 bas-relief on the Royal Chapel in Grenada.

With the marriage of Ferdinand, king of Sicily and heir to the throne of Aragon, to Isabella, heiress to the throne of Castile, on 19 October 1469, the uniting of the Aragonese and Castilian crowns was assured. This political marriage between two important royal families (the bride and groom met only four days prior to the wedding) would eventually unify about 85 percent of Iberia, creating a powerful political and military force. Following the death of Henry IV, king of Castile, in late 1474, Isabella was crowned queen. When John II died in 1479, Ferdinand inherited the crown of Aragon. Ferdinand and Isabella then ruled nearly all of Spain.

Under the nuptial agreement, both Castile and Aragon maintained separate governments under their respective monarchs.

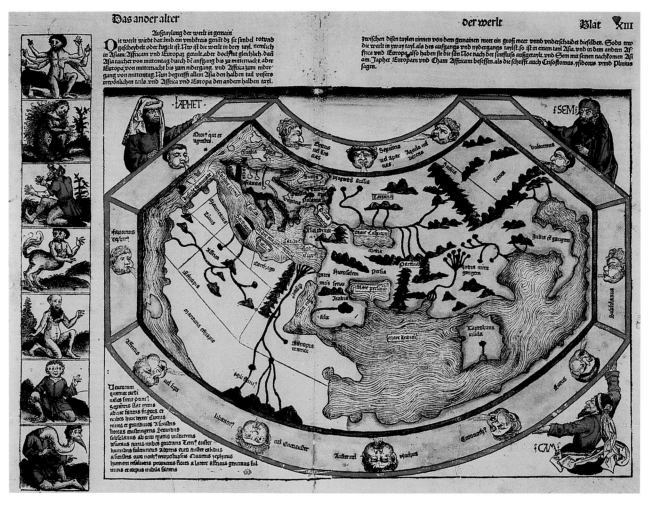

Despite Viking voyages to the coast of Newfoundland, the Western Hemisphere was unknown until Columbus returned to Spain from his first voyage. This Ptolemaic map shows the world as it was known in 1492; Asia is on the right and Africa and Europe on the left.

Nevertheless, the marriage did serve to unify governmental initiatives in military and diplomatic matters. It allowed Isabella and Ferdinand to turn their joint attention to finishing the reconquista in Spain's southern region. On 6 January 1492, the victorious couple marched triumphantly through Granada, celebrating victory over the Moors. Less than four months later the crown of Castile agreed to support Christopher Columbus in his planned voyage to discover a western sea route to Asia.

With the final expulsion of the Moors imminent, the Crown and the church had turned against other groups within Spain, among them the Jews. Nearly all Spanish Jews were *conversos*; they had renounced Judaism and converted to Christianity, at least in name. In 1478 the courts of the Inquisition were established to cleanse Spanish society of heretical elements, including conversos and other individuals whose beliefs were questionable. The day Columbus embarked for the New World, 2 August 1492, was also the day the Spanish crown designated as the deadline for all Jews to leave Spain.

As a result of the reconquest, Spain had developed a land-based military prowess and economic, social, and ideological systems geared to supporting military efforts against the Moors. From these systems developed the social position of *hidalgos*, aristocratic strongmen supported by family wealth who formed a warrior class in Spanish society. Under contracts with the Crown, hidalgos organized armies and fought in the reconquest. Booty secured through military victories was divided between hidalgo and Crown, subsidizing additional military efforts.

Thus, on the eve of Columbus's first voyage, Castile and Aragon had joined together to complete the reconquest and Spain could look beyond its own borders. The social, economic, and ideological systems already in place engendered military expansion through the monarchs' support of the entrepreneurial hidalgos. Columbus's discoveries in the New World would provide the opportunity and the wealth to fuel further expansion.

Columbus's Voyages of Discovery

When Columbus left Spain in 1492, he reasoned that by traveling west from Spain, he would find a sea route to the Indies and their spice-rich islands, lands that were only poorly known to Europeans. No one could have guessed that the Western Hemisphere lay between him and his goal.

After a six-week voyage across the Atlantic from Spain, Columbus made landfall on the island of Guanahani in the Bahamas. He and his crew explored Guanahani and nearby islands before sailing southward through the Bahamas. Archaeologists have not been able to agree on the identification of Guanahani, although most believe that it is present-day San Salvador or a nearby island. Today multidisciplinary research is generating new data and ideas concerning Columbus's landfall (see chapter 2).

Information on Columbus's voyage comes from his letter and from a ship's log in which he recorded his observations and route. His southward heading took him to the north coast of Cuba. He sailed eastward along that coast, crossing the passage between Cuba and Haiti and continuing along the north coast of Haiti on the island of Hispaniola. Sailing east of Cap Haitien on Christmas Eve 1492, the *Santa Maria* ran aground on a coral reef. The ship was abandoned and men and supplies put ashore, with orders to build a fort (named La Navidad) in the village of a native chief, Guacanacaric. This effort was Spain's first attempt to establish a settlement in the New World.

A number of historians have written about the site, but its exact location eluded researchers until the 1970s, when William Hodges found what appears to be Guacanacaric's village. Over the past few years the site, a large fifteenth-century Taíno Indian village adjacent

Columbus and the exploration of the New World were popular themes during the age of exploration. An engraving by Theodore de Bry depicts the first encounter between Columbus and the people of the New World. Like many engravings of New World scenes, it was not based on firsthand observation.

to a small hamlet called En Bas Saline, has been excavated by Kathleen Deagan and her team of archaeologists searching for clues to La Navidad (see chapter 3).

After Columbus's triumphant return to Spain he mounted a second expedition (September 1493–June 1496) to colonize the newly discovered lands. It was made up of seventeen ships carrying animals, supplies, and more than 1,000 men (many of whom brought families). Columbus initially explored islands in the Lesser Antilles (including Dominica and Marie Galante) before sailing on to Puerto Rico and then to Hispaniola. When Columbus returned to the small settlement of La Navidad after almost a year's absence, he found that all of the men left there were dead and their supplies lost.

Columbus began to explore eastern Hispaniola and discovered the gold sources in Cibao. The possibility of accumulating wealth and a desire to hold the land for Spain led to the founding of a town on the northern coast of the modern Dominican Republic; Columbus named the town La Isabela for the sovereign who had sponsored his voyage.

On his second voyage Columbus also returned to Cuba before sailing southward to the island of Jamaica and then on to Guadeloupe. When he was again back in Spain, he provided an account of much that he had seen on the voyage, including the first information on the effects of European diseases on the people of the New World.

Columbus's third voyage (July 1498–November 1500) took him first to Trinidad; then he made landfall on the mainland of South America. He returned to the fledgling colony on Hispaniola to find it in chaos, suffering from hunger, illness, and disagreements among Spanish factions. A representative of the monarchy had been sent to put the colony in order. Columbus and his two brothers, who had helped to govern in his absence, were arrested and returned to Spain.

An important new source of information on the third voyage, one that contains our only detailed knowledge of the *Niña* (one of Columbus's original three ships also used on the third voyage), has been discovered in the Spanish archives by Eugene Lyon. The *Libro de Armadas* contains a detailed report of the ship's cargo, crew, passengers, supplies, and outfitting (see chapter 4).

On his fourth voyage (May 1502–June 1503), Columbus first tried to land at Santo Domingo on Hispaniola to find shelter from a storm, but Nicolas de Ovando, then governor and a successor to Columbus, denied him entry. Turned away, Columbus made landfall on the coast of Honduras and explored the coasts of Nicaragua and Costa Rica. He also reached Panama, where he found gold, then traveled on to Jamaica, where he was marooned for a year. After the fourth

A de Bry engraving recounts the arrest of Columbus in Hispaniola on his third voyage. Despite his titles of viceroy, governor, captain-general, and admiral, Columbus was returned to Spain in disgrace.

voyage, Columbus fell into disfavor with the Spanish Crown. Queen Isabella's death in 1504 further reduced his influence at court. His writings in his later years reflect bitterness and frustration at the turn of events in his life.

Columbus's motives for undertaking his four voyages of discovery were complex. He said that his primary purpose was to convert the natives to Roman Catholicism, but other statements suggest that he had other goals, including the use of natives as laborers and the hope of finding gold and wealth. His ultimate dream may have been to conquer Jerusalem for Christianity, using the wealth of the New World. Columbus was a complex individual whose goals may never be understood fully.

Exploration and Settlement of the Caribbean

Under his original agreement with Queen Isabella, Columbus was to receive the hereditary title of viceroy over all of the lands he discovered, along with the titles of governor, captain-general, and admiral. One-tenth of the royal revenues derived from the lands he discovered were to be his, as were one-eighth of the voyages's revenues (if he financed one-eighth of the expedition's cost). His role as a contracted royal agent followed the tradition of the hidalgo in Spain.

Isabella eventually ignored this original agreement when the enormity of Columbus's discovery became apparent and when he proved to be an unpopular administrator among the Spanish colonists on Hispaniola. Because of his failures, he was officially removed as viceroy and governor of the colony.

By 1503, Nicolas de Ovando, the new governor of Hispaniola, had drawn up a plan for founding a chain of 15 perimeter towns on Hispaniola to subdue the native inhabitants and better control the island. About that same time Spanish settlements were being placed at other locations in the Caribbean to provide bases for economic pursuits. Archaeologists have excavated Puerto Real on Hispaniola, one of the early towns founded by Ovando (see chapter 5).

This portion of the 1502 Cantino map shows the islands of Cuba and Hispaniola as well as part of the Atlantic coast of South America. The identity of the landmass northwest of Cuba remains uncertain. If it is Florida and the Atlantic coast of North America, it indicates Spanish knowledge of that continent prior to Juan Ponce de León's voyage in 1513.

Even before Columbus's second expedition sailed from Cadiz in September 1493, other European powers were dispatching ships to the western lands, responding to the intelligence brought back by Columbus in March of that year. Knowledge that lands across the Ocean Sea (Atlantic) could be reached by ship led to an explosion of expeditions, ranging from voyages of exploration to large colonization efforts. Spain led the way, but England, Portugal, and even France participated. Historians have documented more than eighty such voyages between 1492 and 1504. As geographical knowledge increased, it became clear that the Caribbean islands were only a small part of the New World and that vast uncharted lands lay west and south. Explorations quickly moved in those directions, and colonies followed.

The third and fourth decades of the sixteenth century saw expansion of the Spanish empire through much of Mexico (New Spain and New Galicia), Central America, and Peru and along the northern coast of Brazil. The wealth of the Inca, the Aztec, and other native societies was shipped to Spain as permanent Hispanic colonies were established.

This period of expansion was the time of the conquistadors and *adelantados*. Supported by royal contracts, men like Hernán Cortés and Francisco Pizarro searched for fame and fortune. The lure of gold, land, and slave laborers stimulated dreams of wealth and glory. It is no wonder that Spanish conquistadors vied to be first to gain control of bits of the New World.

Amerigo Vespucci stands next to Martin Waldseemüller's map showing much of South America as well as the Gulf of Mexico and the eastern United States. Published in 1507, five years after the Cantino map, it also suggests that European knowledge of the New World advanced more rapidly than is evident from official correspondence and documents.

Discovery and Exploration of La Florida

Juan Ponce de León, ex-governor of the colony of San Juan (now Puerto Rico), depicted in an eighteenth-century engraving which credits him with the discovery of La Florida. Although his was almost certainly not the first Spanish voyage to reach that land, he was the first to have a royal charter granting permission to search for it.

As sailors, conquistadors, and officials spread Spain's empire to lands south and west of the early settlements on Hispaniola, interest grew in lands to the north and northwest. Indians captured in the Bahamas for use as forced laborers on Hispaniola and elsewhere must have passed on rumors of these lands. Clandestine voyages not sanctioned by the Crown might also have provided information.

In 1512, Juan Ponce de León, the wealthy ex-governor of the island of San Juan (today Puerto Rico), obtained a three-year contract from the Spanish Crown giving him sole right to search for and settle Bimini, a land rumored to lie to the north of the Lucayos (Bahama Islands). He set sail from Puerto Rico on 3 March 1513 on a northwest heading that took him up the outer edge of the Bahama island chain. On the fourteenth he anchored off Guanahani, where Columbus had first touched land in October 1492. That landfall is noted in an account that also says Columbus renamed the island San Salvador. He continued northwest for three weeks before making landfall on the Atlantic coast of Florida north of Cape Canaveral. He then sailed southward around the peninsula, past the Florida Keys, and up the Gulf of Mexico coast.

Even though he traveled along the Gulf coast of Florida, Ponce was not certain whether the new land he had discovered was a large island like Cuba and Hispaniola. Because he had made his discovery during the Easter season, the feast of flowers or *flores*, he named the new land La Florida. That remained the Spanish name for the southern United States throughout the colonial period. It is uncertain if Ponce actually had heard of a Fountain of Youth, a legend prevalent among Indians of southern Florida and the northern Caribbean islands. He certainly never found it. But he did discover a new land and something that would be even more important to Spain's New World exploits: the Gulf Stream. This natural current was to become a major sea highway for Spanish ships returning to Spain from Veracruz and the Caribbean.

In 1521 Ponce returned to the southwest Florida coast with livestock (cows, pigs, horses, and sheep), seeds for planting, and missionary priests. His hopes to found a colony failed, however, and he was mortally wounded in a battle with natives.

In 1517 three ships set sail from Santiago under the captaincy of Hernández de Córdoba. He was made captain because he was said to be good at kidnapping and killing Indians. Originally the expedition was to sail to the Bahamas to take slaves. But Anton de Alaminos, the same pilot who had guided Ponce in 1513, persuaded Hernández to sail west to search for rich lands rumored to lie in that direction.

One of the most extraordinary encounters occurred between the expedition of Hernan Cortés and the Aztec empire in Mexico. The glory of the Aztec capital of Tenochtitlán rivaled any city the Spaniards had seen in Europe.

The expedition explored the north and west coasts of the Yucatan peninsula, where the Spaniards saw Mayan temples and fought several battles. Disheartened by battle losses and short on water, they decided to sail for Florida. Alaminos had sufficient understanding of the region to guide them directly to the bay where he had anchored with Ponce. There they were attacked by aborigines, and Anton and Hernández de Córdoba were wounded. After returning to Cuba, Hernández died.

The voyage made the Spaniards further aware that great wealth could be found in Middle America. It also became evident that great civilizations existed in the region; Spanish voyagers to the coast of Yucatan in 1518 saw a native city said to be as large as Seville, possibly the Mayan town of Tulum.

The Spaniards moved quickly to put their new knowledge to use. A series of voyages and expeditions was planned, including one to Veracruz, Mexico, led by Hernán Cortés in 1519 that eventually reached the heart of the Aztec empire in the Valley of Mexico.

With Cortés established on the Gulf coast of modern Veracruz, preparing to invade the interior of Mexico, other Spaniards sought to establish their own bases on the coast farther north. Governor Francisco de Garay of Jamaica received permission to outfit four ships under the command of Alvarez de Pineda to explore the coast north of Ponce de León's discoveries on Florida's Gulf coast. Among other things, he was to search for a passage between the Gulf and the Pacific Ocean, looking for a northern counterpart to the route discovered by Núñez de Balboa in 1513.

In 1519 Pineda sailed from Jamaica to the Yucatan Channel between Cuba and Mexico, then turned northward and continued until he reached the Gulf coast of Florida. Turning southeast, he followed the coastline, searching for the sea passage that Ponce de León thought might separate the "island" of La Florida from the mainland. Pineda quickly realized that Florida was not an island.

He reversed course and traveled the entire Gulf coast around to Mexico, eventually reaching Cortés's settlement in Veracruz. Although the report from the voyage has been lost, a map survives. It shows Cuba, peninsular Florida, and the entire Gulf of Mexico coast (including the Mississippi River, Yucatan, and the coast of Central America). Two harbors indicated on the coast of peninsular Florida must be Charlotte Harbor and Tampa Bay.

The failure of Ponce's attempt at settlement in 1521 did not deter an even larger venture by Lucas Vásquez de Ayllón in 1526. After sponsoring two voyages in 1520 and 1523 to the Atlantic coast to gather information, Ayllón accepted a royal charter that required him to establish forts and settlements at his own cost. Ayllón, royal judge in Santo Domingo in Hispaniola, tried in 1526 to establish a

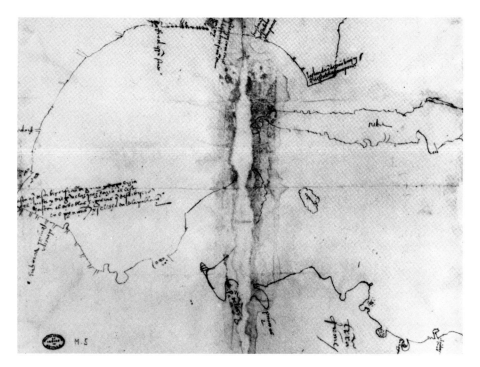

Alvarez de Pineda's voyage of 1519 resulted in a sketch map of the entire Gulf of Mexico coast. Both Tampa Bay and Charlotte Harbor are shown. A translation of the notation written north of Tampa Bay credits Juan Ponce de León with reaching that point. If true, he sailed much farther up the Gulf coast than is generally thought.

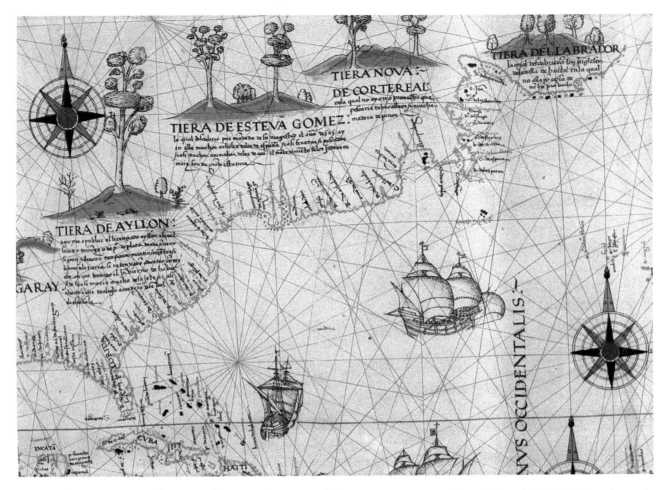

Diego Ribero's 1529 world map reflects the extent of European activities in the New World, including Vásquez de Ayllón's colony on the Atlantic coast. The interior of North America remained unknown.

base settlement of about 600 persons (San Miguel de Gualdape), probably on the coast of Georgia. The colony was an abject failure, lasting only three months. Some of the African slaves taken to the colony may have remained behind after the Spanish left.

Perhaps the worst of the Spanish failures in La Florida was the expedition of Pánfilo de Narváez, a seasoned veteran of the New World but one described by a contemporary as "cruel and stupid" and the "most incompetent" of the New World conquistadors. Narváez had been on Columbus's second voyage and had led armies in Cuba and Mexico. In 1526 the Crown gave him a charter to explore La Florida from the southern tip of the peninsula around the Gulf of Mexico to northern Mexico.

Narváez sailed from Cuba for Florida's Gulf coast in late February 1528 but did not arrive until early April because of a series of mishaps. His force of 400 soldiers and 40 horses landed near Tampa Bay (an equal number of horses having died on the way). After dispatching his ships to locate a more northerly bay to serve as a rendezvous (Bahía de Miruelo, or Apalachee Bay), Narváez and his men marched north. When they reached the Apalachee Indians in northwest Florida, they camped for a short time. But attacks by the Indians forced Narváez and his men to move to Aute on the coast. Archaeologists believe that Aute is the St. Marks Wildlife Refuge site, which has produced a number of Spanish artifacts.

Loss of soldiers and other misfortunes disheartened the army. To escape they made flatboats in which they intended to sail to Mexico. But traversing the Gulf of Mexico in small, open boats proved disastrous. Many, including Narváez, were swept out to sea and lost; others managed to land on the Texas coast where they were enslaved by aboriginal peoples.

Only four members of the expedition managed to escape their Indian captors. Together they walked overland across northern Mexico, where in April 1536, eight years after their arrival in Florida, they were found by Spanish slavers who took them to a safe haven. One of the survivors, Álvar Núñez Cabeza de Vaca, wrote an account of the expedition and its misadventures.

The most ambitious of the Spanish attempts to explore the interior of La Florida was led and financed by Hernando de Soto. De Soto had made a fortune while serving as Pizarro's chief military advisor in Peru, and he funded the Florida expedition with Peruvian gold and silver. His charter was similar to that of Narváez: he was to conquer, pacify, and settle 200 leagues of La Florida's coast, taking with him 500 men and supplies for 18 months. He was required to build three stone forts at his expense; in return he, like Narváez, would receive titles, lands, and a share of the colony's profits.

De Soto's expedition was well planned and well supplied; some of the men had fought with him in Central America and Peru. While being supplied in Cuba, he sent his chief pilot ahead to reconnoiter

The first information on the interior of the United States came from the narrative of Álvar Núñez Cabeza de Vaca, one of the four survivors of the Narváez expedition. *Right*: Cabeza de Vaca's account, the title page of which is reproduced, was first published in 1542, but the information was available earlier to members of Hernándo de Soto's expedition. *Far right*: Francisco Pizarro and a companion, mounted on horses, meet the Inca ruler Atahualpa, who is carried in a litter as befitting his status.

the landing site, Bahía Honda (Tampa Bay), the same bay Narváez had visited on his trek. It is clear that he knew where he wished to land on the Gulf coast of Florida and that he wanted to move north into the interior of the Southeast.

The expedition went ashore at Tampa Bay, established a camp, and unloaded their horses and supplies in late May 1539. Almost immediately they had the good fortune to encounter Juan Ortiz, who, left behind by a ship looking for Narváez, had lived among the Florida Indians for eleven years.

After reconnoitering the surrounding territory and gathering information from various aboriginal groups for six weeks, de Soto, with about 500 people (including craftsmen, friars, and two women) and hundreds of captive Indian bearers, moved inland, heading north. The expedition spent the winter of 1539–1540 at Anhaica, the main town of the Apalachee Indians. That site has been located and excavated by an archaeological team. It provides our most dramatic evidence for the presence of de Soto's expedition in the Southeast (see chapter 8).

In the spring the army broke camp and moved north across Georgia and the Carolinas, crossing the Appalachian Mountains into Tennessee. Evidently the discovery of mineral wealth in the mountains of Peru and Mexico stimulated de Soto to seek the piedmont and mountains.

Once across the mountains, de Soto followed the Tennessee River Valley into Alabama, where a great battle was fought at Mabilia, then reached Mississippi, scene of another battle and where he spent the winter. In the spring of 1541, the Spaniards came to the Mississippi River. Their journey from Tampa Bay had taken a year and a half. The next year was spent in Arkansas, visiting aboriginal villages and unsuccessfully searching the mountainous regions for wealth.

The army returned to the Mississippi River where de Soto became ill and died. The survivors tried to reach New Spain by crossing Texas on foot, but the journey proved too arduous and they again returned to the river where they built boats. They floated downriver to the Gulf of Mexico and then followed the coastline to a Spanish settlement near Tampico, Mexico.

Relative to its charter, the expedition was not a success. Nevertheless, the narratives from the expedition provide a great deal of information on La Florida and its inhabitants. Even today scholars continue to study the de Soto narratives for firsthand information on the sixteenth-century southeastern aborigines (see chapters 6 and 7).

Despite the failures of the Narváez and de Soto expeditions, Spain continued to seek a permanent settlement in La Florida to protect her shipping lanes. The Spanish treasure fleet regularly sailed from

Although the Atlantic coast of the United States was well charted by the 1520s, the Pacific coast remained unexplored. Casper Vopell's 1542 globe connected western North America with Asia.

Veracruz along the Gulf coast, through the straits of Florida, and up the Atlantic coast before turning east to Spain. A base was needed to help protect that route and to provide an opportunity to salvage precious cargoes from ships wrecked off Florida's coasts.

A new colonization effort was organized, funded by the viceroy of New Spain and led by Tristán de Luna y Arellano. In the summer of 1559, de Luna sailed for the Florida panhandle with as many as 13 ships and 1,500 soldiers and settlers. Many of the men were experienced in New World exploits (some were soldiers who had marched with de Soto in La Florida). Luna himself had been with Vásquez de Coronado in the Southwest.

Initially the expedition landed at Mobile Bay, but it moved on to its goal, the port of Ochuse (Pensacola Bay; see chapter 9). Once a camp was established, Luna sent an expedition to explore the interior. His men traveled inland but found the region almost depopulated. When the group returned to Ochuse, they were greeted with the news that a disastrous hurricane had sunk all but three of de Luna's ships, some still loaded with supplies. A number of colonists had drowned. The situation deteriorated further as colonists, hounded by starvation, attempted to secure food at inland aboriginal towns but failed. The colonists finally mutinied, and many of the settlers returned to New Spain.

In March 1561, Ángel de Villafañe arrived at the settlement with orders to take command and move the colony to Santa Elena near Beaufort, South Carolina. He reached the Atlantic coast in May with four ships and 60 people. Failing to find land suitable for settlement, he continued north. When a hurricane sank two of the ships, he had to abandon the effort.

Not all of Spain's efforts in early sixteenth-century La Florida were restricted to the Atlantic and Gulf coasts and the interior of the Southeast. North of Mexico lay a great uncharted land, the southwestern United States, whose boundaries were uncertain (the Pacific coast of California was not mapped until late in the sixteenth century). The four survivors of the Narváez expedition heard rumors of large Indian towns on the upper reaches of the Rio Grande (no doubt a reference to Pueblo villages), raising false hopes that the region contained wealth.

One goal of the first viceroy of New Spain, Antonio de Mendoza, was to explore those northern lands. In 1538, in order to establish a base from which exploration could take place, he named Francisco Vásquez de Coronado governor of the province of New Galicia, a frontier area in northwestern Mexico. The next year a small expedition led by Father Marcos de Niza traveled north from New Spain into the Southwest. Accompanying the friar were Indian servants and a survivor of the Narváez expedition, a black man named Estéban.

When Father Marcos de Niza and his party neared the Cíbola pueblos of Zuñi on the Zuñi River in western New Mexico, Estéban was sent ahead. When he entered the pueblo of Háwikuh, he was killed. The rest of the party returned to New Spain, where their report only fueled rumors of the legendary Seven Golden Cities of Cíbola.

Desiring to find these riches, Coronado organized a second expedition that set out on 23 February 1540. His army of 230 soldiers, 800 Indian bearers, six priests, and sheep, goats, cattle, and horses headed north from Compostela, the capital of New Galicia. They crossed the Gila River and reached Háwikuh, which was taken by force and served Coronado as a headquarters. But no wealth was found among the Zuñi. A smaller expedition headed northwest to the Hopi pueblos, but again no wealth was found, although that expedition did reach the Colorado River and the Grand Canyon.

Coronado then decided to travel eastward to Acoma pueblo and a province called Tiguex on the Rio Grande in Arizona. There he wintered in 1540–1541. Mistreatment of the Indians led to rebellion against the Spaniards; they retaliated, nearly wiping out two pueblos.

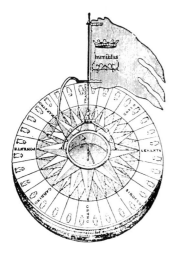

Francisco Vásquez de Coronado's route through the Southwest and into the southern plains. Portions of the route are still uncertain.

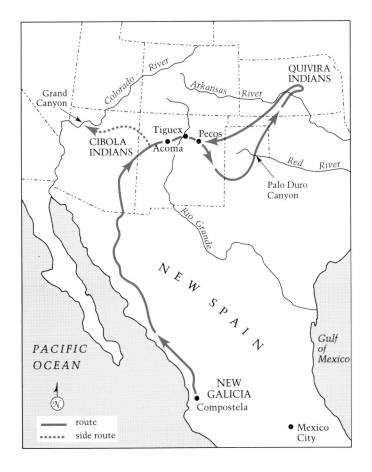

Breaking camp, the army continued eastward, searching for Quivira, another rumored golden kingdom. They had also been told of the huge herds of bison on the Great Plains. By summer 1541, Coronado had reached well into the southern plains, perhaps as far as the Arkansas River. But no gold was discovered, and the expedition began retracing its steps to Mexico, arriving in New Galicia in late summer 1542. Spanish efforts to explore the Southwest would not resume for nearly four decades.

At the same time that Coronado returned to Mexico (the summer of 1542), members of the de Soto expedition in Texas met Indians who told them of having seen other Christians. How different might our history have been if the two armies had met, establishing the sought-after overland route from La Florida to Mexico.

Disease and Depopulation

There is no doubt that the Spanish exploration and settlement of the New World, including the Caribbean and La Florida, infected the Indians with Old World pathogens. Over the two centuries following Columbus's first voyage, these diseases killed millions of aborigines.

Various researchers estimate that the aboriginal population declined by 90–99 percent over that period.

Apparently there were two sources of Old World diseases, Europe and Africa. Population decline in the Caribbean was so great early in the sixteenth century that the Spanish began to bring black slaves from West Africa to work the mines in Hispaniola. Extinction of native peoples from the Lucayos (Bahamas) and Hispaniola occurred rapidly as a result of epidemics made worse by enslavement and mistreatment.

Depopulation in La Florida was also severe, especially among those who suffered both Spanish military actions and epidemics. Unlike the Caribbean, where native populations disappeared in the sixteenth century, many societies in the southeastern United States survived into the seventeenth century, and some into the eighteenth, before succumbing to the effects of disease and raiding by European powers. This was especially true in Florida and along the Georgia coast, regions in which Spanish missions were established. Other southeastern natives, such as the ancestors of modern Creek, Chero-

By 1544, when Sebastian Münster's New World map was published, North America was shown to be separated from Asia, but the exact configuration of the western coastline had not yet been determined.

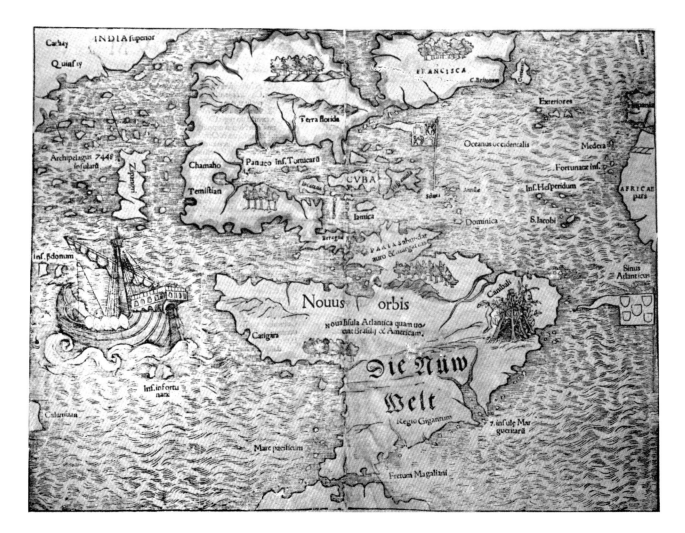

kee, Choctaw, and Chickasaw, were not missionized. Their descendants, greatly reduced from precontact population levels, still live in the Southeast and in Oklahoma.

Depopulation during the sixteenth and seventeenth centuries resulted in many cultural changes among aboriginal peoples in La Florida. Social and political changes occurred as native leaders died; economies were disrupted, and societies reorganized into less centralized systems. Native societies observed in the eighteenth century, at the time of the Creek Confederacy, were quite different from the prehistoric chiefdoms that existed when Hernando de Soto had first passed through the Southeast. Reduced populations caused the development of new cultural institutions as societies tried to adapt and survive.

In chapter 10, Marvin Smith presents archaeological evidence for changes that occurred within the chiefdoms of the Southeast during the early colonial period. It is a horrible irony that although the de Soto and other early Spanish expeditions provide our only views of some native cultures at the time of European contact, it was those same expeditions that introduced the diseases that led to the demise of those cultures.

St. Augustine, the First Successful Colony

Although Spain dominates the story of the early explorations of La Florida, France also played a role. In fact, it was in response to French colonization attempts that Spain again sought to establish a presence in the southeastern United States.

Building on his contacts with the Spanish Crown and his successful exploits as a captain-general charged with protecting Spain's Caribbean settlements and shipping lanes, Pedro Menéndez de Avilés rapidly rose to prominence in the 1550s. It was no quirk that Phillip II summoned Menéndez to court in 1563 for consultation on ousting the French from Spanish lands on the Atlantic coast.

The Frenchman Jean Ribault had founded Charlesfort on Parris Island, South Carolina, in 1562. Although that colony soon failed, René de Laudonnière led a second attempt in 1564, establishing Fort Caroline near the mouth of the St. Johns River. The French left rich written accounts of their activities on the Atlantic coast of La Florida, providing important information on the native peoples of the region.

Armed with a royal charter empowering him to found a colony in La Florida, Pedro Menéndez sailed to the New World and quickly destroyed Fort Caroline, effectively foiling France's attempt to wrest La Florida from Spanish control. Fulfilling the conditions of his royal

F. Delfinum.

Prom Gallicum.

An encounter between the French and native peoples on the southeastern Atlantic coast in the 1560s. De Bry's original engraving was published in black and white; color has been added to this version.

contract, he placed settlements at St. Augustine and Santa Elena (on Parris Island, at the site of the French settlement). Garrisons, some with Jesuit priests, were placed along both coasts of peninsular Florida. In chapter 11, Eugene Lyon recounts the Menéndez plan for settlement of La Florida, and in chapter 12 Edward Chaney and Kathleen Deagan look at the founding of St. Augustine.

Although Menéndez was successful, the Florida colony provided little financial gain for him or other colonists. Most of the outlying garrisons were abandoned after only a few years. Santa Elena survived until 1587. The La Florida colony was never self-sufficient, and it continually had to be supplied from outside.

St. Augustine, a small frontier coastal town, did survive, but Spain's hold on the rest of the vast territory of La Florida was tenuous. Establishing missions among the native population seemed to be the best solution for keeping the territory. Missions would relieve Spain of having to protect her Florida colony from Indian raids, and they were much less costly than building forts or towns in the interior of the Southeast.

After the initial mission efforts by Jesuits from 1565 to the early 1570s met with little success, the Franciscan order established a chain of missions from St. Augustine northward along the Atlantic coast and a second chain extending westward, inland across northern Florida. By the 1700s more than 130 missions had been built.

Spain continued to attempt to learn more about the interior of La Florida and to establish the long-sought overland route to Mexico. Pedro Menéndez, Florida's first governor, sent Juan Pardo to accomplish the task. Between 1566 and 1568, Pardo twice traveled inland from Santa Elena. During his initial journey he and 125 soldiers reached western North Carolina; later he retraced that route before continuing on across the Appalachian Mountains and reaching Tennessee. During the expeditions he located several Indian villages visited by de Soto nearly three decades earlier.

But Pardo never found the route to Mexico. The colony of La Florida and its town of St. Augustine would remain merely outposts, isolated from other Spanish New World settlements and inadequately defended. And although the Franciscans were able to convert thousands of native Guale, Timucuan, Apalachee, and other Indians to Catholicism, the crowding of native peoples into mission towns only increased the spread of disease, continuing the population decimation begun at the time of European contact.

Excavations in St. Augustine under the direction of Kathleen Deagan have documented the late sixteenth-century town under the modern landscape as historical archaeology continues to provide new perspectives on how Europeans adjusted to the New World.

During the English raid on St. Augustine in 1702, mission settlements were sacked and the town itself was burned. Only the stone fort was not taken. Just as military mishaps generate inquiries today, so they did then, and a map of the action was drawn. Amelia Island (Isla de Santa Maria) is at the top. The fort at the bottom was located near the St. Johns River and was supposed to guard the northern approach to St. Augustine.

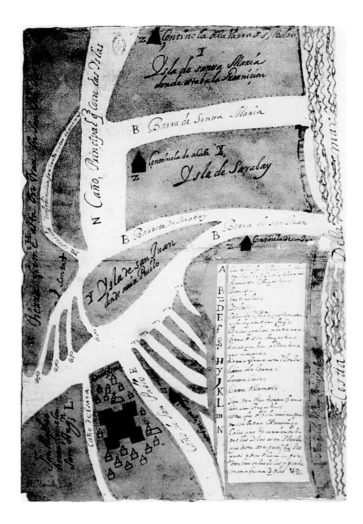

The colony's fragile nature ultimately led to attacks by English colonists aided by native allies. English raids in 1702 and 1704 destroyed the mission system and scattered the mission Indians. Spain's hold on La Florida grew steadily weaker as English colonies crept down the Atlantic seaboard.

Except for the period 1763–1783 when La Florida was ceded to Britain, Spain maintained possession of the colony into the early nineteenth century, although it continued to shrink in size as the French, the English, and later the Americans made inroads. The native people were not as lucky; disease and maltreatment continued to take heavy tolls. By 1763 the indigenous peoples of Florida—Calusa, Timucuan, and others—were completely gone, and Creeks, Cherokees, and other southeastern peoples whose ancestors probably once numbered in the millions were reduced to tens of thousands.

In 1821 what remained of the original Spanish lands became a territory of the United States of America. Spain's three centuries in La Florida, an important chapter in our nation's history, were over.

2 / Columbus's 1492 Voyage and the Search for His Landfall

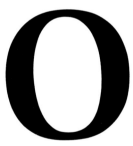On a clear November evening, three weeks after he arrived in the New World, Christopher Columbus stood on the aft deck of the *Santa Maria*, calculating the North Star's altitude with a quadrant. Later that night, he recorded the ship's position in his log as being 42° north of the equator, roughly where Pennsylvania is today. He had been sailing along the coast of a landmass the natives called Colba. "It is certain," he wrote, "that this is tierra firme and that I am off Zayto and Qyinsay a hundred leagues more or less." What Columbus meant is that he had found the Asian continent, that, in particular, two legendary Chinese cities—probably present-day Zhao'an and Hangzhou—lay only about 300 miles away. After traveling for almost two months, he was finally within reach of his destination. Yet, without seeing the Grand Khan or visiting his kingdom or acquiring any riches, Columbus abruptly turned his vessels about and headed in the opposite direction.

Why Columbus reversed his course is a mystery, though if he harbored doubts about his location—a reasonable assumption, considering he had encountered little that resembled the civilization described by Marco Polo—his action would have helped him avoid the truth. Personal motivation aside, wherever the Genovese explorer

In Columbus's day latitude was determined by shooting the sun or the north star at its zenith (determining the angle relative to the horizon) and then reading from a table that listed latitude entries with angle for each day of the year. East-west position (longitude) could not be so calculated and was kept by plotting compass course and estimating speed.

thought he was, he certainly was not near China. Despite his wildly inaccurate estimate of latitude, his log entries describing geographic features, distances traveled, and other aspects of the voyage, when taken together, indicate that "tierra firme" was not a continent but an island—that Colba was Cuba. Indeed, Cuba is the first landmark about which there is some degree of certainty. In contrast, the locations of Columbus's stops before Cuba, including the most historically significant stop of all—the first landfall in the New World, the island Columbus called San Salvador and the natives there called Guanahani—are open to dispute.

Everyone agrees that San Salvador is located in the Bahamas, a chain of hundreds of islands and cays that stretches 760 miles between the southeastern coast of Florida and the eastern tip of Cuba. Facing the Atlantic between the twentieth and twenty-seventh parallels, the islands act as a gateway to the Caribbean for ships approaching from the northeast. Since Columbus did in fact approach from that direction and, three weeks later, sighted Cuba, there is no doubt that he passed through the chain of islands. Nor is there any reason to question Columbus's assertion, in the log, that he went ashore in four places: first San Salvador, then the islands he christened Santa María de la Concepción, Fernandina, and Isabela. But agreement ends there.

During the past 350 years, no fewer than nine sites have been proposed as the first landfall, from Grand Turk Island at the extreme southeastern end of the Bahamas to Egg Island more than 300 miles to the north. One proposal came in 1828, from the American novelist

Washington Irving, who placed the landfall at Cat Island in the northern Bahamas. But he was motivated less by historical fact than by literary whimsy. About the same time, Juan Bautista Muñoz, in the course of writing a history of the New World, reconstructed the voyage and identified Watling Island, midway in the Bahama chain, as San Salvador—an opinion shared by many subsequent investigators. In 1926, the Bahamian government officially renamed Watling "San Salvador." Both terms are used today. Even Abraham Lincoln's assistant secretary of the navy, Gustavus V. Fox, contributed to the debate. A lifelong seaman who had spent many years in the Caribbean, Fox studied the landfall question in the early 1880s, concluding that Columbus first set foot in the New World at Samana Cay, 65 miles southeast of Watling Island. These sundry San Salvadors have been used, in turn, as the jumping-off points for two dozen different passages through the chain. A composite map of the proposed routes looks like the ramblings of a drunk.

All but one of the alleged landfalls fell out of favor in 1942 when Harvard historian Samuel E. Morison published his Pulitzer Prize–winning biography of Columbus in which he reaffirmed Muñoz's position: that the Italian mariner first went ashore at Watling Island.

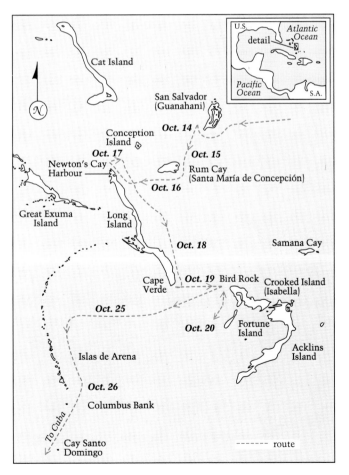

Columbus's initial landfall on the island of Guanahani and his route through the Bahamas are shown. Researchers will probably never agree on a single interpretation of his route.

Christopher Columbus is shown in an early sixteenth-century painting, perhaps the best known portrait of him.

At that time, Morison was not only the world authority on Columbus but a superb seaman with a keen understanding of navigation (he had even sailed the route himself). His view was considered valid for four decades.

But Morison's reconstruction of Columbus's passage through the Bahamas contained gaps and errors—for example, locations of key native villages mentioned in the log—and as these became apparent historians began questioning the Watling landfall. In 1986 a team of National Geographic Society scientists, directed by senior associate editor Joseph Judge, charged that the Morison route was not just flawed but completely wrong. After simulating the geography of the Bahamas with computer models, which made it possible to sail different courses electronically, and reexamining geographic and archaeological data, the team settled on the route suggested by Fox. They concluded that Columbus had landed first at the small emerald-green pendant of sand and trees known as Samana Cay and pronounced the mystery solved. Yet, only a year later, an oceanographer and a computer scientist from the Woods Hole Oceanographic Institution on Cape Cod challenged the team's estimates of wind and water currents and placed Columbus within sight of Watling Island on the morning of 12 October 1492.

Doubtless, the matter would have been settled long ago if not for a lack of information about the voyage. No map has survived, and Columbus's log, written in Castilian Spanish, disappeared soon after he presented it to King Ferdinand and Queen Isabella. To make matters worse, the only copy of the log, which Isabella commissioned, also has been lost. What has survived is a literary hybrid—part paraphrase, part transcription—of the copy made by Bartolomé de Las Casas, a friar who had known Columbus and had himself traveled extensively in the New World, who provided the first full account of the Spanish conquest, the *History of the Indies.* In short, the record of Columbus's voyage that exists is a thirdhand manuscript written in sixteenth-century Spanish.

Not only does Las Casas's manuscript contain outright errors—some, such as the latitude reading off the coast of Cuba or assertions about the proximity of Japan and China, so egregious that they call attention to themselves—but it is also full of ambiguity. Descriptive passages are sometimes so general that they could apply to any number of islands in the Caribbean. San Salvador, for instance, is described as "flat . . . green . . . and [having] a lake in the middle"—a portrait that matches Grand Turk Island, Conception Island, and several others. Certain words have double meanings depending on the context in which they are used, and the log is skimpy on context. An example is the phrase *camino de,* which can mean either "the

In the late 1520s the royal cosmographer of Spain, Alonso de Chaves, compiled a guide to New World navigation. His *Espejo de Navegantes* lists the islands of Samana and Guanahani and gives their latitudes relative to one another and to other islands. He notes that Guanahani is "the island first found when these Indies were discovered."

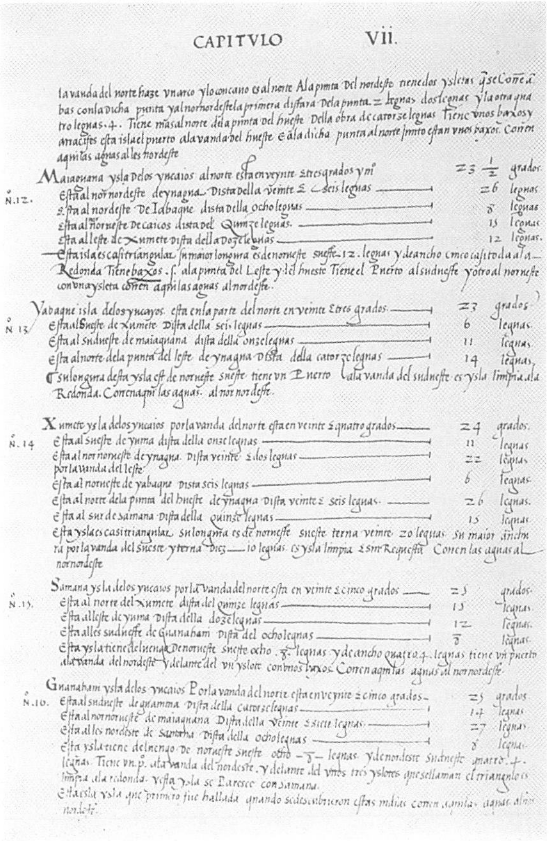
CAPITVLO VII.

way from" or "the way to"—a distinction critical to determining locations. Finally, the Las Casas manuscript has numerous erasures, unusual spellings, and brief illegible passages, as well as marginal notes that the friar intended either for inclusion in the text or as reminders to himself about the transcription. Some of these irregularities—especially those regarding terms of distance— bear directly on the location of San Salvador. Still, apart from notes made years later by one of Columbus's sons, this document is the sole source of information about the European discovery of the Americas.

From the beginning, the ambiguities, errors, and omissions in Las Casas's manuscript have been compounded in translation. In 1981, the Society for the History of Discoveries, a group of Columbus scholars, concluded that all the published editions of the log differed, in varying degrees, from the Las Casas manuscript. The discrepancies were due in part to an insufficient understanding of sixteenth-century Spanish, in part to bias. Regarding passages that permitted more than one interpretation, for example, translators tended to choose the direction, distance covered, and geographic detail that best matched their preconceived notions about the voyage. In Morison's translation, published along with his biography of Columbus, San Salvador simply was identified as Watling Island, without any acknowledgment that the location of the first landfall was in dispute.

A new, unbiased study by Oliver Dunn and James E. Kelley, Jr., *The Diario of Christopher Columbus's First Voyage to America, 1492–1493*, provides thorough historical and linguistic analyses of all the disputed sections of the manuscript, as well as an exact transcription of Las Casas's own words. Their translation, in particular, will help lift the fog that has obscured Columbus's route through the Bahamas.

Indeed, by carefully cross-checking different log entries (regarding sailing directions, island topography, and the location of villages) against the physical characteristics of the islands today, as well as against archaeological evidence uncovered during the past few years, it is now possible to identify San Salvador. After centuries of doubt, it is satisfying to be able to point to the place where the first step was taken.

On 3 August 1492, the *Niña*, the *Pinta*, and the *Santa Maria* sailed south from Spain to the Canary Islands, off the northwest coast of Africa. After stopping there for repairs and provisions, Columbus headed due west, the direction that would bring him, accord-

Published in 1480, *Imago Mundi* (a book on the geography of the world) helped to convince Columbus that the Atlantic Ocean, which was thought to separate Europe from Asia, was about 60 degrees of latitude wide and could be crossed. The book contains notes in his hand in the margins.

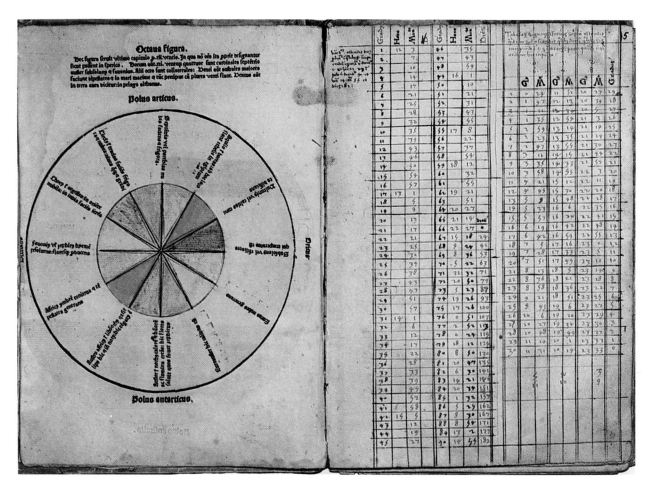

ing to his reckoning, to the Indies. There is disagreement about how far south the three caravels were driven by wind and ocean currents during the 37-day Atlantic crossing, but virtually all modern navigational studies find them, by 12 October, on the eastern side of the central Bahamas—somewhere in an area about 12,000 miles square.

Within this rectangle lie a number of prominent islands, including Watling, Rum Cay, Long Island, Samana Cay, and a horseshoe-shaped cluster consisting of Fortune, Crooked, and Acklins islands. Viewed from above, these variously shaped outcrops suggest an *S*, tipped slightly backward, with the top curve consisting of Watling, Rum Cay, and Long Island, and the bottom curve of the horseshoe cluster, with Samana Cay, smaller than the others, resting outside the figure, just east of the bottom curve.

According to Morison, Columbus followed the path described by the *S*, stopping first at Watling, then Rum Cay, Long Island, and Crooked Island, before heading west to Cuba. Joseph Judge, on the other hand, has Columbus starting his passage through the Bahamas off the *S*, at Samana Cay, and following only its bottom curve—crossing to Crooked Island, then sailing on to Long Island and back to Fortune before leaving the area. So it is here, in the central Bahamas, that the search for San Salvador truly begins. And from this point on, any attempt to retrace Columbus's path depends as much upon correctly interpreting the log as it does upon navigation, geography, and archaeology.

Fortunately, the Las Casas manuscript itself contains clues to how it should be read. Some islands are described more completely than others so their locations are more certain. The site of the fourth and last stopover in the Bahamas, the strip of land Columbus called Isabela, is such a place. Once it is firmly identified, Isabela can serve as a benchmark by which to locate sites about which there is less information in the log. And the evidence strongly suggests that Isabela is the horseshoe-shaped cluster consisting of Crooked, Fortune, and Acklins islands. Columbus came upon this cluster on the morning of 19 October: "We all three ships reached it before noon at the north point where it forms an isleo [small island] and a reef of stone outside of it to the north and another between the isleo and the big island." Just off the northwestern cape of Crooked Island is a lone promontory known today as Bird Rock, which, as the log indicates, is separated from the island by a reef. In honor of the "isleo," Columbus named this location the Cape of the Small Island.

The San Salvadoran natives, called Lucayans, whom Columbus had pressed into service as guides, called the "big island" Saomete. Columbus understood them to say that a city lay some distance inland or on the opposite side (the exact location was unclear) and that

A late sixteenth-century engraving shows a romanticized scene of Columbus bidding farewell to Isabella and Ferdinand as he prepared to sail from the port of Palos in 1492.

the king who lived there ruled all of the neighboring islands and possessed a great deal of gold.

Columbus and his crew sailed south along Isabela's western shore, searching for a way around the island and a passage to the king. Midway down the coast, they anchored at a second cape—Cape Beautiful, so named for its rich array of exotic flora. Although Columbus noted in his log that Cape Beautiful was separated by a narrow bight from another sliver of land, he referred to both islands as Isabela. He continued south to the tip of the second island, then turned and attempted to sail northeast and east but found the water "so shallow that I could not enter or steer for the settlement [Saomete]." For this reason, perhaps, he named Isabela's southernmost tip Cape of the Lagoon.

This description clearly matches the Crooked-Fortune-Acklins cluster. Crooked Island is roughly *L*-shaped, with one side forming the top of the horseshoe and the other the upper half of the western leg, which, in turn is separated by a shallow waterway from the lower half, Fortune Island. Acklins makes up the entire eastern leg. Moreover, the three islands surround the Bight of Acklins, a twenty-mile expanse of shallows that has changed little in five centuries. It is such a "lagoon" that separated the Cape of Lagoon—the southern tip of Fortune—from the region of Isabela (Acklins) where Saomete supposedly lay.

Columbus never reached the El Dorado of which his guides spoke, but there was once a huge Lucayan settlement directly across the bight, on the western side of Acklins. Archaeological studies in 1983 and 1987 uncovered remnants of fire pits, including charred wood and limestone spars (small heat-cracked rocks), and midden deposits containing large quantities of fish bones, in addition to the shells of clams and conchs, which were staples of the Lucayan diet. Also unearthed were numerous fragments of griddles—earthenware platters the Lucayans used for baking cassava bread—which are always associated with permanent habitation. The size of the village and its involvement in long-distance trade would befit only a chief as wealthy and as powerful as the "king" who, according to the log, was supposed to have ruled Saomete. The settlement extends along the shore for more than three miles, at least six times farther than the average Lucayan village. At most sites throughout the Bahamas, less than 1 percent of the excavated pottery shows signs of having been imported from other islands, whereas more than 25 percent of the pottery found at the Acklins settlement originated in the Greater Antilles (specifically, Cuba and Hispaniola).

Having found passage around the southern tip of Isabela impossible, Columbus reversed course and sailed back to the Cape of the Small Island, where he dropped anchor and went ashore. Only a short distance inland, he and several members of his crew passed "some big lakes" and verdant groves with "flocks of parrots that obscure the sun." From the bank of one of the lakes, they spied a "serpent" almost six feet long: "When it saw us it threw itself into the lake and we followed it in, because it was not very deep, until with lances we killed it."

Then, "about half a league from the place where [they were] anchored," they came upon a village whose Lucayan inhabitants had only recently fled into the forest. Before long, the natives conquered their fear and approached the Europeans, who gave them gifts of bells and glass beads. Later Columbus asked the Lucayans to bring water from the lakes to the ships.

There is little doubt that these events took place near the northwestern cape of Crooked Island, just across from Bird Rock. In 1983, archaeologists discovered a village site about two miles (roughly half a league) inland of that point. As described in the log, there is a freshwater lake about a quarter of a mile away. Excavations in 1987 revealed midden deposits, pottery, and house floors. Among the curious items unearthed was a leg bone of a crocodile, a reptile that until then had not been known to inhabit the Bahamas. Since throughout the log Columbus identified various snakes and lizards by name, it

Columbus's coat of arms includes the official emblems of Castile and León (the castle and the lion) and several islands, which represent his New World discoveries.

Columbus and his epic voyage have become symbols of adventure and discovery. In a 1621 engraving Columbus the navigator stands with the tools of his trade beside a globe with the Old World at the top and the New World at the bottom.

Almirante de nauios para las Indias.

is likely that this rather forbidding species was the mysterious serpent he encountered and killed on Isabela.

All of which is to say that there is virtually complete congruency between Columbus's descriptions of Isabella, the fourth landfall, and the cluster of Crooked, Fortune, and Acklins islands. The isleo of the log, which inspired the name Cape of the Small Island, is therefore the benchmark by which the locations of San Salvador, Santa María de la Concepción, and Fernandina should be judged. In short, whatever route is proposed for Columbus's passage through the Bahamas, it must put him within sight of Bird Rock on the morning of 19 October.

Beginning with Columbus's sighting of the isleo (Bird Rock) and, nearby, Isabela (Crooked Island) on the nineteenth and working backward allows us to trace his route and identify San Salvador. Columbus says in the log that the caravels approached the isleo from the northwest, meaning that they started from the coast of Long Island, which lies about 25 miles away and is the only landmass in that direction. Taking him at his word regarding the previous 24-hours' journey ("I followed the wind"), one can see that he could easily have sailed the roughly 60-mile shoreline of Long Island by the time dusk fell on the eighteenth. In other words, Columbus made his third land-fall on the northern end of Long Island.

During the afternoon of the seventeenth, before getting caught in the "dirty" weather that would keep him running far offshore of Fernandina the entire night and the next day, the Spanish fleet had taken "barrels of water" from a freshwater lake near a Lucayan village. Morison's inability to locate this village, or to demonstrate that a native settlement of any kind ever existed on the extreme north-eastern shore of Long Island, was considered a major weakness in his route. In 1984, archaeologists found evidence of 31 Lucayan sites on Long Island, eight of them on the eastern shore, two of which are in the locations described by Columbus. Surface collections at the northernmost of these sites on Newton Cay have turned up evidence of a permanent Lucayan village. Moreover, behind the village site lies a freshwater pond—the same pond, presumably, to which the Span-iards brought their empty barrels 500 years ago. Most important, the pond and the village are close to a prominent shoreline feature that Columbus had passed earlier that day (the seventeenth): "When I was two leagues distant from the end of the island, I found a very wonder-ful harbor with one entrance, although one might say two, because it has an isleo in the middle. . . . I thought that it was the mouth of some river." There is an ideal candidate for the harbor almost exactly where Columbus said it should be—along the northeastern shore. Into this harbor flows a tidal creek whose strength, as it swells and streams through a constricted inlet, makes it seem like a river. As Columbus indicated, an islet rests at the center of the harbor's mouth, and the village and its freshwater pond are within walking distance.

According to the log, Columbus visited one other village on Fernandina, a few miles south of this harbor, a place now called Fish Ponds. In fact, it is the village he set out from, sailing north, on the morning of the seventeenth, after the crew had spent the previous day exchanging trinkets and goods with Lucayans there while Co-lumbus observed whales, parrots, and exotic trees. The remains of a permanent settlement, including griddle sherds and middens, have been unearthed at this site as well. The evidence seems overwhelm-ing that when Columbus spied Fernandina on the horizon, he had before him the northernmost shores of Long Island.

If this is the case, the site of the second landfall, the place that Columbus called Santa María de la Concepción, cannot be other than Rum Cay, 20 miles east of Long Island (and near the peak of the S figure's upper curve), roughly the distance the explorer claimed to have traveled between the two. The log contains little information about Santa María de la Concepción. Columbus did not anchor there

Three late sixteenth-century engravings of Christopher Columbus were all done decades after his death in 1506. At least three cities claim his burial location.

until he had almost passed the island, and his stay was uneventful. Lucayans, who "let us go around the island," were encountered, but no settlements were reported. (As one would expect from the log, village sites have been found everywhere but the western cape, where Columbus went ashore. Midway between two of these sites is a cave in which the Lucayans carved pictures on the walls, a practice the natives followed only in places where they lived.)

Critics have made much of the fact that Rum Cay measures five miles by ten miles, whereas the log describes an island three times that size—five leagues by ten leagues. Morison invented a special terrestrial unit of measure he called an "alongshore league" to account for the discrepancy, but it was an idea that strained the credulity even of his supporters. A better explanation is that Las Casas confused distance terms in this passage. In his manuscript, the friar twelve times canceled out the word *leguas,* meaning leagues, and replaced it with *millas,* meaning miles, whereas the reverse—leagues substituted for miles—never occurs. This discrepancy suggests that Las Casas, or the scribe who preceded him, was for some reason disposed to translate distance figures into leagues. It is likely that in the entry describing Santa María de la Concepción, Las Casas simply chose the wrong word in his transcription. Using either miles or leagues, on a case-by-case basis, the Watling track matches the log in all seven instances in which Columbus specifies a distance.

Harder to explain is Columbus's statement that he saw "so many islands" upon leaving San Salvador that he could not decide to which he should sail first. When one approaches Rum Cay from the northeast, as Columbus says he approached Santa María, the horizon appears relatively empty. But this observation alone is scarcely sufficient evidence for rejecting Rum Cay as the second landfall, especially as it lies dead center between Long Island's northern tip, the third landfall, and Watling Island. Watling is where Columbus

Facing page: The Virgin of the Navigators offers her protection to Columbus, his men, and New World native peoples in a 1505 Spanish painting.

ended his transatlantic crossing, and it matches log descriptions of the first landfall to a greater degree than any other island in the central Bahamas.

The first words Columbus used to describe San Salvador are, "This island is quite big and very flat and with very green trees and much water and a very large lake in the middle and without any mountains; and all of it so green that it is a pleasure to look at." One of the most prominent of Watling's features is a large, centrally located lake. On 14 October, Columbus and some of his crew explored the western coast of San Salvador in longboats: "And in between the reef and shore there was depth and harbor for as many ships as there are in the whole of Christendom, and the entrance to it is very narrow." Watling has a large, protected harbor, exactly like the one described in the log, on its western shore. Later he "saw a piece of land formed like an island, although it was not one, on which there were six houses." Not far from the deep-water harbor is a peninsula—Cut Cay—that is almost separated from the rest of the island. Lucayan pottery has been found on that cay, which suggests (but, alone, does not prove) that it was once inhabited (the "six houses" observed by Columbus). Elsewhere on Watling, Charles Hoffman, an archaeologist at Northern Arizona University, excavating a Lucayan site, uncovered a number of objects that the log specifically states were given to the natives and "in which they took so much pleasure": green and yellow glass beads, broken crockery, a coin, and a belt buckle, objects that have been found nowhere else in the central Bahamas.

These tokens and trifles—the first entries in the archaeological record left behind by Columbus and his crew—heralded the arrival of European civilization in the New World. The Genovese explorer may not have known where he was when he stepped onshore on 12 October 1492, inadvertently inaugurating one of the most dramatic episodes in the history of the Americas, but now we do. And it was Watling Island, today aptly again named San Salvador.

Kathleen A. Deagan

3 / The Search for La Navidad, Columbus's 1492 Settlement

olumbus's voyages of exploration have been compared with good reason to the first explorations of space in the twentieth century. Despite the great changes in technology and society that took place between those two types of exploration, they had a comparable impact on their times. The first major transatlantic explorations and the first space exploration altered and intensified people's understanding of the world in which they live and their place in it. Both also resulted in an explosion of technological advances and scientific inquiries.

The impacts of the encounter between Old World and New were most immediate and devastating to the inhabitants of the Americas. The Spaniards, with a more effective technology, introduced new forms of social control and organization as well as new plants, animals, and methods of using the land that often had great ecological impact. The most visible and tragic result was the terrible decimation of the native American population as a result of disease. As might be the case in any encounter with an alien life form, there was no immunity on either side to the common diseases of the other, and for the Caribbean Indians, who were the first to greet the Europeans, these diseases resulted in almost complete extinction within 50 years of contact.

After sailing aground on a reef, the *Santa Maria* was salvaged by Columbus's men aided by local Arawak Indians. Modern charts record reefs in the general location where the accident is thought to have occurred.

Because of this swift and terrible disappearance of many native cultures from the circumcaribbean area, and because of the relative absence of written documentation about those people before their decline, we know almost nothing about them. One of the great tasks of archaeology is to learn about these native groups and reconstruct their lifeways, since information about them exists mostly in the ground.

The first town in the Americas where Europeans and native Americans lived together, La Navidad, was inadvertently established by Christopher Columbus in 1492, when his flagship, the *Santa Maria*, struck a reef and sank. The documentary accounts of those events and Columbus's first voyage are few and well known. In general, they recount that after a voyage of 42 days, the *Niña*, the *Pinta*, and the *Santa Maria* sighted land. Later the small fleet sailed southward through the Bahamas. By Christmas Eve 1492 the *Santa Maria*, Columbus's own ship, was off the north coast of Haiti near present-day Cap Haitien. Columbus and his men had met some of the local Indian rulers the previous evening and had been up the entire night trading and entertaining them. Only the ship's boy was awake and at the helm. The *Santa Maria* ran aground, settled on a coral reef, and could not be saved.

On Christmas Day, Columbus's men unloaded the cargo and supplies of the *Santa Maria,* assisted by the Arawak Indian chief Guacanacaric, who governed a nearby town. They placed all of the goods in two large houses belonging to the *cacique,* or chief, which he then gave to the Spaniards. The *Santa Maria* was also dismantled above the water table, and the planks and timbers were used to fortify an area that probably incorporated the houses given by the cacique.

The town was reported by Columbus to be about one kilometer distant from the site of the wreck, and the fortification of the chief's structures suggest that the fortress was within the town itself. Within the space of a week a fort was under way, and it was alleged by Columbus in a letter to Ferdinand and Isabella in 1493 that a moat, a palisade, and a cellar for storage were being constructed. Other accounts suggest that a well for water and a watchtower may also have been built.

This tiny settlement was named La Navidad, because it was established at the time of the Nativity. Thirty-nine men were awarded the dubious privilege of remaining there with food and supplies for a year and instructions to trade with the Indians for gold. They included a physician, a gunner, a boat builder, a barrel maker, a caulker, and a tailor. On his second voyage eleven months later Columbus returned to La Navidad to find the settlement and surrounding Indian town burned, all of the men dead, and the supplies dispersed among the Indians over a distance of several kilometers.

What happened to the men of La Navidad? Various accounts indicate that they died as a result of disease, internal fighting, leaving to trade elsewhere, antagonizing their hosts by their greedy behavior concerning women and gold, or an attack from Indians of the interior regions. Columbus investigated the circumstances of the colony's destruction and searched for the gold he believed his men had acquired, but he was unsuccessful in both efforts. He soon left La Navidad and

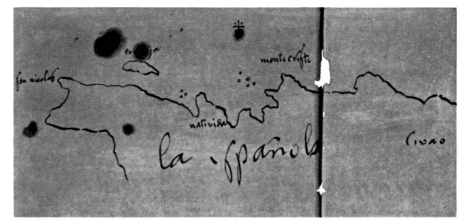

Columbus's sketch map shows the north coast of *la ispanola* (Hispaniola) and his settlement of *nativida*. Saint Nicholas (the western point), the island of Tortuga, and Monte Cristi (to the northeast of La Navidad) all have the same names today.

This engraving, which accompanied the 1493 Basel edition of Columbus's letter describing his first voyage, provides a European view of La Navidad. In reality, construction would have been of wood and much less elaborate than the stone buildings shown in the engraving.

continued westward along the north coast of Hispaniola, to found La Isabela, his first intentional settlement.

The location and fate of La Navidad have captured the imaginations of many scholars over the years but perhaps none so intensely as Samuel Eliot Morison, the Harvard historian, and Dr. William Hodges of the Hospital Le Bon Samaritan in Limbé, Haiti. Dr. Hodges is a medical missionary and avocational archaeologist who has studied the area for more than 30 years. Based on his studies of Columbus's log and other accounts, prevailing sea conditions, knowledge of sailing, and changing shoreline geography, Morison concluded that the site of La Navidad should be within a kilometer of the tiny Haitian fishing village of Limonade Bord de Mer. Excavations commissioned by Morison were conducted there in 1939 but revealed only the remains of an eighteenth-century French blockhouse.

In 1975, Dr. Hodges was led to a remote Indian village site by local farmers, who often brought him artifacts for the small museum he maintains in Limbé. The archaeological site was located about half a kilometer inland from Limonade Bord de Mer, at the edge of a mangrove swamp and saline basin that connect the site with the shore. Today it is occupied by a small Haitian farming community known as En Bas Saline, and that is the name that we gave to the site during our archaeological work.

Analysis of aerial photographs indicates that a tributary of the region's major river, the Grande Rivière du Nord, probably connected the site to the shore as recently as 300 years ago. Now dry, a channel of this tributary can be seen in the photographs, extending along the north part of the site and emptying into the sea at Limonade Bord de Mer. Damming by eighteenth-century French planters considerably altered the northern course of the Grande Rivière and caused a great deal of alluvial deposit along the coast to the west of the site; En Bas Saline itself, however, has been free of such accumulation, as is apparent from the observation that relatively undisturbed archaeological deposits are present only about four inches under the ground. No water-deposited silt lies atop the site. Dr. Hodges carried out preliminary excavations at the site in 1977 and showed, through the

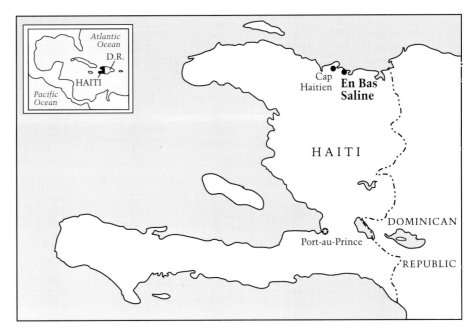

En Bas Saline, the probable site of Chief Guacanacaric's village and La Navidad, is located east of Cape Haitian near the small coastal village of Limonade Bord de Mer.

kinds of Indian pottery he recovered, that it was a densely occupied Indian town during the late fifteenth century. He also located part of a large, deep feature which he hypothesized to have been a well at La Navidad. The site remained undisturbed after that time until University of Florida excavations began in 1983.

We had been working in Haiti since 1979 at the site of Puerto Real, a Spanish town occupied from 1503 until 1579 (see chapter 5). The town's ruins are located less than a mile from En Bas Saline, and it was probably the Spaniards of Puerto Real who were in direct contact with the Indians of Guacanacaric's town and used them as slaves before their extinction in about 1510. We began the search for La Navidad in 1983 and have continued each year since with the sponsorship of the Government of Haiti (Bureau National d'Ethnologie), the Organization of American States, the University of Florida Institute for Early Contact Period Studies, the National Endowment for the Humanities, the National Geographic Society, the Florida Museum of Natural History, and the National Science Foundation.

In addition to finding La Navidad, our objectives included the archaeological study of the culture of the Indians of this region on the eve of European contact and therefore on the eve of their destruction. Changes that they underwent as a result of European contact can be better understood at En Bas Saline, because the site contains a late prehistoric, precontact component, as well as an early contact period occupation. By comparing the ways of life represented in these two occupations, we expect to gain more specific understanding of how European contact initially altered native American social organization.

In order for us to identify La Navidad, certain conditions had to be met and demonstrated. A large Indian town occupied by a chief had to be located within about a mile of the presumed wreck site. Not only did we see that this condition was met at En Bas Saline, but extensive survey and exploration by Hodges and others showed that there is no other similarly large town of the right period within the area around the site. Another necessary condition was that the Indian town had to be occupied at the time of Columbus's arrival. The pottery from the site, as well as the radiocarbon and thermoluminescence dates, shows that it was in fact occupied in 1492.

We then had to predict what should be underground if this were La Navidad. This normal first step is complicated because we are uncertain whether Columbus was telling the truth in his letters to Ferdinand and Isabella and whether his men carried out the orders he said he gave them. If both conditions could be ascertained, it would be necessary to locate buried evidence for structures with some European features, very likely including the stains from a burned chief's

Archaeological excavations at En Bas Saline take place when the local villagers' fields, normally planted with manioc, bananas, and other crops, lie fallow.

house, watchtower posts, palisade posts and a moat, and possibly a cellar and well. The presence of European artifacts alone would not be conclusive, since trading activities could have brought portable items to areas still unseen by Europeans. Even tiny fragments of glass and metal must have seemed as strange and wonderful to the Indians as moonrocks seem to us and would surely have been removed from La Navidad and hoarded or traded by the Indians shortly after its destruction.

What *should* have stayed in the ground were bits of European wood, since some of La Navidad was built from the timbers of the *Santa Maria*, as well as European seeds and European animal bones from the supplies left with the men who stayed in La Navidad. These kinds of things are dropped on the ground and forgotten, but archaeologists have a chance of finding them 500 years later. Our first step toward solving these problems was to set up a program that included topographic mapping, aerial photographs, a spatially controlled collection of material from the ground's surface, an electromagnetic survey, and test excavations. Much of this work has been supervised by Maurice Williams, who has spent a good portion of his research time hacking through banana gardens, cactus, and thorntree thickets.

Because the site is densely covered in garden crops and other vegetation, mapping was a time-consuming activity, requiring three years and 93 transit stations to complete. The map itself was generated by the Surface II topographic mapping program that shows the

An aerial photograph of En Bas Saline shows a portion of the ring of shell and debris delineating the Arawak village occupation. Today the site is crossed with agricultural fields. The one high area within the ring may be the location of the chief's house. Just to the east archaeologists found the well containing European artifacts.

differences in elevation throughout the site, helping us to locate structures and other features.

The contour map shows that the site is an irregular C-shaped earthwork measuring approximately 380 yards in diameter north to south and 325 yards in diameter east to west. The earthwork itself is about 2.4 feet in height, about 22 yards wide, and considerably more pronounced along its eastern side. There is an opening in the southeastern part of the eastern earthwork. The construction is lower and less regular along the west side, which probably faced the river during the site's occupation. The earthwork appears to have been purposefully constructed rather than gradually accrued, in that borrow pits are evident along its inner side. The central part of the annular ring is generally flat and open, except for a small mounded area near the center. The central area may have been a plaza or ball court, which is typical of late prehistoric Caribbean Indian villages, a feature Columbus commented on when he described Guacanacaric's town.

Along with the topographic mapping, we also did an electromagnetic survey of the site at En Bas Saline. It was done with an EM31 terrain conductivity meter, which measures the conductivity of the soil. The machine passes an electrical current through the ground and measures the degree of conduction by the soil at any selected point. When there is a dense object under the ground, there will be a lower level of conductivity; where there is disturbed soil (a filled-in moat, for example), moisture collects and results in higher conductivity levels. We are hoping to locate cellars, a moat, or partial cellars or moats in this way.

The survey was done at intervals of six feet on a grid over the entire site. These results were also generated by the Surface II computer mapping program. Using this technique, we located several interesting anomalies throughout the site, which we intend to excavate as soon as we can return to En Bas Saline. Surface collection of the site has also given us clues about where the chief's and other Indians' residence areas were.

Excavations were carried out in 1984, 1985, and 1986, and attempted in 1987, located according to the results of the topographic and electromagnetic surveys and the results of Dr. Hodges's work in 1977. These excavations provided more specific information about the site's stratigraphy, time of occupation, and inhabitants, although it must be kept in mind that we have covered only a small portion of a large site. More than seven tons of earth, shell, rock, bone, and artifacts have been shipped back to the Florida Museum of Natural History, where they have been cleaned, sorted, identified, and analyzed by a team of archaeologists, zooarchaeologists, wood specialists, computer specialists, malacologists (shell specialists), and physicists.

Radiocarbon dates, thermoluminescence dates, and the presence of European items have allowed us to place the occupation of the site between about A.D. 1300 and A.D. 1500. From the kinds of European items recovered, and from the near certainty that Columbus's men introduced European diseases against which the Indians were defenseless, we suspect that the site was not occupied long into the sixteenth century.

Much of the information from the site is about the Taíno-Arawak Indians who lived there. From the few historical records that exist about these people, we know that they lived in villages of a few hundred to a thousand people and that they had a well-developed political system with chiefs and warfare. They farmed cassava (a root crop) and corn, and they used sea resources heavily. Early accounts frequently mention ritual and religious activity, which emphasized spirits represented by idols. These spirit idols, known as *Zemis*, were made of stone, shell, pottery, bone, wood, and cotton.

Our first excavations in 1984 were done near Dr. Hodges's earlier excavations, in the vicinity of the large hole he thought might have been a well. This area has proven to be the most interesting excava-

Arawak Indian pottery excavated at En Bas Saline *(this page and page 52)*.

tion at the site. It contained nearly all of the European material located, and there is clear evidence in the form of charred posts, charcoal, and burned clay daub that a large structure burned there at a high temperature. The University of Florida Materials Science Department analyzed some curious slag-like material from that area under the supervision of Dr. Dow Whitney. The analyses showed that the material was clay, chemically identical to unburned clay daub fragments found in the same area that had been burned in an extremely hot fire—so hot that the quartz in the clay had crystallized, forming a glass-like slag.

This evidence for a large, burned structure was located close to the large feature found by Dr. Hodges in 1976 that he believed to have been a well. We were able to relocate and excavate this feature and learn more about it. It is a circular hole of about 70 inches in diameter at the top and 6.5 feet deep. It was filled in about 500 years ago with earth, shell, and refuse, although the hole was also used as a grave for an infant; two and a half feet below its surface, Dr. Hodges had found an infant skeleton laid to rest with a circle of conch shells around it.

We got several radiocarbon and thermoluminescence dates from the materials filling the hole, and these provided an overall date of 510 +/- 35 years BP (or A.D. 1405–1475). This date was refined, however, by the presence well down in the hole of the teeth and a jaw fragment from a European pig (*Sus scrofa*) and a rat bone (*Rattus rattus*) identified in the Florida Museum of Natural History's Zooarchaeological Lab under the supervision of Dr. Elizabeth Wing.

Both of these species were unknown in the New World before the arrival of Columbus, and they leave us no doubt that this hole was filled in after 1492. If these animals were associated with La Navidad, they would have to have arrived on Columbus's ships and not been introduced later through other European contact. The most likely source of such later contact was with the town of Puerto Real, which, as we noted, was founded in 1503 less than a mile from Guacanacaric's village.

It is not difficult to explain the presence of the rat. Rats are age-old shipboard passengers, and they were certainly on Columbus's vessels. The pig was more of a problem, because it was represented by a tooth, which is unlikely to have reached the New World in anything but the head of a live pig. There is no manifest or list of goods from the *Santa Maria*, but it is well known that Spanish vessels of that era almost always carried live animals to provide the officers with fresh meat.

To help us interpret our specific pig and rat, we solicited the help of Dr. Jonathan Ericson of the University of California at Irvine, who analyzed the strontium and lead isotopes in the bones. Soils in specific parts of the world have characteristic patterns of such isotopes as strontium, nitrogen, carbon, and lead. Plants that grow in those soils absorb the same isotope profile, and these profiles are in turn passed along to the animals who eat the plants and reside in the bone in the original profile configuration. When the isotopes in animal bones are identified, they can be compared to known soil isotope profiles to suggest where the animal grew up. Analyses to date show an Old World pig, with stable isotope elements most closely matching those of Seville, Spain. This information supports our notion that the pig came to Hispaniola from the Old World rather than from another, later site in the Caribbean.

The Old World origins of the pig also suggest that it came with Columbus, since few Old World pigs would have been present at Puerto Real. Documents of the era are specific about the population explosion of pigs in Hispaniola within five years of the establishment of La Isabela in 1493. Columbus brought pigs on his second voyage, and they multiplied so rapidly that they became a nuisance. Licenses were issued in 1508 to hunt them down because they were such garden pests, so it is unlikely that they would have been imported at great expense from Spain even in 1503, when they were so abundant in Hispaniola at that time.

The analysis of animal and plant remains—often recovered through chemical separation of soil—has provided the best evidence for European presence at En Bas Saline in the late fifteenth century. Only 18 European artifacts dating to the era of Columbus have been found; they include pottery, glass, and metal fragments. Although these represent only about .001 percent of the artifacts from the site, they establish that the site was indeed occupied around 1492. Their small number and limited variety suggest that European presence was not intense or of long duration and probably occurred early after 1492.

This last suggestion is supported by the fact that traditional Taíno-Arawak crafts and material culture had not yet been eliminated by disease-related population losses when the European animals and plants were deposited at the site. We can support this fact with the large quantities of elaborate and highly sophisticated pottery found at the site in post-1492 contexts, as well as such ritual and ornamental items as Zemi spirit symbols, tobacco pipes, lip

plugs, pendants, and tubes for ingesting snuff or hallucinogens. The presence of these items suggests that European presence or influence at En Bas Saline took place early in the historic period.

Excavations in other parts of the site, away from the mounded area in the central plaza, have contributed information about housing, cooking, and trash disposal among the Indians. Small circular houses were built of posts and thatch, although in the central mound area the structure—the possible cacique's house—seems to have been made of wattle and daub. Hearths were located near some of the structures, and trash was found both scattered around them and in pits.

In 1985 we excavated the flat central part of the site in the vicinity of a stratigraphic and electromagnetic anomaly, hoping that it was a moat. It turned out to be a series of deep, straight-sided trenches, packed with ash, pottery, bones, food remains, and shells. Radiocarbon data indicate that the holes were filled in about A.D. 1300. We cannot yet determine the function with confidence, but the contents suggest that they might have been a communal cooking pit. A great quantity of animal bone and shells represents the diet of the people of En Bas Saline: a wide variety of fishes, lizards, turtles, snakes, and small rodents. The use of cassava, the staple horticultural crop, is reflected in the presence of clay and stone griddles, rough coral graters, and tiny chert microliths, probably set into wood and used for grating the hard cassava roots.

Continuing detailed analysis of the artifacts and faunal and floral remains from the site will provide a basis for a better understanding of late fifteenth-century Taíno cultural patterns and the changes in them after contact.

Meanwhile, the search for La Navidad will continue, and we believe that En Bas Saline is a strong candidate for that site. The evidence for suggesting that it is indeed the town of Guacanacaric, and therefore the host village for La Navidad, is strong.

1. The site is located precisely where independent and detailed documentary research by Morison and others suggested that La Navidad should be, suggestions made well before the presence of the Indian town at En Bas Saline was known.

2. Documentary accounts make it clear that La Navidad was in or adjacent to a large Indian town occupied by a chief, and there has been no other such town located in the possible area within which La Navidad could have been located.

3. The size and layout of the site, the mangrove growth patterns, and relationships of the site to the shore correspond closely to information in the Columbus accounts.

4. Radiocarbon, thermoluminescence, animal bone, and artifact

dates show that the site was occupied from about A.D. 1300 to A.D. 1500 and that people were living there in 1492.

5. The tooth of a pig from Spain suggests that the animal was unloaded from a ship at La Navidad, almost certainly before 1503 when Puerto Real was founded. No ships other than those of Columbus are known to have unloaded at La Navidad, which was obviously not a good port.

Although we cannot state that we have, in fact, located the fortress of La Navidad itself, we have located some promising areas within the Indian town. The most promising of these is the central mound with the large hole, the large burned structure, and the European materials, where we intend to continue excavations.

We will also continue the recovery and analysis of archaeological remains that should inform us about the Taíno-Arawak Indians who first encountered the European intruders—perhaps a more fitting quincentenary focus than even Columbus. The arrival of Europeans in 1492 at La Navidad marked the beginning of the end for the Taíno Indians, whose culture was extinct within 30 years. To observe that event, we could do little better than to try and reconstruct the lives and culture of those unfortunate native Americans.

Eugene Lyon

4 / *Niña,* Ship of Discovery

When I first opened the *Libro de Armadas* in Seville, in Spain's Archive of the Indies, its contents were daunting: more than 400 pages of accounts, ration lists, and shipping information written in an early and difficult script. I put the bundle of documents aside but was compelled to return and read it in detail; it contained information on fleets sent from Spain to the New World during the period 1495–1500, soon after Christopher Columbus's second voyage.

Two-thirds through the *Libro,* I found a receipt by Pedro Francés, master of a caravel (a small sailing ship). It described how, in preparation for a voyage to Hispaniola in 1498, he had received the vessel along with its sails, rigging, tackle, and other equipment. The name of the caravel was given as the *Niña,* also known as *Santa Clara.* Suddenly, the question blazed: could this be Christopher Columbus's favorite ship, the historic *Niña?* Did this document refer to the staunch little caravel that brought the Admiral of the Ocean Sea safely home from his momentous sea voyage in 1492?

Were there other documents in the *Libro* that could tell us how the *Niña* looked? There has been much conjecture about the appearance of Columbus's vessels, and several markedly different sailing models of the *Niña* have been built over the years. Francés's inven-

Caravels in port are shown in a 1594 engraving. Eugene Lyon's research indicates that the *Niña* had four sails rather than three.

tory might yield important new clues about the *Niña*. The description on the receipt seem to point to a kind of sailing rig quite different from that on any of the reconstructions made to date.

The *Libro* proved to be an archival treasure trove. On other pages I found Columbus's contract with the shipmaster of 1498, the manifest for the cargo loaded on the *Niña* in that year, and lists of passengers who sailed aboard.

Information contained in the pages of the *Libro* and in the vast Columbus literature published over the years allows us to reconstruct *Niña*'s story. Through the mists of almost 500 years we can glimpse this small but sturdy ship of discovery. And with her story comes new information on Columbus's voyages and the nature of Spain's initial attempts to explore and settle the New World.

The *Niña* was first mentioned in the summer of 1492 beside the River Tinto in Andalusia, Spain. The town of Palos was required by royal decree to furnish two caravels for Columbus's first voyage, and it was there that the outfitting of ships for the expedition took place. *Niña*'s owner was Juan Niño, a resident of nearby Moguer, where the caravel had been built. *Niña* was a nickname meaning "little girl"; the ship was more formally called *Santa Clara*, after the patroness saint of Moguer.

Caravels were first used by the Portuguese in their discovery of the Madeira and Azores islands and their explorations along the African coasts. Spanish shipbuilders adopted and modified the caravel type from those Portuguese vessels. The ships were small, light, and nimble, usually rigged with lanteen (triangular) sails that made them ideal for work in coastal waters.

Columbus's famous fleet—*Niña*, *Pinta*, and *Santa Maria*— sailed from Palos on August 1492. Captain Vicente Yáñez Pinzón of that town commanded the *Niña*, whose crew also included Juan Niño. A brother, Martín Alonzo Pinzón, captained the *Pinta*. The fleet sailed to the Canary Islands, where the *Niña* apparently underwent a change of sails from full lanteen to partial square sails in anticipation of the ocean voyage.

Niña soon proved herself seaworthy, a quality commented on by Columbus. After landfall on Guanahani (San Salvador) in the Bahamas, *Niña* and *Pinta* were often sent ahead of the slower and more clumsy *Santa Maria* on scouting duties. When the *Santa Maria* sank at Hispaniola, Columbus sailed home aboard *Niña*.

On the return voyage, the caravel was crowded with her own crew and those survivors of the *Santa Maria* who had not remained at the settlement of La Navidad. In February 1493, in mid-Atlantic, *Niña* was struck by a severe Atlantic storm, but the seaworthy vessel weathered it and returned them first to Portugal, then back to the Rio Tinto near Palos. That first journey ended 15 March 1493.

Columbus's second voyage, in contrast to the first, featured a large flotilla. Among the seventeen ships and caravels that left Cadiz in September 1493 was the faithful *Niña*.

Some historians believe, however, that the first-voyage *Niña* and the second-voyage *Niña* were not the same, that there may have been two. I believe that the evidence, including some documents from the *Libro de Armadas*, points to their being the same ship. There is certainly little doubt of our ability to trace *Niña* from 1493 onward.

When Columbus arrived once again in Hispaniola, he found no survivors at La Navidad. Moving eastward he founded another town, Isabella. He then purchased two of the caravels in the fleet and sent the rest of the vessels home. Columbus still sought the realms of Asia and sailed westward in April 1494 upon his next expedition of discovery in his small caravel fleet. Its lead ship was the *Niña.*

After discovering Jamaica, Columbus coasted to Cuba, where, "aboard the Caravel *Niña,* also named *Santa Clara,*" on 12 June he made the fleet's crewmen swear that they also believed they had reached the mainland of Asia.

Seriously ill, Columbus returned with his little fleet to Isabella. In the fall of 1495, Juan Aguado's fleet, sent out with supplies for Columbus, was caught with three other caravels in Isabella's open roadstead by what may have been a hurricane. Six caravels were destroyed; only the sturdy *Niña* rode out the storm. From the wood of the other vessels, another caravel, *Santa Cruz,* was built. Under Columbus's command, the two caravels made the passage back to Spain, where they were refitted.

The *Niña* had yet another adventure: under the command of master Alonso Medel, *Niña* was sent by Bishop Juan de Fonseca (and without Columbus's approval) on a commercial voyage to Rome during the Lenten season of 1497. On the return journey, a fleet of six French corsairs captured the little caravel as she left Sardinia. The pirates stripped the ship, removed her crew, and anchored for the night. But Medel bribed three of the corsairs with 30 gold ducats to let the Spaniards escape. Diving into the sea, they swam to the *Niña,* woke the sleeping French guards, and pushed them overboard. Then they cut the anchor lines and set sail for Spain. Columbus, furious at this misadventure, filed a lawsuit to reclaim the *Niña,* successfully recovered her, and sent her, together with the *Santa Cruz,* for final preparation for another Indies voyage.

Much of the earlier enthusiasm in Spain for New World expeditions had evaporated by then, and it took Columbus almost two years to overcome the obstacles he met in preparing his third voyage. At last Ferdinand and Isabella assented, and in October 1497, they ordered funds made available out of revenues owed them by two Italian merchant-bankers, Pantaleon Italico and Martin Centurion.

Concerned by the delay, Columbus decided to dispatch an early contingent of two caravels in order to send much-needed supplies to Hispaniola. For this purpose he assigned *Niña* and *Santa Cruz* and

commissioned Pedro Fernández Coronel to serve as fleet commander.

But there came an immediate crisis. Many of Columbus's seamen, unpaid for past services, had told him that they would not go to the Indies unless they were paid. The king and queen were unable to help any further. Fearing that he would find no crews for the voyage, Columbus solved the problem by using some of the money he carried for expenses in Hispaniola to pay his crews, hoping to make restitution from gold that might be found in the Indies. The *Libro de Armadas* describes how Columbus paid Coronel and others their back pay from the 1493 voyage.

As Columbus prepared for his third voyage, it continued to be urgently necessary to supply colonists in Hispaniola. He was, moreover, permitted to take 330 additional salaried colonists to the Indies. The first contingent of vessels, consisting of *Niña* and *Santa Cruz*, was to leave early in 1498. The outlines for the funding of the enterprise were contained in his Crown contract of April 1497. Monies due the Crown from Italico and Centurion were to be remitted to Fonesca and Columbus to underwrite the expedition (Fonesca handled Columbus's account for the Crown).

The *Libro* discloses more information about these two caravels than others listed because *Niña* and *Santa Cruz* were jointly owned by the Crown and Columbus. Thus shipmaster Pedro Francés had to sign, acknowledging receipt of the *Niña*'s hull, masts, yards, and rigging with her other accoutrements. The *Libro* provides a great deal of information about the *Niña*. Certainly she was small: I calculate about 67 feet in length on the weather deck, with a beam of 21 feet, a draft of just under 7 feet, and a lading capacity of 58–60 *toneladas* (about 52 tons). She had a bowsprit, and two *botalos* (boomlets), one fore and one aft. For the 1498 voyage, *Niña*'s sails were a fore, main, mizzen and countermizzen, with two bonnets for the main and a bonnet for the foresail. She also carried another set of sails: a new main and foresails, with new bonnets for each. These sails meant the caravel had four masts, not the two or three previously thought.

She featured six shrouds on each side of the mainmast, four on each side of the foremast, and for the mizzen three per side. *Niña* loaded 2,517 pounds of new hemp rigging line for cables, sheet-ropes, tie-runners, bowlines, and lifts. Her rigging also featured preventer-sheets, main-runners, pendants, and dead-eye lanyards. She had rope ladders and 68 pulleys and blocks of varying sizes.

Niña's major weapons were listed as ten *bombardas*, with breech-blocks, wedges, and a hammer for the wedges. Bombarda could be the breech-loaded lombard, but the description went on to include the word *molynetes*. The question then is whether these were lombards

The *Niña* is rebuilt under the masterful hands of Robert Leavy, using information from the *Libro de Armadas* and other sources.

or falconets. Clearly the answer had implications for ship size, as the siting and serving of ten lombards would require substantial deck space. The question was at least partly solved by finding the word *molynete* in a description of later sixteenth-century falconets (translated by Paul Hoffman of Louisiana State University), giving the impression of a turning cylinder or yoke. It appears therefore that the guns were swivel guns, to be fitted upon the gunwales. A 1496 enactment had required each caravel to carry 10 bombardas on each Indies journey. *Niña* also carried 80 lead balls for the guns, 54 long and 20 short lances, a template for measuring the balls, and 100 pounds of gunpowder. She was equipped with axe, adze, saw, and caulking iron; she carried one large and two small anchors, a boathook, and a funnel.

On her 1498 journey, the *Niña* sailed laden with wheat and flour, wine, sea biscuit, olive oil, garbanzos, cheese, salt pork, vinegar, fatback, sardines, and raisins (see list below). Some of the cargo was carried for the Crown's account, some for individuals.

Her human cargo and that of her sister caravel, *Santa Cruz*, was comprised of colorful individuals. The fleet was commanded by one of Columbus's most trusted associates, Pedro Fernández Coronel, who had served the admiral as a regent on his council at Isabella in 1494 and as *alguacil* on Hispaniola. The two caravels carried 90 persons on royal salary, including 18 farmers, 50 crossbowmen, and a surgeon. Ten convicted murderers, freed in compliance with a Crown decree that allowed such persons to emigrate to the Indies, went aboard. Two of them, Maria and Catalina, were Gypsy women.

The *Libro* provides other information about the *Niña*. Cooking aboard was done in large copper kettles over a fire or fires kindled with vineshoots (*gavillas de sarmientos*) and fed with olivewood. Between fire and cookery, with garlic, fatback, olive oil, salt meat, beans, and bread baking, the *Niña* must have been a fragrant ship to leeward. Brought from as far as Estremadura, washed with heated lye from the Triana soapworks, the pieces of fatback were rubbed with red clay and bran to create a protective crust, marked with an iron, and packed in panniers to load aboard the caravels.

The *Niña* and *Santa Cruz*, sent on ahead of the other ships, successfully crossed the Atlantic and arrived in Hispaniola. Columbus followed, sailing from Spain on 30 May with his second contingent of ships. On that voyage he first discovered the mainland of South America (near Trinidad), then sailed back northward, eventually arriving at Santo Domingo in Hispaniola, where among other troubles, he found a rebellion. On 28 September 1499, Columbus had to sign a humiliating settlement with the rebel leader. Shortly after, on 9 October, according to a marginal note in the *Libro de Armadas*, Co-

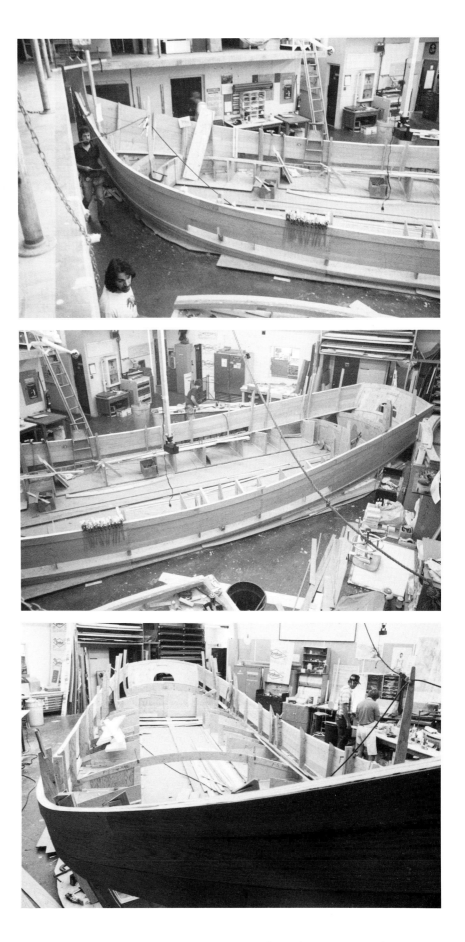

At the Florida Museum of Natural History, carpenters and preparators use Leavy's model of the *Niña* to construct a two-thirds scale replica for the *First Encounters* exhibit. They faced a problem that the original shipbuilders never had: their *Niña* must come apart in sections small and light enough so the ship can travel with the exhibit.

lumbus ordered Pedro Francés to turn the *Niña* over to one Diego Ortiz. This transaction may have been a forced sale, for the admiral later complained that he had put to sea at Christmas 1499 with only one caravel. At that point the *Niña* disappears from the archival records.

Niña, Columbus's ship of discovery that made three voyages to the New World, was among the smallest of the caravels. But her ability to cross the Atlantic was proven. Her sturdy seaworthiness is undeniable. Perhaps the only thing more remarkable than these caravels were the men who sailed them.

Cargo of the *Niña,* on the 1498 Voyage
Year of 98
Copy of a Receipt which Pedro Francés master of the caravel *Niña* named *Santa Clara,* made of the things which he received in his caravel

The things which I, Pedro Francés, master of the caravel *Niña,* received—by order of the King and of the Queen, Our Lords, to carry in the said caravel to the islands of the Indies, which things I will give there to whoever, by Their Highnesses' [order] should receive them—are the following:

> Wheat: 34 *cahizes*
> Wine: 31 pipes
> Biscuit: 100 *quintals*
> Olive oil: 2 *cuartos de tonel* (or tun)
> Garbanzos: 2 *cahizes*
> Cheeses: 665, which weighed 2377 lb.
> Flour: 18 large burlap sacks, which weighed 4375 lb.
> Salt pork: 12 pannier-baskets and one pannier-basket
>   of garlic, which all weighs 2450 lb.
> Oakum: 1 large bale; it weighed 182 lb.
> Tuns: 3 for water
> Mats: 21, for the hold-compartments

The things which I also received, in addition to those of the King, which are of some private persons, are the following:

Of Valdenebro
> Wine: Three pipes
> Olive oil: a *cuarto de tonel* and 80 *botijas,* filled
> Wine: also 3 *cuartos de tonel*
> Vinegar: 1 *cuarto de tonel*
> Pig's feet: 3 pannier-baskets which weighed 625 lb.
> Cheese: 1,500 lb.

Garlic: 1 sack
Olive oil: 1 barrel of 400 lb.
Beans and garbanzos: 6 *fanegas*

For Rafael Cataño
 Biscuit: 1 pannier-basket and 2 small barrels,
  which all weighed 150 lb.

For Bartolomé de Mesta
 Biscuit, cheese and fatback: 100 lb.

Gil Delgadillo
 Cheese: 3 pannier-baskets; 346 lb.
 Sardines: 1 *cuarto* (*de tonel*)

Diego Descobar
 Sardines: 1 tun
 Cheese and raisins: one-half tun
 He also carried 45 (?) bundles of willow-withes

[Signed and dated 23 January 1498 in Seville]

Note: The cargo totaled 52.84 *toneles machos* (about 46.7 tons), close to the cargo carried by the caravel on her trip to Rome the year before. Two pipes equaled one *tonel*; with wheat, barley and other similar commodities, two *cahizes* equaled one *tonel*. *Cuartos* and *barriles* were smaller containers than the tun. *Niña's* supplies were largely paid for by the Spanish Crown and sent as supplies for the colonists on Hispaniola. Private persons were permitted to send their own shipments to the Indies aboard.

Charles R. Ewen

Maurice W. Williams

5 / Puerto Real: Archaeology of an Early Spanish Town

ocated on the northwest coast of Hispaniola, Puerto Real was one of the earliest Spanish colonial settlements in the New World. Founded in 1504, just over a decade after Columbus's first voyage of discovery, the town is one of only a few such early settlements in the Caribbean that has been systematically studied by archaeologists. Such sites provide the opportunity to understand the initial Spanish adaptations to the New World and the development of a Hispanic-American colonial tradition.

At Puerto Real it is possible to identify the elements of the Columbian exchange. What beliefs and behavior and habits were brought from the Old World to the New? How did the Spanish colonists adapt those traits to new social, economic, and environmental conditions? Combining historical archival research with archaeological excavations is generally an ideal way to study the Columbian exchange. The Spanish Crown kept meticulous records of all its activities, including its colonization efforts in the Caribbean. The documentary record for the settlement of Hispaniola during the sixteenth century is fairly extensive. Archival materials relative to Puerto Real are included in this documentary paper trail first assembled by Dr. William Hodges of Limbé, Haiti. Many were recently dis-

Puerto Real, established in 1504, was located just south of La Navidad. In the eighteenth century a French geographer evidently found the ruins and thought the site was La Navidad. When it was rediscovered by William Hodges in 1974, nothing remained above ground level.

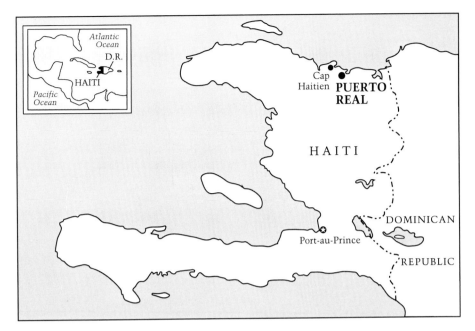

covered in Spain's Archive of the Indies by Eugene Lyon, who has interpreted them for archaeological use.

To understand the history of Puerto Real—why it was founded, why it was neglected by the Crown and then forcibly evacuated less than a century after its founding—it is necessary to look beyond the city limits. To put events at Puerto Real in their proper perspective, it is essential to know what was happening elsewhere in the Caribbean during the sixteenth century.

Columbus's second voyage (in 1493) was made specifically to settle the island of Hispaniola, and he was successful, after a fashion, founding the town of La Isabela. His third and fourth voyages were exploratory ventures that moved well beyond his colony on Hispaniola. If Columbus was adept at exploration, he was equally inept at the administration of what he had discovered. In his absence first his brother and then others governed Hispaniola. The Columbus family was ultimately removed, and the Crown appointed Nicolas Ovando as governor.

It was during Ovando's governorship (1502–1509) that the complete subjugation of the island occurred. Spanish administrative sway was extended throughout the entire island through Ovando's founding of 15 towns. This act served a twofold purpose; it satisfied the royal instruction to establish proper new settlements on the island, and it ensured Spanish control of the natives. Puerto Real was one of these new communities.

Around 1504, Rodrigo de Mexía, a lieutenant of Governor Ovando, led a group of settlers to the north coast of Hispaniola to found one of the new cities. The location chosen for this northern

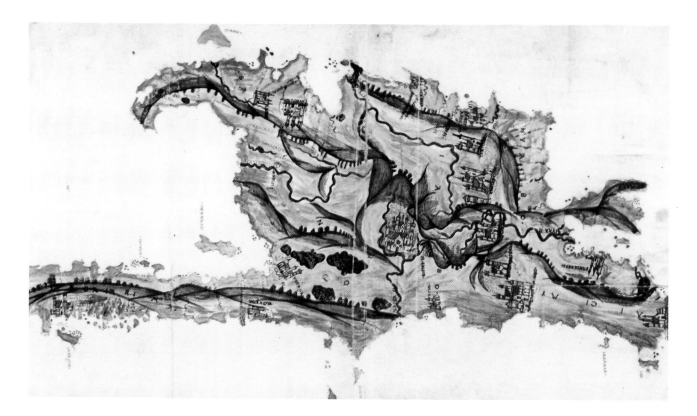

The towns established by Spain on the island of Hispaniola in the early sixteenth century are shown on this map drawn in 1508. Puerto Real is represented by an upside-down town symbol in the northwest part of the island. Its name (also upside down) is written under the symbol.

settlement, christened Puerto Real (Port Royal) because of its excellent riverine harbor, was close to the site of La Navidad. This time, instead of being massacred by the native inhabitants, the Spanish turned the tables.

How was the settlement of Hispaniola accomplished so quickly? When the Spanish came to the Caribbean, they did not find an unpopulated, fertile land waiting to be developed by industrious Europeans but rather a land already populated by hundreds of thousands of native peoples. When the Spanish began to exploit their discoveries through mining, farming, and other activities, they did little of the actual physical work themselves. It was left to be done by the native inhabitants through the systems of *repartimiento* and *encomienda*. The repartimiento was essentially a division of spoils consisting of land and Indians given to the colonists. Though technically free, the native Arawaks on Hispaniola were obliged to provide the colonists with labor and services. The second practice, encomienda, was in theory more benign. It was supposed to be a reciprocal relationship with the natives providing a limited amount of labor in return for protection and Christian instruction. However, both systems were thin disguises for de facto slavery. Forced labor and disease cut a swath of death through the native population.

Puerto Real was originally envisioned as a mining colony. The Spanish hunt for gold prompted a brief flurry of mining activity in the mountainous hinterland near the town, but no gold was found and existing copper deposits proved disappointing. The area around Puerto Real did, however, serve as a source of labor for the more productive mining districts elsewhere on the island.

The town's early years were its best. In the first decade of the sixteenth century, Puerto Real was a thriving community of about 100 households. In 1508 the Crown granted the town its own coat of arms, a golden ship sailing a wavy sea on a field of blue, recalling the arrival of Christopher Columbus in the area in 1492.

The decline in native population coupled with a rise in demand for labor prompted slave raids on nearby islands. To the north, the Bahamas were completely depopulated of their Lucayan inhabitants by slave raiders and disease. More than 40,000 Indians were unloaded at the two ports servicing these slaving operations, Puerto Real and Puerto Plata to the east. As these enslaved Indians also succumbed to disease and harsh labor conditions, African slaves were brought in. The end of the Lucayan slave trade about 1514 signaled the beginning of a general decline in the towns on the north coast of Hispaniola.

At Puerto Real, as at other early Caribbean settlements, Spaniards formed only a comparatively small part of the population in the first decade of the sixteenth century. The repartimiento of 1514 illustrates the imbalance of the population at Puerto Real. There were only 20 *vecinos* (registered male colonists); three had Castilian wives and two had native wives. Also mentioned are 18 other residents who held Indians; the status of these other residents is uncertain, but the adult Spanish population must have numbered less than 50. On the other hand, 839 Indians are listed, 540 of whom were Indios de Servicio, part of the original encomienda Indians of the island. The other Indians were classified as *naborias* or lifetime serfs. These Indians were not even technically free and may have been Lucayans taken in slave raids. Spain's Caribbean successes were built on the backs and bodies of the native peoples.

A continuing decline in the economy of the northern coast of Hispaniola prompted the abandonment of the neighboring town of Llares de Guahaba, and its citizens moved to Puerto Real. For a brief time, the Hispanic population may have increased.

The eventual failure of the northern towns corresponds with the economic decline of the island as a whole, which can be traced directly to the Spanish desire to obtain silver and gold. After the initial frenzy to find gold on Hispaniola had died down, the island at first became a base for further exploration. But when vast mineral wealth was discovered on the Central American mainland, a real population drain began on Hispaniola. The mainland gold rush did more than just draw off manpower; it also diverted shipping from the less profitable island ports.

The convoy system of shipping, first implemented in 1542, was designed to ensure that precious metals from Central and South America arrived safely in Spain. All ships were required to sail in convoy and could visit only approved ports on the convoy's route. Puerto Real was well away from the Carrera de las Indias, as the route of fleets was called, and was not a port where fleets anchored. The citizens were thus denied access to goods brought by the fleet, and Puerto Real and the other neglected island ports turned to the *rescate* (illegal trade) for goods.

Meanwhile Puerto Real had to contend with other problems on land. A smallpox epidemic that swept the island in 1518–1519 nearly wiped out the Arawak Indian population, and Puerto Real came to depend more upon imported African labor. So great was the demand for labor that by 1520 African slaves had become the dominant element in the work force.

In 1519 there was a revolt of the remaining native peoples around the environs of Puerto Real, and they joined the larger revolt led by the cacique Enrique. As late as 1532, hostilities persisted when a vecino, his wife, two children, and 14 of his Indian slaves were killed. Peace was finally achieved the following year, and in an attempt by Spain to strengthen its hold on the north coast, 60 new colonists arrived in Santo Domingo to repopulate Puerto Real and Monte Christi, a town to the east.

By this time the economy of the Caribbean islands in general was based upon the trade in cowhide. Leather was much in demand in Europe, and the Indies had an abundance of cattle. The mercantile policies of Spain decreed that all colonial commerce, including hides, should be conducted exclusively with the mother country. But with no access to the Spanish fleet, Puerto Real's citizens who had cowhides to market had no way to sell them. Nor could bulky hides compete with silver and gold for the limited cargo space of the fleets, if access could be gained.

Such was the paradox that confronted the citizens of Puerto Real. They could obey the law and do without even the barest necessities, or they could trade with smugglers and enjoy European goods unavailable to them by other means. And since some smugglers were not above transacting business at gunpoint, often the choice would be to trade with the corsairs or risk having the town sacked and burned. In 1566 the French corsair Jean Bontemps entered Monte Christi, Puerto Real, and La Yaguana. He seized 12 vessels and burned Puerto Real. It is not surprising that most of the hides produced at Puerto Real found their way into the illegal trade system.

The chief perpetrators of the rescate changed throughout the sixteenth century. Prior to the mid-sixteenth century most of the for-

Olive jars are ubiquitous on Spanish colonial archaeological sites in the New World, including Puerto Real. The cardboard boxes of the day, they were initially used to ship olives, olive oil, and other products and were often recycled or used in other ways.

eign interlopers were Portuguese who dealt mainly in slaves. The French, present as early as 1535, were heavily involved in smuggling after 1548. John Hawkins, the renowned corsair, and other Englishmen were operating in the islands after 1560. The Dutch did not become important in the rescate until the end of the century, but their presence eventually forced the abandonment of the western half of Hispaniola.

Meanwhile Puerto Real was suffering from both natural and economic disasters. An earthquake rocked the north coast of Hispaniola in 1562, followed in 1566 by the incident with the French corsairs. In that year, Spain ordered a cessation of registry of ships at Puerto Real due to its smuggling activities. Puerto Real sued and had its registry temporarily restored, but this move only delayed the inevitable.

Ironically, it was not the loss of revenue that worried the Spanish Crown. The economic importance of the hide trade was negligible: Kenneth Andrews has noted that "hides were the virtual offal of the Indies, left for Lutherans and mulattoes to haggle over by Spaniards occupied with transactions of a higher order—sugar, dyes, and precious metals." Rather, the main concern of the Crown was the presence of these foreign interlopers, not the hides they diverted from Spain. They presented threats to Spain's New World empire.

In the ports of northern and western Hispaniola most of the population was involved in smuggling. Spain could not stop the smuggling (her own Crown-appointed town officials were heavily involved), but she was unable to supply these outpost settlements with access to adequate shipping.

In 1578, the settlement of Bayaha was established midway between Puerto Real and Monte Christi and forcibly populated with the citizens of those two towns, in the belief that it would be easier to stop smuggling at a single point than all along the coast. But it was not the case, and smuggling continued with the collusion of the town officials. Spain's ultimate response was the depopulation of the western third of the island in 1605, which left it open to French settlement.

Archaeological Investigations

Puerto Real, abandoned in 1578, was rediscovered in 1974, nearly 400 years after its abandonment, by Dr. William Hodges, a medical missionary and historian who has lived in Haiti for many years. He has studied intensively the history of the north coast of Haiti, combining his research with archaeological investigations. While following up leads concerning the location of La Navidad, Columbus's 1492 settlement, Hodges came across an area rich in sixteenth-century artifacts.

Mapping and excavations at Puerto Real uncovered the central cathedral and pinpointed a number of buildings associated with individuals of various social status.

The cathedral must have been quite elaborate. It had three stone gargoyles on its western side. The two end ones served as drain spouts; this one, in the center, was intentionally stopped up so it would not work. Perhaps the cascade of water was annoying.

His discovery proved to be Puerto Real, the only known settlement in that area at that time.

After notifying the Haitian government, Hodges contacted Charles Fairbanks, University of Florida archaeologist, who also recognized the significance of the site. Field investigations by Hodges and Raymond Willis, then a graduate student, began in 1979.

The first field season located the central cathedral of Puerto Real, prompting a larger field effort in 1980. The cathedral was completely excavated, the cemetery was discovered, and efforts were begun to delineate the site and identify activity areas within it. Exploratory efforts also identified outlying areas, which were investigated during the third field season.

In the 1981 season, work was done at three different parts of the town. One, located next to the cathedral, was a thick-walled building which might have been a tower or secure warehouse located on the town plaza. In the second was uncovered part of the early sixteenth-century residence of a Puerto Real citizen of high status. The third yielded crude, locally produced pottery and a large amount of cattle bone, refuse from skinning and activities to make tallow and other cattle by-products, dramatic evidence for the cowhide trade.

The following year Kathleen Deagan, of the Florida Museum of Natural History, assumed direction of the project. A complete topographic map of the site was made and a systematic sampling of artifacts across the town completed by museum archaeologist Maurice Williams. Computer analysis produced a map of the town delineating local Spanish residential and civic areas and native houses.

The topographic map shows features such as an eighteenth-century French canal that runs east to west across the center of the site. The former bed of the Fosse River is also apparent. Other more subtle changes in relief indicate the remains of masonry buildings. Depressions associated with some concentrations of masonry material probably reflect the dismantling and robbing of stone from buildings and their foundations by French planters, a practice known to have occurred at the site during the eighteenth century.

The main part of Puerto Real seems to measure about 540 yards north-south and 330–435 yards east-west. Although it is not possible to identify with confidence those areas of the town that functioned as roadways, a grid pattern extending out from the central area is likely. Such a pattern would follow Spanish city planning in the New World. Legal norms established in the second half of the sixteenth century organized towns on a grid format around the central plaza which contained public, administrative, and religious structures. Evidence indicates that this grid plan was in use at Puerto Real before it was mandated by the Spanish Crown.

Buried masonry building rubble was not distributed evenly across the site but was clearly nonrandomly clustered. Each concentration was designated a "locus," reflecting past activity probably related to a building. Our maps then could be used to identify potential individual residences and other buildings.

Another objective of the fieldwork was to examine the relationships among groups of artifacts found associated with the masonry debris loci. Were certain types of artifacts always found with other types? If so, what did this fact say about the associated building and its occupants? If the economic status of occupants of individual structures could be determined, it might be possible to delineate economically stratified neighborhoods within the town.

A factor analysis of the excavated artifacts was done to determine

Facing page: Spanish sixteenth-century majolica pottery—tin-glazed earthenware common at Spanish colonial sites—were collected by William Hodges at Puerto Real.

The distribution of artifacts recovered from the systematic coring of the site was plotted by using a SYMAPS computer program. This map shows the distribution of masonry rubble. Each concentration is probably the location of one or more Spanish structures. The same technique was used to map Spanish and non-Spanish artifacts. The resulting map of much of the town allowed archaeologists to make informed decisions about where to carry out extensive excavations.

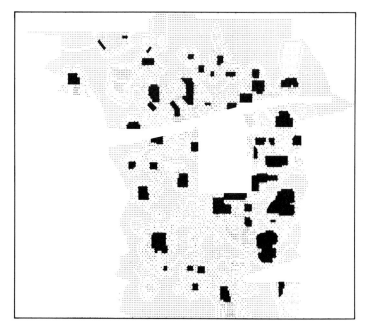

possible statistically significant correlations between different types of artifacts, and maps were generated showing the distribution of these types across the site. The results did define distinct associations of artifacts. It was possible, by correlating consistent groupings of artifacts, to identify areas associated with specific occupations and specialized craft or commercial activities. The town was beginning to emerge.

It was also possible to interpret the site more specifically by studying those artifacts that could be associated with masonry buildings. By using the data recovered from the survey and comparing it with patterns known at other Hispanic sites, three basic types of occupation were defined: the dwellings of Spanish colonists, the households of either native Arawaks or lower status individuals, possibly African slaves, and nonresidential structures, possibly areas of commercial activity. Finally, we began to look for townwide patterns. It appeared, on the basis of independently documented models from other Spanish sites, that lower, middle, and upper status neighborhoods could be delineated.

Archaeological analysis had brought Puerto Real back to life. We have an excellent idea of its layout, its neighborhoods, and even the ways its occupants adjusted Old World life-styles to New World conditions. It was at Puerto Real and other similar island towns that the unique life-styles that have developed in much of Latin America first appeared.

Charles Hudson

Chester B. DePratter

Marvin T. Smith

6 / Hernando de Soto's Expedition through the Southern United States

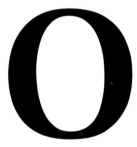On Sunday, 25 May 1539, a fleet of five ships, two caravels, and two brigantines sighted the western coast of Florida and cast their anchors. During the next four years, Hernando de Soto and his army would explore much of the interior of the southern United States, from Florida to Texas.

As an episode in the age of European New World exploration, the de Soto expedition was equal in historical significance to Francisco Vásquez de Coronado's 1540–1542 exploration of the southwestern United States. When judged in terms of the bravery, endurance, and intrepidness of the participants and the cruelty with which they treated the Indians, the expedition is comparable to those of Hernán Cortés and Francisco Pizarro. The difference was that Cortés and Pizarro succeeded in discovering complex native societies which possessed precious metals and had large populations of people who could be exploited for mining and food production; de Soto failed to discover any such societies, for in North America there were none.

The importance of the de Soto expedition, however, is not to be measured merely in terms of whether it can stand comparison with similar adventures by contemporaries. It also is important for what it reveals about the native societies that dominated the sixteenth-

Hernándo de Soto, shown as he was portrayed by a late eighteenth-century artist, was born in Spain about 1500. He went to Central America in 1514, where he received the training and experience that would serve him on the expeditions to Peru in the early 1530s and to La Florida.

De Soto's odyssey through the southern United States has always caught the public's fancy. Streets, parks, towns, counties, physiographic formations, caverns, shopping malls, and even automobiles have been named after him, but few people know the details of his excursion into La Florida and its impact on the native peoples.

century South. De Soto and his comrades were the first Europeans to encounter the large Indian chiefdoms in the interior South, and they were also virtually the last to see them at the apex of their social development.

Within a few decades after the survivors of de Soto's army made their way down the Mississippi River to the Gulf of Mexico and New Spain (Mexico), these southern chiefdoms declined and ultimately collapsed in terms of both population and social structure. Their collapse was caused in part by the economic and social impact of the de Soto expedition but even more by the introduction of germs and viruses for which the Indians had almost no immunity.

In 1559–1561 members of the Tristán de Luna expedition visited some of the towns that de Soto had visited in Alabama, Georgia, and Tennessee, and in 1566–1568 Juan Pardo visited some of the same towns that de Soto had visited in South Carolina, North Carolina, and Tennessee. In both cases, these later Spanish explorers found the Indian societies reduced in numbers and probably afflicted with serious political and economic problems.

Beyond these two expeditions, with negligible exceptions, it was over a hundred years before Europeans again visited places where de Soto had been. When they did, they found far fewer Indians than de Soto had reported, and nowhere did they find the large, bellicose chiefdoms that de Soto had encountered. In some cases the Indians had forgotten the level of social complexity that their ancestors had attained. For example, James Adair, one of the outstanding eighteenth-century authorities on southern Indians, says that those he knew insisted that in their societies the only path to status was by achievement and that there had been no "red emperors" in America. Since the Indians themselves had no memory of their ancestors' attainments, it is little wonder that in the nineteenth-century American intellectuals created an elaborate mound-builder myth to explain the existence of the great earthen mounds and finely made artifacts that dot the southern landscape—mounds and artifacts manufactured by the people of the southern chiefdoms.

The history of the South may be said to begin with the de Soto expedition, but to realize the full value of the documentary record of the expedition it is first necessary that the route he followed be reconstructed precisely. While it has been relatively easy to reconstruct the general route of the expedition, it has been difficult to do it precisely. By "precisely" we mean the identification of particular archaeological sites as having been named towns on de Soto's itinerary and the identification of the particular trails and old roads that the expedition followed.

As we have worked at figuring out where de Soto went, we have

Near Plains, Georgia, this pecan store is located close to the route of de Soto and his army, but many other places named for him are nowhere near the correct route. His trail will probably continue to be a subject of contention, much like the identification of Columbus's landing site.

come to understand that precise reconstruction of the route has required us to use five different kinds of information. *All* of these sources of information have been essential. The first and most important is the documents produced by the expedition and its aftermath, particularly the narratives by the participants. The second is modern maps that reflect accurately the topography of the South. The third is documentation from other sixteenth-century Spanish expeditions into the South, particularly those of Tristán de Luna and Juan Pardo. The fourth source has been accumulated patiently by archaeologists for several decades as they have built up an increasingly full record of late prehistoric Indian societies in the South. Finally, the fifth source is historical geography, needed because the landscape of the South has been modified drastically by human use during the past several centuries.

These five sources of information have become available to scholars at different times over 400 years. Four narratives of the de Soto expedition are known to have survived: a detailed, day-by-day account of all but the last year of the expedition by Rodrigo Ranjel, de Soto's secretary; a detailed but not thoroughly day-by-day account by an anonymous Portuguese Gentleman of Elvas; a brief but valuable recollection by Luys Hernández de Biedma, factor for the expedition; and a floridly written secondhand account by Garcilaso de la Vega, son of an Inca mother and a Spanish father, who drew upon stories told him by participants in the expedition as well as upon two written accounts, by Alonso de Carmona and Juan Coles, which are not known to have survived.

Two of these narratives were published soon after the expedition occurred. The account by the Gentleman of Elvas was published in Portugal in 1557 and that by Garcilaso de la Vega was published in Lisbon in 1605. On almost all particulars of the expedition the work of Elvas is more accurate than that of Garcilaso, but so long as only these two accounts were available it was difficult for scholars to choose between them. More than one scholar was beguiled by the superior literary quality of Garcilaso.

Rodrigo Ranjel's account was first published in Gonzalo Fernández de Oviedo's *Historia General y Natural de las Indias* in 1851, and Biedma's account (the only one whose original manuscript has survived) was first published by Buckingham Smith in 1857. When the accounts by Ranjel and Biedma became available to scholars, it became clear that Elvas's account was preferable to Garcilaso's.

For a precise reconstruction of the route, these narratives had little value until they could be used in conjunction with accurate maps. The first reasonably accurate maps of the Southeast were produced by French and English cartographers in the eighteenth century. But maps that accurately represent the topography of the Southeast—showing elevations and river systems in detail—were not available until the late nineteenth and early twentieth centuries.

A printed form of the documents from the Luna and Pardo expeditions was likewise slow to become available. The major documents of the Luna expedition were collected by Herbert I. Priestly and published in 1928. Some of Luna's men visited several of the same towns that de Soto visited, but because the Luna documents contained no day-by-day itineraries it was difficult to reconstruct accurately the travels of Luna's colony (see chapter 9).

Three brief accounts of the Juan Pardo expedition were published in the second half of the nineteenth century. Mary Ross attempted to reconstruct Pardo's route using these documents, but again they contained too little detail for an accurate reconstruction.

By the late 1930s, much of the information essential for a reconstruction of the de Soto route was available to scholars. Several had proposed reconstructions of the route before that time; in fact, the names of some Indian towns visited by de Soto appear on sixteenth-century maps. The earliest one to include such names was the 1584 map of La Florida by Abraham Ortelius and Gerónimo de Chaves. But the place-names on this and similar maps are little more than ornaments, like the trees that dot the landscape and the monsters that decorate the edges of the maps.

The first known attempt to reconstruct the entire route of the de Soto expedition was by the French cartographer Guillaume Delisle. The route is shown in his 1718 map of eastern North America, a map influential in early eighteenth-century cartography. Considering the limited information that he had at his disposal, his reconstruction of the route is an impressive achievement. His spellings of de Soto place-names suggest that Elvas's narrative was the source of his information. Ironically, Delisle located one of the large chiefdoms—the province of Cofitachequi—far more accurately than later scholars until the work of Stephen Baker and ourselves.

The most ambitious reconstruction of the de Soto route, and today the most authoritative, is the report of the U.S. de Soto Expedition Commission, published in 1939. This commission was created by a congressional resolution, approved 26 August 1935, to provide information to prepare for a celebration of the four-hundredth anniversary of the expedition. Chaired by John R. Swanton of the Smithsonian Institution, it began work in 1936 with meetings in Washington, Tampa, and Tuscaloosa, Alabama.

The commission's route begins at Tampa Bay; it goes north to the Indian province of Apalachee in and around present Tallahassee, where de Soto spent the first winter, and then through Georgia—

Looking toward 1939, the 400th anniversary of de Soto's landing, the U.S. Congress appointed a de Soto Commission to study the route. John R. Swanton of the Smithsonian Institution prepared the final report, which led to the placement of many historical markers, like this one near Bradenton, Florida. Today, aided by archaeological evidence not available to Swanton, scholars are again tracing the route.

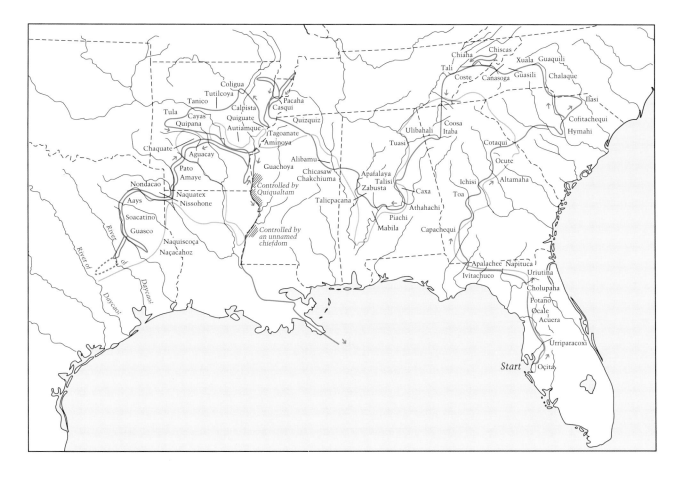

Swanton's reconstruction of the route (in light blue) failed to show the expedition crossing the Appalachian Mountains into Tennessee or reaching the complex native societies now known to have lived in northeast Arkansas. The route as reconstructed by Charles Hudson and his associates is in blue. Much archaeological data, both the distribution of artifacts and knowledge of the locations of major aboriginal populations, have been combined with geographical and historical information to produce the reconstruction. The route provides major clues to understanding the social geography of native groups in the sixteenth century.

through the provinces of Ichisi on the Flint River, Ocute on the Ocmulgee River, and Cofitachequi at Silver Bluff on the Savannah River. The route then goes north up the eastern side of the Savannah River through Xuala, located near Walhalla, South Carolina, north and west through the western tip of North Carolina, and to present Chattanooga, where the Indian town of Chiaha was located on Burns Island in the Tennessee River. From here it goes downriver to Coste on Pine Island, which is thought to have been inhabited by the Koasati in the eighteenth century, then south to Coosa in Alabama on the Coosa River, at the site where Old Coosa Town was located in the eighteenth century, and to the Tallapoosa River. The route swings far to the south in Alabama through Talisi near Selma and Mabila not far from present Mobile, then north again and west into Mississippi where the province of Chicaça is placed in the Tupelo vicinity, where the Chickasaws were located in the eighteenth and nineteenth centuries. Here de Soto spent the winter of 1540–1541.

From Chicaça the route continues west and crosses the Mississippi into Arkansas, passing through a densely populated area with many chiefdoms and then through sparser populations as the aridity of the land increases. Finally, after going as far west as Caddo Gap, Arkansas, the expedition turned back to the southeast, spending the winter of 1541–1542 on the Ouachita River, and returning to the Mississippi River in the spring. Here at the Indian town of Guachoya, which the commission places just upriver from Natchez, Mississippi, de Soto died. Now under the command of Luys de Moscoso de Alvarado, the expedition turned west again, hoping to find an overland route to New Spain. The commission route takes them as far west as the Trinity River in Texas, where the harshness of the land and the sparseness of Indian populations forced them to give up this attempt, and they returned once again to the Mississippi River, where they spent the winter of 1542–1543 building boats. In the following summer they made their escape by water.

Except for their route through Florida, which is reasonably accurate, our research indicates that the remainder of the route of the de Soto Commission is almost wholly inaccurate. In part, the commission failed to achieve an accurate reconstruction of the route because the archaeology of the late prehistoric South was only in its infancy in the 1930s. But it also erred repeatedly as a consequence of assuming that place-names were attached to the same locations in the eighteenth and nineteenth centuries as in the sixteenth. One of our earliest lessons was that using eighteenth- and nineteenth-century place-names to reconstruct the route can be misleading.

What the commission and all earlier scholars lacked was independent verification for a location of any of the towns de Soto encountered in the interior. With no firm interior points of reference, it was possible to take de Soto almost anywhere. We were able to locate firmly several interior towns by reconstructing the route of Juan Pardo's expedition of 1566–1568. In addition to the three short accounts of the expedition mentioned, we relied heavily on a remarkably detailed document, little used by earlier scholars, by Juan de la Bandera, who was notary for the second Pardo expedition. Bandera included in his report detailed information on directions, distances traveled, features of topography, the activities of Pardo and his men, and the names of Indians. With this document we were able to reconstruct Pardo's route with considerable accuracy.

Pardo visited five and possibly six of the same towns that de Soto visited, and he encountered them in the same order as de Soto had. They were Guiomae (de Soto's Aymay or Hymahi), at the junction of the Congaree and Wateree rivers; Cofitachequi, near Camden, South Carolina; Ilasi (de Soto's Ilapi), near Cheraw, South Carolina; Guaquiri (de Soto's Guaquili), near Hickory, North Carolina; Joara (de Soto's Xuala), near Marion, North Carolina; and Chiaha, on Zimmerman's Island in the French Broad River, near present Dandridge, Tennessee. In addition, the town of Cauchi, which Pardo encountered near Marshall, North Carolina, may have been the same

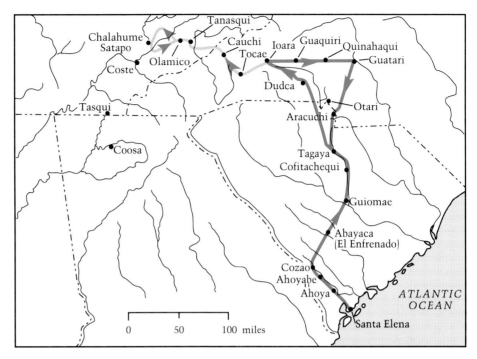

Interpretation of the route of the two Juan Pardo expeditions provided key evidence for tracing de Soto's route. Pardo's men revisited some of the same aboriginal towns that de Soto had reached nearly two decades earlier. On his first trip Pardo reached Joara at the foot of the mountains (in blue). Less than a year later he retraced his steps and then traveled farther west to Satapo (in red), just south of Knoxville.

as de Soto's Guasili. We found all of these towns located many miles to the northeast of where they were in the de Soto Commission reconstruction.

In addition to giving us interior points of reference, our experience with the Pardo expedition helped us to understand de Soto's way of operating. For example, it is clear that Pardo and his foot-soldiers (he had no cavalry) were able to travel regularly five leagues per day. By examining actual distances on modern maps we established that Pardo's men were measuring these distance using the *legua comun* (3.46 miles to the league) instead of the *legua legal* (2.63 miles to the league), the unit of measurement used by the commission. When de Soto traveled the territory, his expedition had on occasion traveled at the same rate of speed as Pardo's. De Soto had cavalry, and he regularly sent them out in advance of his main force, but the expedition could move no faster than his people on foot. In general, however, the de Soto expedition traveled a little more slowly than the Pardo expedition.

Another advantage we have is the monumental advances made by archaeologists in reconstructing the social and cultural entities that existed in the late prehistoric Southeast. Virtually all that is known about these societies has been learned in the past 50 years and much of it in the past 20, when archaeologists have been able to say where Indians were living in the sixteenth century and, equally important, where they were not. There were, for example, no people living along the middle and lower courses of the Savannah River in the middle of the sixteenth century, so the area where the

Title page of Alonso de Chaves's *Espejo de Navegantes*, ca. 1530. A compilation of information on New World navigation, including the Gulf coast of La Florida, this rutter or *derrotero* describes both Bahía Honda (Tampa Bay) and the more southerly Bahía de Juan Ponce (Charlotte Harbor). Firsthand narratives of the de Soto expedition state that the expedition landed at Bahia Honda and distinguish that harbor from Bahia de Juan Ponce, leaving no doubt that Tampa Bay was the landing site.

de Soto Commission placed the grand chiefdom of Cofitachequi was in fact vacant at the time of the expedition.

However, even though archaeologists are able to date particular prehistoric sites to within a few decades, they are seldom able to date a site accurately enough to satisfy a historian. While engaged in this research, Marvin Smith succeeded in isolating a series of sixteenth-century European artifacts which make it possible to date certain sites far more accurately than has previously been possible. One approach Smith used was to compare European artifacts found in archaeological sites in the South with similar artifacts found in sites elsewhere in the world whose precise dates of occupation are known. For example, at several sites in the South a small number of tubular blue glass beads have been found that are identical to beads found at a pearl fishery at Nueva Cadiz, Venezuela, where Spaniards lived for a short period between 1509 and 1545. And since these Nueva Cadiz beads were manufactured in Europe for only a short period of time, a site where one is found can confidently be dated to the time of the de Soto expedition.

Smith has also examined the documents of sixteenth-century exploration in the South to learn what kinds of artifacts the Spaniards carried and used, particularly what kinds of artifacts they gave and traded to the Indians. Juan Pardo, for example, gave many iron chisels and wedges to Indian chiefs, and a surprising number of them have been recovered from archaeological sites in the South.

We have reconstructed the route of the de Soto expedition from beginning to end, though we are more confident of some parts of it than of others. Some segments can be verified or improved through archaeological research, and we expect adjustments to be made for some years to come.

1539–1540

De Soto landed his men at Tampa Bay, establishing his camp at Oçita near the mouth of the Little Manatee River. They traveled northeast from this camp to the vicinity of present Lakeland, Florida, then northwest, following a trail that lay to the west of the Withlacoochee River. With difficulty they crossed the Cove of the Withlacoochee, a large wetland that includes the Withlacoochee River itself, and came to the chiefdom of Cale on the north side of the river.

Proceeding north, they passed near present Gainesville and crossed the Santa Fe River, which they spanned with a bridge, to arrive on the other side at the Indian town of Aguacaleyquen. They then turned west, crossed the Suwannee River, and reached the chiefdom of Uzachile.

Above: Sixteenth-century Spanish artifacts found in the Cove of the Withlacoochee, a large wetland region in west-central Florida, have been related to de Soto's crossing of the area in late July 1539. In testimony taken in Spain on 12 June 1560, Ana Méndez, the lone Spanish woman to survive the expedition, remembered "crossing that swamp, there being water in it in places reaching to the knee, in others to the waist, and thence over the head, which they went through with much labor in three days." It was only about six miles across the swamp, but their actual route could have been three times that distance. *Right*: A mid-nineteenth-century rendition of de Soto's landing at Tampa Bay.

Between Uzachile and the Aucilla River they crossed the first of the uninhabited buffer zones they would encounter in their travels. These zones were no-man's-lands between societies at war with each other. At the Aucilla River the expedition came to the chiefdom of Apalachee. Crossing the river, they found the main town of Apalachee, at present Tallahassee, where they spent the first winter.

1540-1541

The following spring they set out to the north. Crossing the Flint River they encountered the chiefdom of Capachequi. They traveled up the western side of the Flint, crossed it again, and arrived at a town of the chiefdom of Toa. Turning east they came to the Ocmulgee River, where they encountered the chiefdom of Ichisi, whose central town was near present Macon, Georgia.

From Ichisi they went east to the Oconee River, where they visited several towns of the chiefdom of Ocute. Departing from Ocute, still headed east, they entered the most extensive buffer zone in all their travels, crossing the Savannah, Saluda, and Broad rivers. Not until they swung south to the junction of the Congaree and Wateree rivers did they come to the town of Hymahi or Aymay, where they encountered the first people on the other side of the "desert of Ocute." The straight-line distance from Ocute to Hymahi is about 130 miles—farther, of course, by trail.

Proceeding north from Hymahi, they came to the main town of the chiefdom of Cofitachequi, in the vicinity of Camden, South Carolina. Because food was in short supply in Cofitachequi, de Soto sent a large detachment of men to a tributary town of the chiefdom, Ilapi, which was in the vicinity of Cheraw, South Carolina.

Leaving Cofitachequi and Ilapi, they headed north along the Catawba River and then west to Xuala in the vicinity of present Marion, North Carolina. From here they ascended into the Blue Ridge Mountains, going through Swannanoa Gap and down the Swannanoa River to its junction with the French Broad River at present Asheville. They followed a trail that ran near the French Broad River through the high mountains into the Tennessee Valley, where they found the Indian town of Chiaha on the north end of Zimmerman's Island in the French Broad River.

While they were resting in Chiaha, de Soto sent two soldiers north to the country of the Chiscas, who were reputed to mine copper and perhaps gold. The Chiscas lived on the upper Nolichucky River and in adjacent areas.

When de Soto left Chiaha, he followed a trail that paralleled the French Broad and Tennessee rivers to Coste, a town located on Bussel

Island in the mouth of the Little Tennessee River. From Coste they went south through the ridge and valley province to the town of Coosa, on the Coosawattee River near Carters, Georgia. Coosa was the capital town of a large chiefdom whose influence extended as far north as Chiaha.

From Coosa they headed south, through Itaba, at the Etowah archaeological site, and Ulibahali, at present Rome, Georgia. They continued down the Coosa River to a small town, which was probably the King site, and then went on to Talisi, near present Childersburg, Alabama. Talisi was the southernmost town under the sway of Coosa.

They continued south from Talisi, crossing the Tallapoosa River, and came to the chiefdom of Tascaluza. Now they swung west, following the Alabama River to Piachi and on to Mabila, a small, heavily fortified town belonging to Chief Tascaluza, located in the vicinity of the lower Cahaba River. Here, on 18 October 1540, de Soto's forces were struck by a large force of Indians in a carefully planned attack, the greatest battle fought by de Soto and his men.

From Mabila, de Soto could have led his men south to ships waiting for him at Pensacola Bay, where they could have been resupplied

Little in this early eighteenth-century portrayal, "The Hernando de Soto Expedition Encounters Chief Tascaluza," is ethnographically correct.

"De Soto's Discovery of the Mississippi," published in 1888. De Soto called it Rio Grande, the great river, but he was not its European discoverer. Earlier Spaniards had certainly located the mouth of the Mississippi River and even Lake Pontchartrain. In Chaves's *Espejo de Navegantes* (ca. 1530), the river is called Espíritu Santo and is said to be the "largest on all this coast."

or simply evacuated. But de Soto, facing ruin, wanted to continue the expedition. He set out toward the northwest, where he came to the chiefdom of Apafalaya on the Black Warrior River. The enormous Moundville site may have still been occupied at that time by a small population, but the most powerful town of the chiefdom appears to have been farther upriver.

From Apafalaya they continued northwest, entering present Mississippi and coming to the chiefdoms of Chicaça, whose towns lay in the vicinity of Tibbee Creek and its tributaries. They spent the second winter in Chicaça.

1541–1542

In the spring of 1541 they continued northwest. For eight and a half days they traveled through an uninhabited area in northern Mississippi until they came to the chiefdom of Quizquiz on the Mississippi River, a few miles south of present Memphis, in a densely populated part of the Mississippi valley. Here they built four large flatboats (*pi-*

raguas) in which they crossed the river. They went northwest to Casqui, which was probably at the Parkin archaeological site, on the St. Francis River, just below the mouth of the Tyronza River.

From Casqui they went northeast to Pacaha, the most powerful town in this region. It was located near the Mississippi River, possibly in the vicinity of Wapanocca Lake. De Soto remained here for some time and sent out two parties to explore to the north. These men certainly reached as far as northern Arkansas, and they may have penetrated just into present Missouri.

From Pacaha, de Soto turned back and crossed the St. Francis River. On the lower St. Francis they came to the large town of Quiguate, which some said was the largest town they had seen in all of La Florida.

At Quiguate, de Soto decided that their luck might change if they went to a mountainous country, where they would stand a better chance of finding precious metals. They set out toward the northwest through uninhabited, swampy country and came to the town of Coligua in the vicinity of present Batesville, at the edge of the Ozark Mountains.

From Coligua they turned southwest, reaching the River of Cayas, the Arkansas River. Here they came to the town of Tanico, where the people lived in a dispersed settlement pattern, quite different from that of the people they had just visited.

From Tanico they went to Tula, in present Yell County, which was apparently the first Caddoan-speaking town they encountered. Here, for the first time the Spaniards found plentiful supplies of bison meat and skins.

From Tula they headed south and then turned back to the east where they followed along the Ouachita River. Leaving the Ouachita and continuing east, they came again to the Arkansas River, where they spent the third winter at the town of Autiamque, a few miles downriver from present Little Rock.

1542–1543

When spring came, de Soto led his men down the Arkansas River to the Mississippi, where they found the chiefdom of Guachoya and where de Soto died of illness.

Moscoso assumed command. The main object of the expedition now was to find a way back to New Spain, though the hope still flickered that they might come upon a wealthy Indian land along the way. Thus their first attempt was overland. In early summer 1542 they left Guachoya, heading northwest, crossing through Arkansas to Chaguate in the vicinity of Arkadelphia, then skirting the southern

Ouachita Mountains. They came to the province of Naguatex in the Great Bend region of the Red River. Like the people of Tula the Naguatex were Caddoan-speaking.

From the Red River they traveled generally southwest, passing through several Indian territories (Nissohone, Lacane, Aays, and Soacatino) and coming finally to the chiefdom of Guasco on the Neches River. From Guasco, Moscoso continued toward the southwest, where he sent out a small party of cavalry. They came upon some people who possessed hardly any corn. These people lived on the River of Daycao, probably the Trinity River. The Spaniards captured some of these Indians and brought them back, but none of their Indian interpreters could understand their language.

Because they knew that they would not be able to procure enough food if they continued in the direction they were going and that they would not be able to communicate with the Indians beyond the Trinity River, they decided to return to the Mississippi River, build boats, and attempt to escape to New Spain by water.

They retraced their route and spent the fourth winter at Aminoya on the bank of the Mississippi River, where they built seven brigantines. On 2 June 1543, they set out downriver. For two days they were attacked day and night by a fleet of large canoes belonging to the chiefdom of Quigualtam. A fleet from the next chiefdom downriver took over the attack for two more days. After that, with the domains of the large chiefdoms behind them, they continued without harassment.

On 18 July they sailed out of the mouth of the Mississippi River into the Gulf of Mexico. They reached the River of Panuco in New Spain on 10 September. Of the original force of about 600 Spaniards, 311 survived. None of the chroniclers tells how many of their Indian slaves survived.

So went de Soto's route as we understand it. How can we be sure that we have gotten any of it right? We can never be absolutely certain, only confident that the route is consistent with all the sources of information we have listed. Constraints of space do not allow us to cite all of the evidence that supports our interpretation of the route, but we can illustrate our modus operandi by discussing in some detail a segment of the route about which we are confident— the part from Chiaha to the territory of the chiefdom of Coosa. Apparently, de Soto first heard of this chiefdom when he was in Ocute, on the upper Oconee River in Georgia, and he heard of it again when he was in Cofitachequi, just before he crossed the Blue Ridge Mountains to come to the island town of Chiaha, one of the northernmost towns under the power of Coosa. As de Soto traveled south from Chiaha, he was on the trail for 12 days before reaching the capital town of Coosa in northwest Georgia, and when he left there he traveled another 12 days before coming to the southernmost town of Coosa. When we plotted the territory of this chiefdom on a map, we were surprised at how large it actually was.

But how do we really know we have located that territory in the right place? In the first instance, we believe that our route from Chiaha to Mabila is accurate because we are starting from a fairly firm location, the town of Chiaha, which was one of the towns visited by Juan Pardo, for whose travels we have such ample documentation. Next, we have plotted the day-by-day progress of the expedition, making sure that the line of march that we propose fits both the locations of protohistoric archaeological sites as well as topographic features. Of course, the United States de Soto Commission also thought that their route satisfied these requirements, but it did not plot day-by-day movements, and there are discrepancies between information in the documents and the actuality of the commission's route.

Another reason we believe this part of the route to be accurate is that the chiefdom of Coosa, as we have plotted it on a map, coincides neatly with three interrelated protohistoric archaeological phases. That is, each of these phases represents a distinguishable "way of life" as reconstructed by archaeologists from artifacts and other material remains from excavated sites. The archaeological phase of Coosa proper was the Barnett phase. But the grand chief of Coosa also held sway over Dallas phase towns along the Tennessee River and the French Broad River to the north, and he exercised a less certain power over Kymulga phase towns southward into Alabama.

Our case is also strengthened by the fact that a number of sixteenth-century European artifacts have been recovered from sites throughout the area of the chiefdom of Coosa. Some of these artifacts no doubt came from the Luna and Pardo expeditions, but some of them seem to have come from de Soto's.

A Nueva Cadiz plain bead found at the Little Egypt site (i.e., at the main town of Coosa) almost certainly came from de Soto's trip. Other sites near Little Egypt have turned up iron celts and wedges and a small steel dirk. Similar artifacts have been found at several Dallas sites to the north and several at Kymulga phase sites to the south. A bead or iron chisel does not, of course, prove where de Soto slept, but their presence strongly indicates that these sites were occupied at the time of the Spanish explorations in the sixteenth century.

A far more dramatic artifact is almost certainly from the de Soto expedition. A sixteenth-century two-edged sword has been found at the King site, the last town that de Soto visited before leaving the Coosa River and heading south into what is now Alabama. In addi-

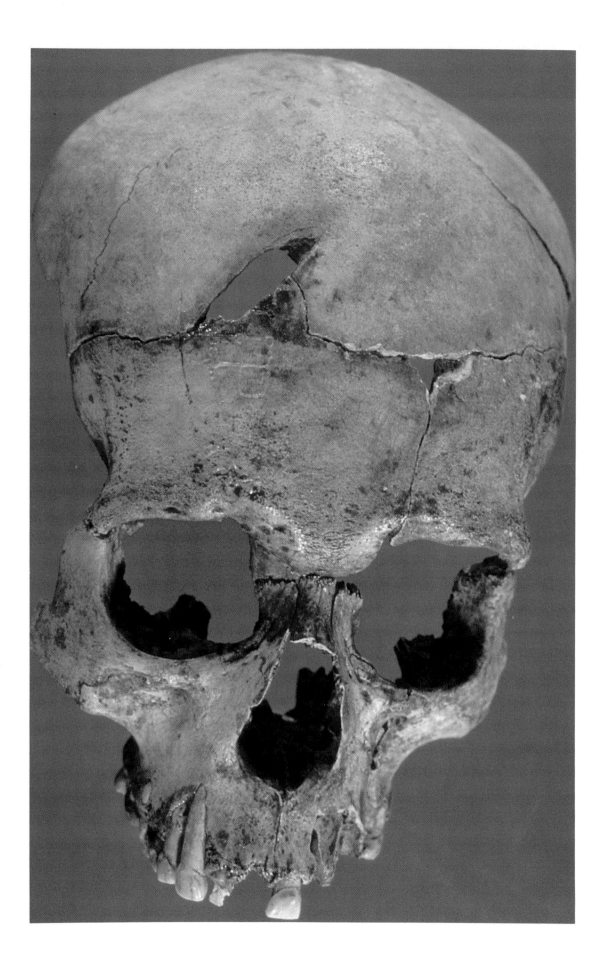

Dramatic evidence of military contact between Spaniards and native Americans is displayed on human skeletal remains from the King site in northwest Georgia, excavated by Patrick Garrow and David Hally of the University of Georgia. The site is possibly a small village within the province of Coosa visited by the expedition in September 1540. David Mathews, working under Robert Blakely of Georgia State University, has determined that this skull (*left*) is from a man in his fifties who received a fatal sword wound on top of his head above the right eye. The thigh bone of an elderly woman (*above*) displayed three sword cuts, also fatal. Others suffered similar wounds.

tion to the presence of this sword, a large number of Indian burials from the King site analyzed by Robert Blakely and his students at Georgia State University show evidence of wounds inflicted by European weapons—swords and lances. The incidence and nature of these wounds are similar to those found on victims of medieval warfare in Europe. Since Pardo did not visit the King site, and since Luna was on friendly terms with the Indians, we are confident that these people were wounded and killed by de Soto's soldiers. The only question is whether the wounds were inflicted at or near the King site or in the battle of Mabila, from which the victims, who would have been slaves taken by the Spaniards, would have either walked home or, in the case of the dead and badly wounded, been carried there by their kinsmen.

Another kind of information less compelling than the evidence already mentioned is nonetheless noteworthy: the coincidence of place-names. We deliberately did not use place-names in reconstructing the route, but when our reconstruction was finished a series of interesting place-names emerged. (1) The capital town of Coosa was on the Coosawattee River, whose name is derived from the Cherokee word *kusawetiyi*, which means "old Coosa place." Cherokee speakers occupied this site in the late eighteenth and nineteenth centuries, after the Muskogean-speaking Coosas had abandoned it. (2) De Soto found the town of Itaba at the famous Etowah archaeological site on the Etowah River near Cartersville, Georgia. Both "Itaba" and "Etowah" are European attempts to spell an Indian place-name. (3) Coste was on an island in the Tennessee River. On a 1715 manuscript map in the British Public Record Office, the Tennessee River is called the "Cusatees" River.

Our interest goes beyond discovering the footprints of de Soto's soldiers and getting the highway markers and bronze plaques and place-names in their right locations. Once the entire route is precisely drawn, we hope to combine information in the documents with archaeological and geographical information to reconstruct a social geography of the South in the second half of the sixteenth century—to locate particular named Indian towns on particular creeks and rivers and to delineate, as far as possible, the territories of most of the great protohistoric southern chiefdoms.

If we succeed—and we have already begun to work, most notably in the instance of Coosa—we will have a historical baseline from which to move both forward and backward in time. We will be able to move back into prehistory to shed light on the social antecedents of the South that de Soto explored. For example, in the middle of the vast "wilderness of Ocute" between the Oconee River and the Wateree River lay the Savannah River where, a hundred or so years earlier, many people lived. Where had they gone by 1540? What explains

This sixteenth-century map, often referred to as the de Soto map, shows the interior rivers and many of the aboriginal villages encountered by de Soto's army. The Appalachians and the various river drainage systems (with some exceptions) are shown with remarkable accuracy, and it is clear that the expedition crossed the Appalachians. Names for coastal bays and rivers are from Chaves's *Espejo de Navegantes* (including Espíritu Santo, the Mississippi). A note on the southwest part of the map says "from Quivira to here are immense herds of bison," indicating that the map maker included information from the Coronado expedition.

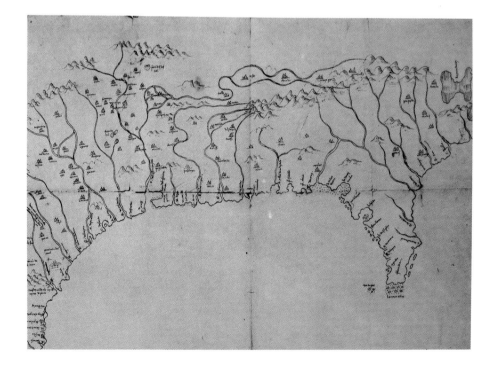

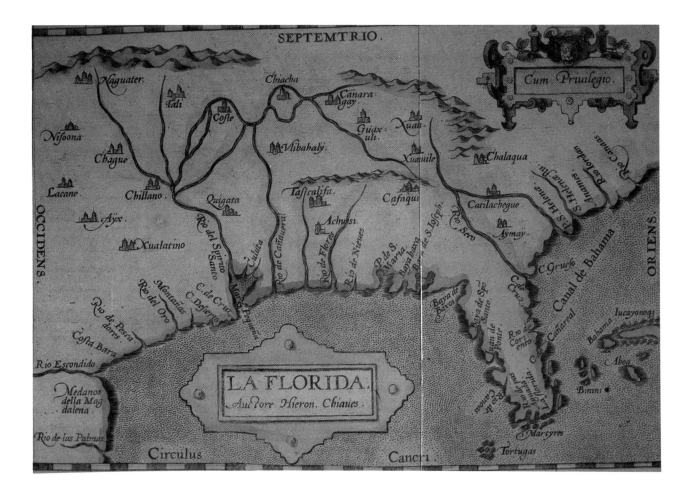

Gerónimo de Chaves's map of La Florida, believed to date from the second half of the sixteenth century, appears to be a simplified version of the de Soto map. It is puzzling that neither one provides any place-names for the interior of the state of Florida.

this exodus from the Savannah River? Information from the de Soto expedition about the chiefdoms on either side of this vacant zone may help archaeologists to answer this question.

In at least one instance our route has already cleared up a stubborn problem in prehistory. One of the controversies in the Tennessee Valley is whether the people of the Dallas archaeological phase were directly ancestral to the Overhill Cherokees who lived on the Little Tennessee River in the eighteenth century. We know that they were not because the Indians who lived in Dallas towns when de Soto and Pardo came through spoke Muskogean languages, and the Cherokees occupied these towns after the original inhabitants had moved away.

One intriguing problem in finding prehistoric antecedents for our map is to discover why so many of the large prehistoric centers were in evident decline at the time of the de Soto expedition. Some, such as Ocmulgee, near Macon, Georgia, had been long abandoned. Some were still occupied—for example, Etowah, and perhaps Moundville—but in the sixteenth century neither of them was the great center it had been. Was there something in the structure of these chiefdoms,

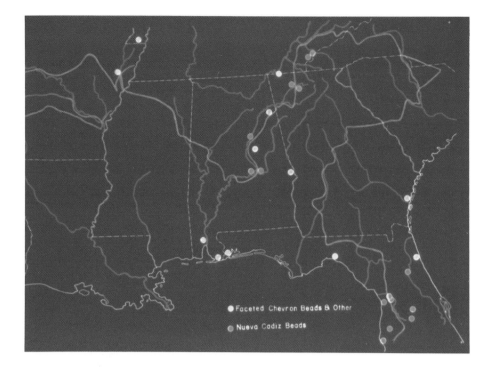

either social or economic, that caused their population centers to rise and fall?

Once we have reconstructed the social geography of the sixteenth-century South, we want to reconstruct what happened to these societies. In his recently published study of what happened along the segment of the route in present Georgia, Tennessee, and northern Alabama, Marvin Smith has evidence that the chiefdoms of Ichisi, Ocute, and Coosa crumbled rapidly after the de Soto, Luna, and Pardo expeditions. For many years anthropologists and historians have known generally that Old World diseases took a terrible toll, but Smith has been able to show how quickly they took their toll and what effect they had on movements of population and on the social transformation of these people. The people who were Toa, Ichisi, Ocute, Chiaha, Coosa, and Talisi in the sixteenth century were Creeks in the eighteenth century. It is fairly clear that they ceased building mounds within a few decades after de Soto's expedition, and this fact is evidence that the upper echelons of the chiefdoms had lost their power.

Finally, a precise reconstruction of the de Soto route will add poignancy and immediacy to particular events that occurred in the course of the expedition.

• When de Soto and his men reached the Ocmulgee River in central Georgia in March 1540, the people of Ichisi were taken completely by surprise. The chief of Ichisi sent out an emissary to ask these men from another world three measured questions: Who are you? What do you want? Where are you going?

Left and right: Marvin Smith has compiled information on the distribution of sixteenth-century metal artifacts and glass beads thought to be associated with the de Soto and other early expeditions. Although for some regions we have little information because of a dearth of archaeological research, the artifact distributions provide strong evidence for the de Soto landing site (Tampa Bay) and the route through Coosa to Mabila.

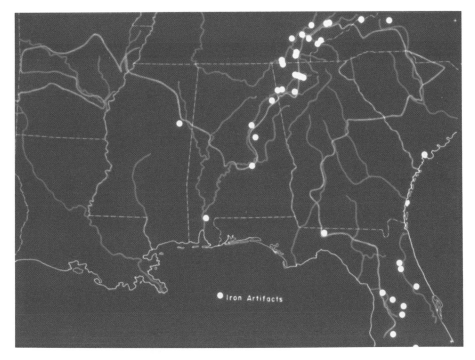

Iron Artifacts

• When de Soto left the town of Coosa, he forced the Grand Chief of Coosa and other important Indians to go with him as hostages. On 18 September 1540, the army reached Talisi, in the vicinity of present Childersburg, Alabama, the last town in Coosa's province. Here de Soto released the chief but refused to release his sister. The man went away weeping for the loss of his sister and for having been taken so far from the center of his social universe, where he belonged.

• Early in the morning of 18 October 1540, de Soto and a small advance party entered Mabila, a heavily fortified frontier town of the chiefdom of Tascaluza in the vicinity of the lower Cahaba River, west or southwest of present Selma, Alabama. Following his usual procedure, de Soto had forced chief Tascaluza to accompany him as a hostage. But after they entered the gates of Mabila, Tascaluza slipped away on a pretext and took refuge in one of the large houses surrounding the plaza of the town. When de Soto attempted to force him to come out, thousands of Indian warriors burst from concealment in the houses and launched a fierce attack. They succeeded in killing several members of de Soto's advance party and forced the rest to flee outside the gates of the town.

But the Indians at Mabila made two fatal errors. They underestimated the military advantages of de Soto's cavalry and defensive arms, and they overestimated the strength of the palisade around their town. At Mabila, Spaniards and Indians fought desperately for the entire day. Only a few Indians were able to escape de Soto's mounted lancers. When the day ended, 22 Spaniards had been killed and about 150 wounded, but as many as 3,000 Indians had been killed. The last surviving Indian warrior attempted to escape by climbing up the log palisade that surrounded the town, but when he got to the top he saw that the town was surrounded. He took the string from his bow and hung himself from a tree that formed part of the palisade.

• On 4 July 1543, the survivors of the expedition fled down the Mississippi River, pursued by a large fleet of Chief Quigualtam's huge canoes, some of them holding as many as 60 or 70 warriors. Such showers of arrows fell upon the Spaniards that no one could man the rudders, and the brigantines spun crazily down the channel of the river. Then, around noon the next day, in the vicinity of present Vicksburg, the Indians' fleet reached the edge of their territory and stopped. They turned their canoes around and started back upriver with the warriors shouting exultantly, "Quigualtam! Quigualtam! Quigualtam!"

As the Spaniards' little fleet of boats approached the mouth of the Mississippi River, a large, dark Indian stood in his canoe shouting and gesturing at the Spaniards. One of the Indian slaves could understand his language. The man was shouting: "If we possessed such. large canoes as yours. . . . we would follow you to your land and conquer it, for we too are men like yourselves."

Jeffrey M. Mitchem

7 / Artifacts of Exploration: Archaeological Evidence from Florida

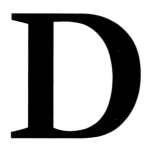oes physical evidence of the Pánfilo de Narváez and Hernando de Soto expeditions exist? Can we confidently correlate specific artifacts found in Florida with those Spanish armies that marched north from Tampa Bay more than four centuries ago?

The answer to those questions in the 1960s would have been no, but today investigations at Spanish–native American contact sites in the New World have led to the development of typologies of European artifacts from the early sixteenth century. Many of the artifacts are now well dated and known to be associated with the Narváez and de Soto entradas. The presence and distribution of these artifacts—objects made of glass or metal and some that are ceramic—can help document the expeditions in La Florida. So yes, we do have excellent evidence of these and other Spanish endeavors, and some of the best evidence comes from several archaeological sites in Florida.

The first site is near the coast of northwest Florida close to Apalachee Bay. When the 1528 Narváez expedition arrived in the territory of the Apalachee Indians which surrounds Tallahassee, they first stayed at a village called Apalachen for almost a month. Then they traveled south to another village called Aute where many of the soldiers became ill and where the Spaniards were under additional

Location of several archaeological sites containing European artifacts associated with the Pánfilo de Narváez and Hernándo de Soto expeditions.

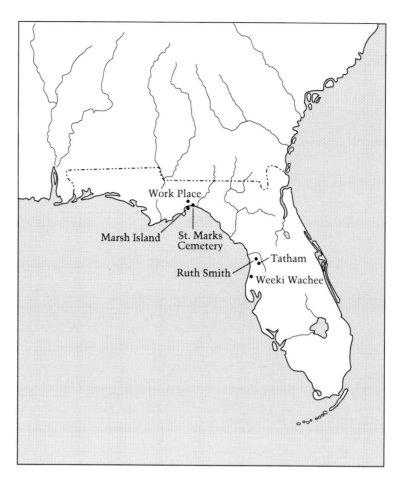

stress from hunger and Indian attacks. Their desperate condition led the Spaniards to the disastrous decision to build bargelike boats to attempt to reach New Spain by sea.

Cabeza de Vaca's account of the Narváez expedition indicates that Aute was located eight or nine days' march from Apalachen, the largest settlement in the region. An inlet was found less than a day's march from Aute, but the account says that the open seacoast was a long way from this inlet. Narváez and his men moved from Aute to the inlet, where they built the boats. They constructed a makeshift bellows and furnace and melted down their stirrups, spurs, crossbows, and other metal items to make nails, axes, and other tools. Many of their horses were killed for food during the building of the barges, and their bones were found 11 years later by members of the de Soto expedition who had traveled south to the coast from Anhaica, their winter camp among the Apalachee (see chapter 8).

Narváez named the inlet the Bay of Horses. Cabeza de Vaca indicated that they had to travel seven days through waist-deep sounds, perhaps down a river, before reaching the open gulf.

The recent discovery of Anhaica in Tallahassee provides an important clue to the location of Aute and the Bay of Horses. Both should be to the south, and Aute should be some distance from the gulf, probably on a river that leads to the open water.

The most likely location for Aute is on the Wakulla River, which meets the St. Marks River just before that river empties into the Gulf of Mexico almost due south of Tallahassee. Aute is likely the Work Place archaeological site, a village on the east bank of the Wakulla. The nearby Marsh Island mound, excavated by archaeologists around 1900, contained over a hundred burials. Several had European materials in direct association, among them iron scissors and other iron tools, glass seed beads, brass bells, and sheet brass beads and bracelets.

The best evidence for the Narváez expedition comes from the St. Marks Wildlife Refuge Cemetery site first discovered in the 1930s and located downriver from the Work Place village site. Local boys excavated portions of the site and recovered metal and glass artifacts of European origin, many in direct association with burials. A number of others have also excavated at the site, and artifacts have ended up in several private collections and in museums. The largest collections are housed in the Florida Museum of Natural History and the South Florida Museum in Bradenton.

Metal artifacts make up the bulk of the collections, including over 800 small silver disc beads. Forty-two of the beads tested were found to be made of .999 pure silver, suggesting they were made from silver being shipped back to Spain from South America. Possibly they were salvaged by the Florida Indians from a shipwreck on the Gulf coast. There are a large number of perforated discs of brass, gold, and silver in the St. Marks collections, several of which appear to have been attached to clothing as decoration, and a few pendants of copper (or brass) and silver. Unfortunately, these objects are of little use for documenting the presence of either Narváez or de Soto. But other objects provide the needed evidence.

For firm evidence there are several brass bells, all identified as Clarksdale bells, a type consistently found in early sixteenth-century Spanish contact sites in the southeastern United States and the Caribbean. The account of the Narváez expedition specifically mentions a gift of bells to a Florida Indian chief, and archaeological evidence from outside of Florida indicates that Clarksdale bells were probably also carried by the de Soto entrada.

In the Florida Museum of Natural History collection from St. Marks, there is a cast of an incised copper pendant, the original of which was destroyed in a fire after it was excavated. Apparently cut from a larger copper piece, it depicts the lower half of the body of a European, along with a dog or stag.

For the purpose of dating the St. Marks Cemetery site, the glass

Small brass hawk-bells were given to Florida's native peoples by both the Narváez and the de Soto expeditions. Specific manufacturing attributes allow archaeologists to separate an early sixteenth-century type, called the Clarksdale bell after an archaeological site in Mississippi, from later varieties. Of these early Clarksdale bells, all except the one on the lower right came from the St. Marks Cemetery site; the sixth bell, about three-quarters of an inch in diameter, is from South Florida.

beads are important. Most of them are faceted chevron beads, a type common on sixteenth-century Spanish-Indian contact sites. Several varieties were found at St. Marks. A few examples of a transparent purple type of bead were also recovered, and they too are good sixteenth-century time markers.

Two other types of glass beads from the site provide strong evidence for an early sixteenth-century date. One type is olive-shaped striped beads of various combinations of white with red, blue, or black glass, excavated from well-dated early sixteenth-century contexts in Florida. The other type is a distinctive oblong bead, square in cross section, designated Nueva Cadiz beads after an archaeological site in Venezuela where they were first found. These beads are considered the best evidence for early sixteenth-century contact because they have been found in New World contexts *only* in sites dating before 1550. Later sixteenth-century contact is suggested by two Florida Cut Crystal beads, which were of Spanish origin, recovered from sites dating to the period 1550–1600. Several gold artifacts are of South American origin. A cast gold figurine now in the South Florida Museum appears to be of the Quimbaya style from Colombia. Some beads were made from gold alloyed with copper, a material called *tumbaga,* made in the Caribbean region and Peru. These objects are either materials salvaged from Spanish shipwrecks return-

Old World ports or the personal property of members of either the Narváez or de Soto entradas. They provide good evidence that the St. Marks site is associated with those early Spanish expeditions.

Apalachee Bay, at the mouth of the St. Marks River, is most likely Narváez's Bay of Horses. The village of Aute (or Ochete, as it is called in the de Soto narratives) could be located at the Work Place site. The St. Marks Cemetery probably served as a burial place for aboriginal groups in the immediate area. European artifacts from the cemetery certainly indicate contact during the period of the Narváez and de Soto expeditions. The absence of other, similar early contact sites along this portion of the coast strengthens the arguments as does the geographical setting of the two sites.

Beyond the simple "Narváez was here" kind of historical reconstruction, this research allows us to examine questions of anthropological significance about the aboriginal societies in this part of Florida. The account of the Narváez trek clearly indicates that the town of Apalachen was the capital of an aboriginal province and the home of the chief. He apparently controlled surrounding lands for a considerable distance, and the inhabitants lived in scattered small hamlets. The village of Aute seems to have been outside of the Apalachee chiefdom, though its inhabitants were friendly with the Apalachee people.

The account also indicates that the subsistence of the people in the area was based heavily on the cultivation of maize, beans, and squashes. Such information can now be used to stimulate additional research in that region. Locating the early Spanish explorers allows us to apply the information from the expeditions to the proper native American group.

Farther south in Florida three other aboriginal sites have yielded large amounts of definite early sixteenth-century contact material: the Weeki Wachee, Ruth Smith, and Tatham mounds, all located north of Tampa Bay in west-central Florida. The sites are associated with the Safety Harbor archaeological culture that extended from south of Charlotte Harbor to the Withlacoochee River, centered around Tampa Bay.

The Weeki Wachee Mound, excavated in 1970, produced 127 glass beads, 151 silver beads, and one amber bead. Glass beads include several varieties of faceted chevron, Nueva Cadiz, and striped oval, all excellent early sixteenth-century time markers. Analysis has revealed that the silver beads are composed primarily of silver and copper, in proportions roughly corresponding to coin silver, probably produced by native artisans using silver obtained from shipwrecks or directly from the Spaniards.

The Ruth Smith Mound was dug into by many different persons

Nueva Cadiz beads excavated by Robert Allen from the Weeki Wachee Mound. These distinctive square-in-cross-section beads, which vary in length from less than half an inch to more than an inch, are excellent markers for the de Soto expedition.

over several decades and eventually destroyed by a bulldozer in the late 1970s. Luckily, several collectors who had material from the site agreed to loan artifacts for study. We were able to examine 32 glass beads, including several varieties of Nueva Cadiz and faceted chevrons. Fifty-one silver beads, two gold beads, a large iron chisel or celt, three rolled iron tubes, three interlocking brass rings, and a sherd of Green Bacín (Spanish) pottery were also recorded. The brass rings are probably a fragment of chain mail, and evidence from a nearby site, the Tatham Mound, suggests that the rolled iron tubes may have been made from armor fragments. Green Bacín pottery, a Spanish-made ceramic, occurs in sites dating from 1490 to 1600, while iron celts are found in early sixteenth-century contexts in many parts of the Southeast.

The assemblage of beads was remarkably similar to those from Weeki Wachee and probably represents contact with the same Spanish expedition. The two sites are in the general region where both the Narváez and de Soto expeditions are commonly supposed to have traveled on their journeys north from Tampa Bay.

The discovery of the Tatham Mound in 1984 added more information about early sixteenth-century contact in the area. This mound, located just a few miles south of the Ruth Smith Mound, was completely excavated in the late 1980s.

Several hundred human burials, including many with European artifacts in direct association, were found, as were 153 early sixteenth-century glass beads, including varieties of faceted chevron, Nueva Cadiz, and other early types. Many objects of silver were encountered, including a variety of shapes and sizes of beads, a celtiform pendant, and a dome-shaped disc with possible leather remnants adhering to the concave surface.

Excavations also uncovered a few small gold objects and several iron implements. One of the iron objects was held in the hand of an elderly female and has been identified as a plate from Spanish armor. A piece of the armor had been broken off and rolled into a tube that was worn as a bead on the woman's neck. Three similar tube beads were found in the Ruth Smith Mound.

The assemblage of beads from the Tatham Mound greatly resembles those from the Weeki Wachee and Ruth Smith mounds. Contact with the same Spanish expedition is suggested by the fact that four of the Nueva Cadiz bead varieties have been found in North America only at these sites. In addition, one variety of faceted chevron beads has been found only at these three sites, the Poarch Farm site in

Excavations at the Tatham Mound, located in the Cove of the Withlacoochee, a wetland area in west-central Florida. Numerous artifacts related to de Soto came from the upper mound, which was built atop an earlier prehistoric mound. Parachute cloth shields the excavators and the site from the hot, drying sun.

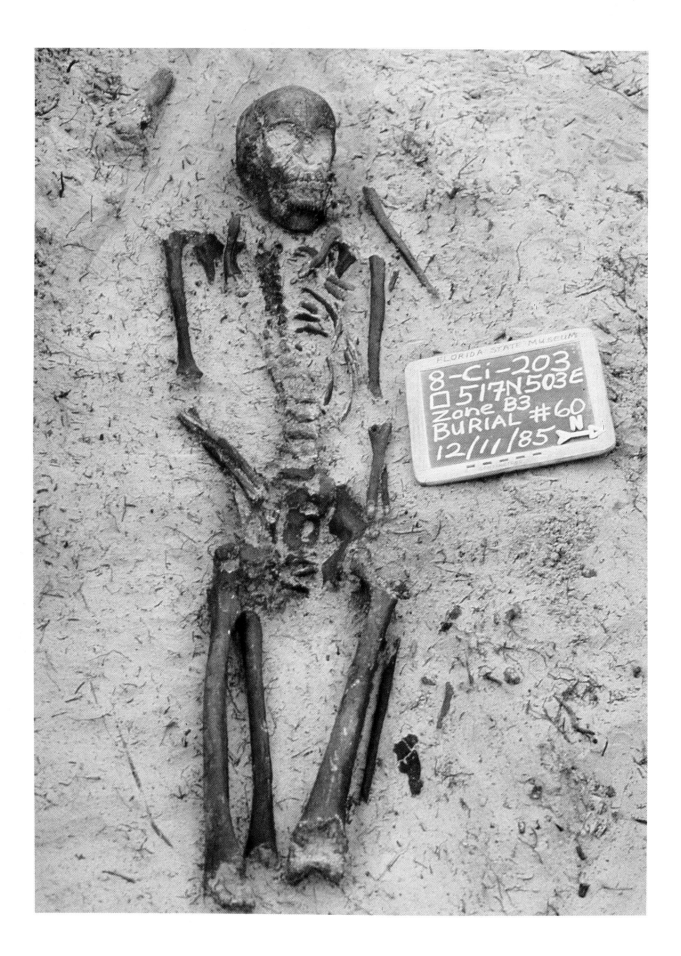

Facing page: One of more than seventy human burials from Tatham Mound, found in the upper mound. The bodies were interred at the same time and are thought to have died from a disease epidemic brought by the de Soto expedition. *Top right*: These large, barrel-shaped silver beads, also from the Tatham Mound, were presumably made by the native peoples from salvaged silver. The one on the lower left is made from rolled, flattened metal. *Middle right*: Distinctive faceted chevron beads, early sixteenth-century markers, have been found at contact sites throughout the New World. These specimens from the Tatham Mound are about a quarter of an inch in diameter and are possibly the glass beads referred in the de Soto narratives as *margaritas* or *margaridetas*. Similar subtypes of faceted chevron beads have been found at several southeastern archaeological sites thought to have been visited by de Soto's army. *Bottom right*: The people associated with the Tatham Mound used large pieces of silver to manufacture a two-inch-long celtiform pendant (*top*) and a long, rodlike bead. Silver is not native to Florida and must have come from mines elsewhere in the New World. This silver, which is .999 pure, was likely salvaged from a Spanish ship that wrecked along the Florida coast. The pendant is made from a small ingot.

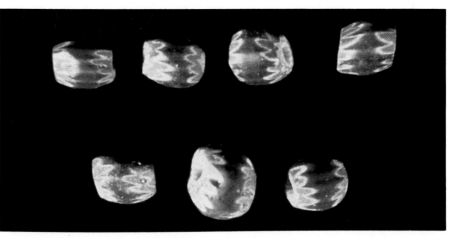

Wrought-iron chisels, such as these from the Tatham Mound, were given to the people of La Florida by the de Soto and Juan Pardo expeditions. Specimens similar to the top chisel (about 5.5 inches in length) have come from contact sites elsewhere in the southeastern United States.

northwest Georgia (believed to be a de Soto contact site), the Fountain of Youth Park in St. Augustine (believed to be Pedro Menéndez's original St. Augustine settlement; see chapter 12), and the St. Marks Wildlife Refuge Cemetery site. Another chevron bead variety has been recovered only from Tatham, St. Marks, and Anhaica, the de Soto winter camp in Tallahassee.

The Weeki Wachee, Ruth Smith, and Tatham mounds, along with the St. Marks and Anhaica sites, offer some of our best evidence for early sixteenth-century European contact with Florida native groups. Direct Indian-Spanish contact is best demonstrated at the Tatham Mound, where at least two human bones display sword wounds, presumably the result of warfare with the Spaniards. The mound also contained more than 74 people who had died and were buried during a short period, probably as a result of a European-introduced epidemic.

Spanish artifacts from Weeki Wachee, Ruth Smith, and Tatham mounds provide clues that may aid in identifying the source of the European objects from these sites. The iron objects recovered from Ruth Smith and Tatham are of particular interest because one firsthand account from the de Soto expedition mentions burying a large number of iron implements and other supplies at the aboriginal town of Cale, believed to be located not far northeast from the two mounds. The people of Cale might well have dug the objects up and traded some of them to neighboring groups.

It is intriguing that more than four centuries after the armies of Narváez and de Soto passed through the Southeast, we not only can find evidence of their presence but can begin to understand the impact of these first encounters on the native peoples of La Florida.

The Spaniards left more than trinkets behind when they crossed the swamp that is today the Cove of the Withlacoochee. One individual (*top*) had the left upper arm severed by a sword blow. Another (*bottom*) was fatally wounded when a sword cut through the right shoulder blade near where it articulates with the upper arm. Lack of immunity to European diseases and fighting against European weapons must have been devastating to the native peoples. It is possible that small populations, like those living in and around the cove, did not recover and were wiped out entirely.

Charles R. Ewen

8 / Anhaica: Discovery of Hernando de Soto's 1539–1540 Winter Camp

In October 1539, Hernando de Soto and his expedition of more than 600 Spaniards established their winter camp at an Apalachee Indian village in the environs of what is now Tallahassee, Florida. Coming fewer than 50 years after Columbus's first voyage, it was the first wintering on the longest overland Spanish reconnaissance of the United States in the sixteenth century.

The expedition occupied the Apalachee encampment for five months, until early March 1540. When the camp was abandoned by de Soto and his army in 1540, its location was lost. Nearly 450 years later, in spring 1987, an archaeologist accidently discovered the site, providing us with the first undeniable evidence for the expedition's presence.

De Soto and his army landed with horses, supplies, and equipment at Tampa Bay in May 1539. After marching north through the Florida peninsula, they crossed the Aucilla River and entered the territory of the Apalachee Indians. For several days they moved west from one Indian town to another.

The Apalachee were among the most powerful and agriculturally productive of the native groups encountered by de Soto's expedition in Florida. Organized into a complex chiefdom (a socially stratified

The Martin site, in the heart of Tallahassee north of the Work Place and St. Marks Cemetery sites, was found by B. Calvin Jones while he was searching for a seventeenth-century Spanish mission. Excavations have left no doubt that the Martin site is the Apalachee Indian town of Anhaica where de Soto's army wintered from October 1539 to March 1540.

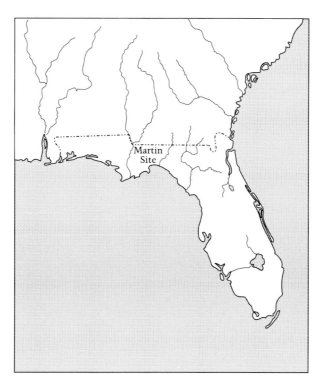

society with chiefs, a noble elite, and commoners), the Apalachee controlled the territory in the Florida panhandle between the Aucilla River and the Ochlockonee River valley. They possessed a large, proud population. Rodrigo Ranjel, de Soto's secretary, described them: "Not one of them, for fear of death, denied that he belonged to the Apalachee; and when they were taken and were asked from whence they were they replied proudly: 'From whence am I? I am an Indian of Apalachee.' And they gave one to understand that they would be insulted if they were thought to be of any other tribe than the Apalachee."

Among the Apalachee the Spanish were met with fierce resistance. A soldier in the expedition, Alonso de Carmona, was impressed by their prowess: "The Indians of Apalachee are very tall, very valiant and full of spirit; since, just as they showed themselves, they kept flying in our faces everyday and we had daily brushes with them."

The Indians practiced a scorched earth policy on their village of Ivitachuco so that it did not fall into Spanish hands, thus denying its food supplies to the army. The expedition advanced to the principal Apalachee town of Anhaica, which had been abandoned but left intact. Seizing the opportunity, de Soto occupied the village and used it as a base. He then reinforced and resupplied the expedition, sending for men and provisions that he had left at the landing camp on Tampa Bay.

Anhaica is described in the de Soto narratives as consisting of "two hundred and fifty large and good houses." The Spaniards were put up in these houses, and others were built as well. The entire village was fortified to guard against raids by the Apalachee.

The five months at Anhaica (October 1539 to early March 1540) were spent under siege conditions. On two occasions the Indians succeeded in burning part of the encampment, and none of the Spaniards ventured far from the camp alone or unarmed.

While encamped at Anhaica, de Soto sent out scouting parties to locate the riches of La Florida. An Indian boy taken captive told the Spaniards of a land to the east where gold was to be found in quantity. He described the processes of mining and smelting ore so accurately that de Soto's men believed every word. On 3 March 1540 the entrada broke camp and traveled north across Georgia in a vain quest for gold and glory.

The exact location of de Soto's first winter encampment has been the subject of considerable debate. It has been generally agreed that the site must be in or around the present city of Tallahassee, but there agreement ended. It was not until the discovery of sixteenth-

Excavation of a portion of the Martin site was done under the shadow of impending development, but a large portion has been purchased by the State of Florida and will be preserved.

Pottery made by the native peoples who lived at Anhaica prior to the de Soto expedition's occupation.

century Spanish artifacts less than a mile from Florida's capitol building that the definitive location of Anhaica was established.

Called the Martin site, Anhaica was discovered by B. Calvin Jones, an archaeologist with the Florida Bureau of Archaeological Research, while he was searching for a seventeenth-century Spanish-Apalachee mission site. Jones had suspected for some time that a ridgetop just east of the capitol was the site of the mission called La Purificación de la Tama, but he did not excavate because it was in a residential neighborhood.

In March 1987, noticing that this ridge was slated for commercial development, Jones asked for and received permission to do some exploratory excavation. Initial testing uncovered aboriginal and Spanish artifacts, evidence that a Spanish site had indeed been located. Yet in many ways the artifact assemblage was atypical of a seventeenth-century mission site. Artifacts recovered included sixteenth-century Spanish olive jar fragments, Fort Walton period aboriginal pottery, small links of iron, and blown glass beads, all of which tend to predate the seventeenth-century mission period. In addition, the artifact assemblage lacked the Spanish tin-glazed majolica plates and bowls and types of aboriginal ceramics that characterize Florida mission sites. It became apparent that the Spanish artifacts were probably from the de Soto expedition rather than from a mission.

The Martin site is named for a previous owner, Governor John Martin, who in the 1930s built a brick mansion which still stands on the property. To confirm the identification of the Martin site as de Soto's encampment, extensive excavations were undertaken. Working from April to December 1987 in the shadow of an office development, the crew recovered evidence suggesting the identification of the site as de Soto's winter camp. Much of 1988 was spent analyzing the artifacts found, and enough information was gathered to prove that the Martin site is indeed the location of de Soto's first winter encampment.

Most of the aboriginal pottery recovered dated from the late prehistoric and premission historic periods, from about 1450 to 1600. Aboriginal materials account for about 90 percent of the artifacts excavated, which is not surprising when one considers that de Soto spent the winter in the village of the Apalachee.

Spanish ceramics, as might be expected of a military, exploratory expedition, are rare at the Martin site. The most common Spanish ware is the utilitarian olive jar, used to transport wine, water, olive oil, and a variety of other commodities. Fragments of these jars recovered at the site are both glazed and unglazed, and the rim types are known to date from the period A.D. 1490–1570. A few fragments of Spanish majolica pottery identified as Columbia Plain (A.D. 1490–1650), Caparra Blue (A.D. 1490–1600), and possibly some unglazed Bizcocho ware (A.D. 1500–1550) have also been recovered.

Glass beads of European manufacture have been found, and some can be used to help date the site and tie it to other de Soto contact sites in the Southeast. Although a few of these glass beads could not be assigned to any tightly dated time span, several clear blown glass beads, a faceted amber bead, a dozen faceted glass chevron beads, and a single Nueva Cadiz bead are known to date to the early sixteenth century.

A 1988 conference on the artifacts of the Hernando de Soto expedition in La Florida brought together items from many sites in the Southeast suspected of being associated with the de Soto entrada. It was discovered that two varieties of the red, white, and blue chevron beads found at the Martin site also appear in the assemblages of sites around Tampa Bay, Apalachee Bay (where de Soto may have resupplied), Tennessee, and Alabama. A type of Nueva Cadiz bead similar to the type found at the Martin site was also recovered at the Ruth Smith Mound, an aboriginal burial mound north of Tampa Bay. Beads, of various types, are proving to be the single most useful artifact for identification of sites associated with the de Soto expedition.

A large number of a small variety of Spanish iron artifacts were found at the Martin site. Dozens of wrought iron nails of several varieties have been recovered. One unusual type has also been reported from a site in New Mexico possibly associated with the Francisco Coronado expedition, which was exploring the Southwest at the same time that de Soto was exploring the Southeast. These nails vary greatly in size and probably were used for a variety of purposes.

Most intriguing of the iron artifacts were many small—less than one centimeter—iron links. At first, only scattered fragments of twisted links were found. Taken separately they were difficult to interpret. However, when a clump of 14 interconnected links was found, it became apparent that these were fragments of chain mail, a type of personal body armor worn by de Soto's army. Designed to counter blows from edged weapons, the iron mail armor proved to be of little utility against Apalachee arrows. A written account from the expedition notes that this type of armor was "thrown aside" after an Apalachee archer demonstrated that he could put an arrow

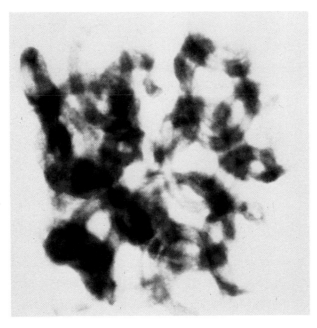

Bottom: These tiny S-shaped and curved pieces of metal, the largest of which are three-quarters of an inch long, were thought to be pieces of chain mail. This supposition proved to be correct when one rusted clump of links was X-rayed (top) and a portion of intact mail could be seen. Similar links have been found in the Tatham Mound and other contact sites in Florida.

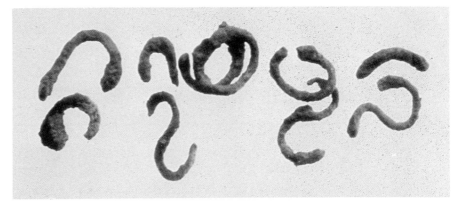

The crossbow was a deadly weapon. Archaeologists at the Martin site found this 1.75-inch metal point that had been used to tip one of the crossbow darts. In the 1930s similar dart points were found in New Mexico at a site believed to have been an encampment of the Coronado expedition at about the same time that de Soto wintered at Anhaica.

through two shirts of mail at a distance of 50 paces. The chain mail armor was replaced by a quilted cloth doublet which, apart from being a more effective defense against arrows, was probably more comfortable to wear in Florida's subtropical climate.

It seems unlikely that the chain mail armor was simply "thrown aside." Each link was connected to four other links and closed by a small rivet. A single shirt would have had thousands of links requiring an enormous expenditure of labor. Rather than being discarded, the armor was probably added to the load of the Indian bearers. The presence of the many scattered links at the Martin site attests to the ravages of Florida's humid, rainy weather on the iron mail.

A crossbow quarrel (dart tip) is another type of iron artifact found at the Martin site. Crossbows are known to have been among the principal weapons of the de Soto expedition, but they were not in general use when the Spanish returned to the Florida panhandle in the seventeenth century.

The artifacts that could be closely dated were the copper coins. Five coins were recovered, of which two have been positively identified. Both date between 1505 and 1517. The first one is a four *maravedi* copper coin (*moneda de vellon*) minted in Spain between 1505 and 1517 for the colony of Santo Domingo. The second is a one maravedi, also copper, minted in Spain between 1505 and 1517, also for use in the Caribbean. The other three, due to their poor state of preservation, can only be identified as Portuguese *ceitils* dating to the sixteenth century or even earlier. A more precise date cannot be given.

In addition to the artifacts, the remains of at least two native dwellings have been found as well as several trash/storage pits and hearths. These remains appear as soil discolorations in the ground and can be easily distinguished from natural disturbances. Apalachee

A four-maravedi coin was one of several coins excavated at the Martin site. All date prior to the time of the de Soto expedition.

houses were constructed using the wattle and daub technique. It consisted of setting posts vertically in the ground, weaving branches (wattles) between the upright posts and plastering this framework with clay that hardened in the sun (daub). Archaeologically, these structures were recognized by a circular pattern of postmolds (soil discolorations caused by the decomposition or burning of the wooden posts) accompanied by a concentration of wall daub.

There is no doubt that the Martin site provides evidence of Spanish-Indian contact in the early sixteenth century, but is this contact necessarily associated with the de Soto expedition? There is only one other historically known candidate, the ill-fated Pánfilo de Narváez expedition of 1528. There is no other major Spanish activity documented for the region during the sixteenth century.

Artifact comparisons, however, leave little doubt that the site is de Soto's. The blown glass beads from the Martin site are distinctive. The only other site reported in North America with beads of similar manufacture is the Poarch Farm site in northern Georgia, also associated with the de Soto expedition. The several dozen wrought iron nails and the large number of discarded iron artifacts recovered at the Martin site also suggest an association with the de Soto expedition since it is recorded that Narváez's men had to melt their stirrups, spurs, and crossbows in order to make nails and tools with which to build boats.

Just before the close of the 1987 field season, a discovery was made that further identified the site with de Soto's entrada. A pig mandible was recovered in a good sixteenth-century context. All of the chronicles of the de Soto expedition mention that swine were included as livestock, transported as food on the hoof. Pigs were not taken on the earlier Narváez expedition.

The site of Hernando de Soto's 1539–1540 winter encampment is significant for archaeological as well as historical reasons. It represents a solid chronological marker for artifacts of the Apalachee Indians in 1539, information that can be used to help date other Apalachee sites precisely. The Martin site, with its known date of occupation, is a yardstick for understanding the changes that occurred in Apalachee culture as a result of contact with Spaniards.

Spanish artifacts recovered from the Martin site can and are being used for comparative purposes by de Soto researchers elsewhere in the Southeast. The artifacts provide our first positive look at what we can expect to find at other de Soto sites, providing concrete correlations between the names of towns visited by the expedition and known archaeological sites. Four hundred and fifty years later, Hernando de Soto's expedition is, again, a reality.

Charles Hudson

Marvin T. Smith

Chester B. DePratter

Emilia Kelley

9 / The Tristán de Luna Expedition, 1559–1561

Twenty years after Hernando de Soto explored the interior of the southeastern United States, Don Luis de Velasco, viceroy of New Spain, charged Tristán de Luna y Arellano with the task of establishing a colony in the territory that de Soto had explored. Luna failed in this attempt, but the documentary record of his exploration sheds light on the social geography of the sixteenth-century southeastern native peoples, and it gives some indication of the changes among those people that the de Soto expedition set in motion.

The motives behind Luna's colony were somewhat contradictory. One was the plan by the Franciscan friar Andrés de Olmos to establish a series of missions on the coast of the Gulf of Mexico that would both make it possible to convert the Indians to Christianity and give refuge to Spaniards who were shipwrecked on the coast. Luna could also satisfy the promptings of some of the survivors of the de Soto expedition who advocated establishing a colony at Coosa, an Indian chiefdom in the interior, as well as the Dominicans who wanted a colony founded in the legendary land of Chicora on the South Carolina coast where there was said to be precious gems. Velasco was also hopeful that silver, gold, and mercury (used in the processing of silver) would be discovered. He knew of several individuals who, it was said, had bartered for gold with Indians. Presumably these men had been members of the de Soto expedition.

Finally, such a colony would prevent the French from validating their claim to this land and would prevent other European states from establishing any claim. In the sixteenth century the geography of interior North America was poorly known. The Spaniards, for example, were afraid that if another European power succeeded in establishing a colony in North America, they might succeed in finding a road to the recently discovered, fabulously rich silver mines in Zacatecas (in northern Mexico) and in the mythical native province of Copala, believed to lie to the north of Zacatecas. Such a road did not exist, of course, and even if it had the distance from the Atlantic Coast to Zacatecas was much greater than the Spaniards imagined.

The Spaniards knew from members of the de Soto expedition that a good port, Ochuse, lay to the west of the bay that lay near the chiefdom of Apalachee, where de Soto spent his first winter. After arriving at Apalachee, de Soto ordered Francisco Maldonado to explore the coast in two brigantines. Allowing two months, de Soto ordered him to explore the entrance of every creek and river.

Maldonado returned to report that he had found a sheltered bay with deep water 60 leagues to the west. He brought back an Indian chief of a village of Ochuse, located somewhere on that bay, whom he had captured there, and also a "sable" blanket of better quality than the Spaniards had yet seen. According to Garcilaso de la Vega, this harbor was sheltered from all winds, and its water was so deep near its shore that Maldonado was able to bring his brigantines close enough to land to disembark "without opening the hatch."

Although Maldonado probably drew a map of his soundings, the information just cited is all that appears in the de Soto chronicles. The description of Maldonado's Ochuse would seem to fit both Mobile Bay and Pensacola Bay, but the distance of 60 leagues from Apalachee Bay falls closer to Pensacola than to Mobile. From the western margin of Apalachee Bay to the entrance to Pensacola Bay is about 210 miles. Using the nautical league of 3.19 miles to the league, this comes to about 65.8 leagues. Distance to the entrance of Mobile Bay is approximately 80 leagues. The two months allowed him may have made it possible for Malonado to continue his exploration to Mobile Bay, but there is no evidence that he explored two large bays.

In addition to Ochuse, another harbor was known to sixteenth-century Spaniards. From survivors of Lucas Vásquez de Ayllón's 1526 colony, the Spaniards learned that there was a good port at the Punta de Santa Elena on the southern Atlantic coast, although this port was poorly described and its exact location unknown. When de Soto made his looping expedition north from Apalachee, he visited the town of

With modern maps and charts and navigation buoys and instruments, it is relatively easy to find specific harbors and bays on the Gulf coast of Florida and locate the passages into them. In sixteenth-century Spanish Florida it was not easy because entrances were often obscured by barrier islands. Just as de Soto's expedition had a difficult time finding the entrance to Tampa Bay, so did de Luna's expedition have trouble finding Pensacola Bay.

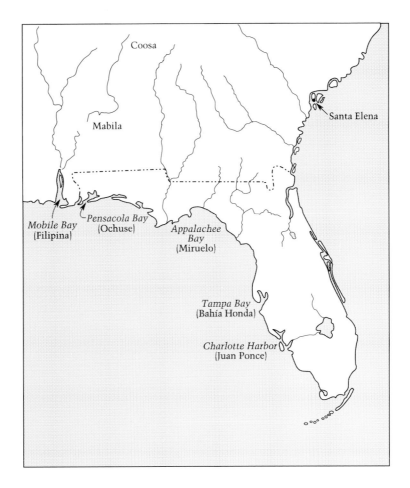

Cofitachequi, where he found European axes and glass rosary beads which the Spaniards inferred had been obtained from members of the Ayllón expedition. From information obtained from the Indians, they estimated that Cofitachequi was 30 leagues from the Atlantic coast, where the encounter with Ayllón had occurred. After leaving Cofitachequi, de Soto's army traveled north to Xuala and across the mountains to Chiaha and the chiefdom of Coosa, where they were well received and well fed by the Indians. Coosa—dominating the Ridge and Valley province in eastern Tennessee, northwestern Georgia, and northern Alabama—seemed to de Soto's men to be one of the finest provinces in all of La Florida. From Coosa, de Soto went on to Athahachi in the vicinity of present Montgomery, Alabama, then continued downriver to the towns of Piachi and Mabila.

It was at Mabila that de Soto fought the greatest military action of his expedition. The Spaniards suffered great injury, but the Indians in and around Mabila were utterly devastated. While at Mabila, de Soto learned from an Indian that Maldonado (as prearranged) was waiting for him with ships at the Bay of Ochuse. One of de Soto's men estimated that Ochuse was 40 leagues from Mabila, and another estimated that from Mabila to Ochuse it was six days' travel time.

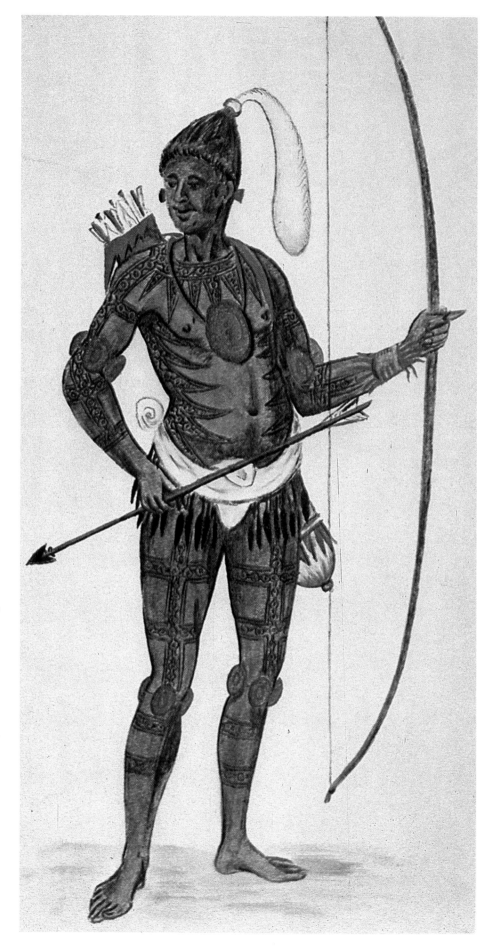

John White's sixteenth-century drawings of Florida natives were probably based on paintings done by the Frenchman Jacques le Moyne. White's pictures provide some of the best visual information available on how the people looked and what they wore. But the native peoples of La Florida were not homogenous. They spoke various languages, some as different from one another as Russian from English. They did share one unfortunate trait: a lack of immunities to the diseases brought to La Florida from the Old World. Records of the de Luna expedition describe the dramatic changes occurring in Coosa in the two decades since de Soto's army had passed through the province.

It is possible that this estimate of distance and travel time was obtained from the captured chief of Ochuse, who had traveled with the expedition all the way from Apalachee. While they were at Mabila, de Soto released the chief of Ochuse, and presumably this man returned home.

A plan of colonization evolved in which Luna would first found a town at Ochuse, then a colony inland at Coosa, and finally a colony at Santa Elena, all three to be connected by a road. Sailors and soldiers who had been with de Soto had told Don Luis de Velasco that from the Gulf coast it was only 80 leagues overland to Punta de Santa Elena. The actual straight-line distance would have been about 350 miles, or about 100 leagues, over difficult terrain with many stream crossings. Velasco also possessed a painted map which indicated incorrectly that Coosa was not far from Santa Elena.

Luna's knowledge of the Southeast probably was based upon Velasco's map, which he must have seen, and on at least two narratives of the de Soto expedition, which he could have read. Also, he appears to have had a number of men with him who had been members of the de Soto expedition. And, finally, he had with him at least one woman from Coosa who had been enslaved by de Soto and taken to Mexico by the survivors of the expedition. This women was to serve as translator when they reached Coosa.

The Expedition Reaches Ochuse

In September 1558, Velasco sent Guido de las Bazares with three small vessels to reconnoiter the Gulf coast and to discover a good port. His pilot was Bernaldo Peloso, a veteran of the de Soto expedition. Peloso reached the Gulf coast and reported that he had sighted land at latitude 29°30' on a coast running east and west. The land was an island about four leagues from the mainland. He then ran between this island and the mainland, but he found the coast to be shallow and not good for a settlement. He named this area Bahía de Bajos (Bay of Shoals). But ten leagues directly east of this bay he discovered a larger one that he named Bahía Filipina. Its entrance was between the point of an island which was seven leagues long, running east and west, and a point of the mainland.

From Bazares's description it is clear that his Bahía Filipina was Mobile Bay. His landfall then was Ship Island (about 12 miles from the coast) or Horn Island (about 9 miles from the coast). His Bahía de Bajos was probably Pascagoula Bay, which was about 38 miles from the entrance to Mobile Bay.

Bazares attempted to explore further eastward on the Gulf coast on two occasions, but on both he was turned back by contrary winds.

He claims to have gone 20 leagues farther, to a point where the coast takes a southeasterly turn. If it is true, he may have reached as far as present Fort Walton, and the distance he traveled was closer to 29 nautical leagues. He evidently missed the entrance to Pensacola Bay.

On 11 June 1559, Luna set sail from San Juan de Ulua on the Mexican Gulf coast with a fleet of 13 ships. He had about 500 soldiers plus 1,000 colonists and servants, including a substantial number of Mexican Indians. He started out with 240 horses, but about 100 died during the voyage. Thirty-one days later he made landfall at a place they believed to be eight leagues west from Bahía de Miruleo, at that time a name sometimes applied to Apalachee Bay. Here they anchored to take on water, wood, and food for the horses.

From the Bahía de Miruelo they sailed west looking for Ochuse with a frigate out in advance of the fleet. But the pilot in the frigate missed the entrance to Ochuse and continued on to Bahía Filipina (Mobile Bay), which they entered on 17 July. Because Luna believed—presumably from information collected by Maldonado—that Ochuse was the best and most secure port on the coast, he sent the frigate out to find it. When the frigate returned it was reported that Ochuse was about 20 leagues (64 statute miles) from Bahía Filipina and about 35 leagues from Bahía de Miruelo (112 statute miles). Both distances are reasonably correct for Pensacola, located as it is between Mobile Bay and Apalachee Bay.

Luna put some of his men and all of his horses ashore at Mobile Bay. The fleet then set sail for Ochuse while the men who were put ashore and the horses traveled overland. Because the fleet both

In the early sixteenth century, horses transported aboard ships were suspended in slings that kept their feet from touching the deck and thus prevented broken legbones in rough seas. A winch was used to hoist the animals aboard. Unfortunately, the horses did not travel well in this manner, and significant numbers died before they could be taken ashore.

departed and arrived on 14 August, the eve of the Assumption of the Virgin, Luna renamed Ochuse the Bahía Filipina del Puerto de Santa María, though it was more commonly called Bahía de Santa María Filipina. Members of the expedition, however, at first referred to it as Ochuse, though in time they more often referred to it as Polonza (also Apolonza). The reason for their changing the name from Ochuse to Polonza is not given, though it may reflect Indian usage. Presumably Polonza is the namesake of Pensacola.

The precise location of Luna's settlement has not yet been discovered. There are two bits of information in the documents that may help pinpoint its location. One is that they laid out their town on a high point of land that sloped down to the anchorage of their ships. This anchorage had from four to five fathoms of water only a crossbow shot (200 yards or less) from land, and the numbers agree with information from the de Soto expedition. The other clue is that after they were struck by a hurricane—soon to be described—they found some boxes of food floating in a creek near their town. This occurrence suggests that Luna's town was located near Tartar Point and that the creek was Bayou Grande. A map of Pensacola Bay made in 1822 by Major James Kearney shows 24 feet of water at a distance of about 150 feet from Tartar Point.

The Expedition to Nanipacana

Luna found only a few Indian fishermen around Pensacola Bay. Later a cornfield was found, but there was no large population of farmers in the area. The Indians thereabouts had few possessions, and if they were mistreated they would run away.

Luna sent out two parties of men to explore the area around Pensacola Bay. One party, under the command of Álvar Nieto and Gonzalo Sanchez de Aguilar, traveled by land, and at a distance of about ten leagues from the camp they found an Indian village where they captured a woman named Lacsohe. They almost certainly explored northward from Pensacola Bay, and the Indian village they discovered may have been located on Pine Barren Creek or Canoe Creek. They explored for ten leagues beyond this town, perhaps into present Escambia County, Alabama, but they found no more towns.

The second expedition, under the command of Don Alonso de Castilla and Baltazar Sotelo, went by boat up a river emptying into the Bay of Ochuse, a river whose channel they found to be narrow, winding, and sparsely populated. The description of this river, which flows into Pensacola Bay, is consistent with the Escambia River but not at all with the Mobile River.

Because there were so few Indians living around Pensacola Bay,

The route of de Luna's men inland from the bay to the province of Coosa. With them were men and probably native peoples who had been in Coosa with de Soto in 1540.

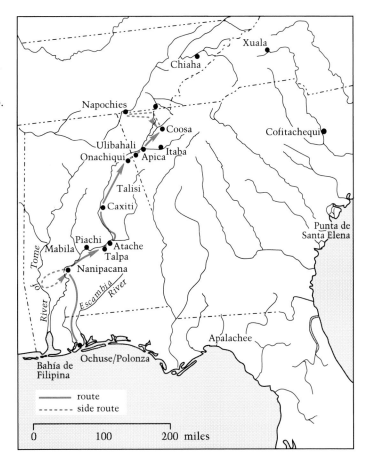

Luna could not obtain supplies of food from the natives, a necessity if the Spaniards were to survive. His problems became truly severe when a hurricane struck just five days after the fleet arrived. Of Luna's fleet of twelve ships (one had been sent back to New Spain with the news of their landing), all except three were sunk or run ashore. About half of their supplies, including food, were lost, and an unreported number of colonists were killed.

As his colonists faced starvation, Luna realized that he would have to move most of his people to Indian towns in the interior, where native food could be obtained. The problem of starvation—and many other problems—was intensified because Luna had taken along too many people.

From the de Soto documents and from the soldiers who had been on the de Soto expedition, Luna would have learned that Mabila and Piachi were 40 leagues to the north. There is not a single reference to the town of Mabila in the Luna documents, no doubt because the soldiers knew that in the course of the battle fought there by de Soto and his army, Mabila had been destroyed and burned to the ground. But they knew that just before de Soto reached Mabila, he had come to the town of Piachi, which lay beside a large river. At some time before 24 September 1559, Luna sent Mateo del Sauz and Don Cristóbal Ramírez de Arellano and a party of 150 to 200 men north to search for Piachi and the River of Piachi.

This detachment marched across 40 leagues of difficult terrain and arrived exhausted and hungry at the River of Piachi—the Alabama River. This distance, it should be noted, agrees exactly with the estimate of de Soto's men who were at Mabila. The detachment searched along the south bank of the river, where they discovered several small towns and one large one, Nanipacana, which had 80 houses. Luna conferred on it the grand name Santa Cruz de Nanipacana. Utchile appears to have been the name of one of the smaller towns. Some of the buildings at Nanipacana had been destroyed and its people fled when Luna's men approached, but they were enticed back with gifts of ribbons and glass beads. They said that their town had once been great but that some Spaniards had come there earlier (the de Soto expedition) and had made Nanipacana the way it was. It is possible that these houses were destroyed by de Soto's men, but because it was the custom in some parts of the Southeast to burn down the house of a man who had died, it is also possible that the houses were destroyed by the people of Nanipacana themselves. Luna decided to move his coastal colony inland to Nanipacana, where food could be obtained.

The move from Polonza to Nanipacana was delayed when Luna came down with a fever and apparently began hallucinating. When he came to his senses, he gave the order to move. Leaving about 50 men at Polonza, Luna moved his starving colonists northward from Pensacola Bay to Nanipacana, sending some of them to row two brigantines and two barks to Mobile Bay and then up the Alabama River, which Luna had reason to believe was the River of Piachi. The others went by trail.

Before Luna and the other colonists arrived, the Indians fled from Nanipacana to the opposite side of the river, taking with them most of their stores of food. Then they began a scorched earth strategy, destroying the food growing in their fields. Luna sent out exploring parties up and down the river near Nanipacana, but all the Indians had fled. He also sent an exploring party to the "River of Tome," which must have been the Tombigbee, but here too the Indians had destroyed their crops and had fled.

Next Luna sent upstream from Nanipacana a detachment of about 100 men in the two brigantines and the two barks to look for Indians and food. They reported having spent 26–28 days going 60–70 leagues upriver and then returning. For the first 30–35 leagues of the river, they reported finding Indian houses and fields, but the people had fled. For the next 30–35 leagues they crossed a depopulated wilderness.

At the end of their journey they came to the province of Atache, which they specifically said was at the head of navigation, i.e., near the falls of the Coosa River or the Tallapoosa River. One of Luna's men, Alonso de Montalván, refers to Atache as "the province of Taxcalusa." The people of Atache had fled, so little is said in the Luna documents about this area. Presumably the expedition returned to Nanipacana.

The Expedition to Coosa

As soon as the supplies of corn were exhausted at Nanipacana, Luna's colonists again faced starvation. Although deer were said to be plentiful around Mobile Bay, they were scarce near Nanipacana, perhaps indicating that they had been overhunted. The Spaniards began to eat acorns, the leaves of trees, and the roots of wild plants, some of which were poisonous. The Indians would appear, shoot a few arrows at the Spaniards, and then disappear.

Luna ordered Mateo del Sauz to take about 40 cavalry, 100 infantry, and two friars and go in search of Coosa, the inland chiefdom in which de Soto had found ample food. This detachment left Nanipacana on 15 April 1560. Because they were starving and because they lacked good guides, they traveled remarkably slowly. Also, after the devastation wreaked by the de Soto expedition, it is possible that the trails were overgrown and indistinct.

After leaving Nanipacana they traveled for 25 or 26 days before reaching Atache (Athahachi in the de Soto chronicles), and "the province of Taxcaluça." The direct distance by land may have been no more than about 80 miles. They found no corn at Atache, implying that the people had run away and had taken their food with them. For many days they had only blackberries and acorns. They wore out their shoes, and their horses were so starved they could hardly travel a league a day.

On 18 May they reached the town of Caxiti. All the people had run away from Caxiti, but the Spaniards found some corn they had hidden, the first corn they had found since Nanipacana. They detailed five men to take 35–40 *fanegas* of corn in three canoes and some rafts back to their starving comrades at Nanipacana.

It is impossible to know what trail they followed north from Caxiti, but it may have been the same one that de Soto had followed in 1540. After leaving Caxiti, they traveled for ten days through an uninhabited area before coming to the town of Onachiqui, which they estimated was 90–100 leagues from Nanipacana. They reached

Onachiqui 57 days after leaving Nanipacana. Members of the party specifically said that it was the first town of Coosa, the major province that was their destination.

The next town Sauz's detachment came to was Apica, which was said to have been five or six leagues from Ulibahali. Since Ulibahali is known to have been located at present Rome, Georgia, Apica must have been to the west or southwest of Rome. Apica could have been the Johnstone Farm site, though this site is somewhat less than five or six leagues from Rome and Ulibahali. It is also possible that Apica could have been at the King site or some less well known site in the area. Both the King and Johnstone Farm sites have produced European artifacts typical of the mid-sixteenth century, such as iron chisels, a sword, and other iron objects. From Apica they went to Ulibahali, where they remained for several days before going farther into Coosa, whose main town was at the Little Egypt archaeological site near Carters, Georgia. Coosa itself consisted of eight towns in an area about two leagues across (6.9 miles). Five were smaller than the main town, two were larger. Because Coosa was one of the places where Luna planned to found a town, and because Sauz's detachment remained there for several months, the Luna documents contain considerable descriptive information on the area. The geographical fea-

Probable evidence of the de Luna expedition, (*above*) two horseshoes were excavated by archaeologists at the High-tower Farm site in Tal-laedaga County, Alabama (near Sylacauga), and (*facing page*) a brass candlestick holder and brass cup were found at the Pine Log Creek site about 25 miles north of Mobile Bay.

tures accord well with the Little Egypt site: the main town was located where two small streams united—the Coosawattee River and Talking Rock Creek—and to the north of the town there was a range of mountains, the Cohuttas.

Several aspects of the culture described by Luna's men are verified by archaeological and historical information. For example, each town of Coosa is said to have had a plaza in which was located a tall pole. Both features are known to have been present at the King site, and both were present in Creek towns in the eighteenth and nineteenth centuries and, indeed, at Creek dance grounds in modern times. Some towns of Coosa had a post to which prisoners and criminals were tied for punishment or torture and to which the scalps of dead enemies were tied. The people of Coosa built summer and winter houses, the latter covered with earth, so that plants grew on top of them. Some, but evidently not all, of the towns were surrounded by defensive palisades.

The Spaniards made some comparisons between Coosa and Nanipacana. The towns were said to have been larger at Nanipacana than at Coosa, but the towns and settlements of Coosa were closer together. Population was denser at Coosa than at Nanipacana or

Atache, but no Coosa town had as many as 150 houses, and few had more than 40 or 50. The people of Nanipacana impressed the Spaniards as being in some sense more civil than those of Coosa—perhaps because the men of Coosa went naked or nearly so, and the temples at Coosa were smaller than those of Nanipacana and were not much frequented by the people. Also, the Spaniards say, the languages of Nanipacana and Coosa were different, although they had some words in common. This report is consistent with the fact that the people of Coosa and Nanipacana are thought to have spoken two different languages belonging to the Muskogean language family—Creek or Koasati (probably) in Coosa and Choctaw (probably) in Nanipacana.

The statements of those who went to Coosa give some idea of how much Coosa had declined in the 20 years since the de Soto expedition. Partly because of the things said by those who knew the Coosa, the Spaniards expected to find a large and wealthy society. But when they got there, it was clear that the Coosa they saw were not as expected. The decline was said to be due to the excesses of a "certain captain," i.e., de Soto. Those who had spoken of Coosa in grand terms said they must have been bewitched for the country to have seemed to them to be so rich and populous. What they found was so at variance with what de Soto had found that Don Luis de Velasco concluded that they had not reached the country that de Soto had explored. Velasco was wrong; they had reached it.

While Sauz and his men were in Coosa, an incident occurred that reveals interesting information about aboriginal politics. Some of the principal men of Coosa asked the Spaniards to go with them on a raid

"We must have been bewitched": de Soto's men who revisited Coosa with the de Luna expedition could not believe that the once rich and populous province had declined so much in the twenty years since their first visit. They laid partial blame on the brutality of a "certain captain," Hernándo de Soto. The cruelty of his army toward the native peoples of La Florida must have been severe. A late sixteenth-century engraving depicts one European's view.

An extraordinary artifact recovered from northwest Georgia provides poignant evidence of the de Luna expedition. A young Coosa girl held a five-inch copper plate depicting a religious scene, perhaps the appearance of Our Lady of Guadalupe in Mexico City in 1531. Probably made by Christian Indians in New Spain, the plate may have been on the cover of a book given to the girl by one of several priests from Mexico who accompanied the expedition to Coosa.

against a neighboring group of Indians, the Napochies. As a way of compensating the people of Coosa for feeding them, Sauz ordered 25 of his cavalry and 25 infantry to go along with a party of 300 Coosa warriors on this punitive raid. Since "ancient times," the people of Coosa said, the Napochies had been their tributaries, but recently the population of Coosa had grown smaller than that of the Napochies and the latter had broken away from their tributary relationship. They had begun killing Coosa and had cut lines of communication to the north.

Near the end of their first day of travel to the country of the Napochies, the Spanish-Coosa army came to what the Spaniards called a stage or theater nine cubits high (12.7–16.5 feet) with crude steps leading up to it. It was situated in an open savannah, and it could have been a mound, perhaps in an abandoned town that had once belonged to or was a tributary to Coosa. While his men sat on the ground around this "stage or theater," the paramount chief of Coosa climbed up on top of it and exhorted his men to remember the injuries done to them by the Napochies and to acquit themselves valiantly in battle.

At the end of the second day, they camped near the first Napochie village, not far from a large river that the Indians called Oquechiton—which the Spaniards said meant "the great water"—the Tennessee River. Early the next morning, when they attacked the village, they found that the inhabitants had learned from spies that their army was coming to attack them and had fled.

The Coosas soon deduced where the Napochie villagers had gone.

The Spaniards and Coosas went directly to the bank of the Tennessee River at a place where the river was wide and shallow enough to ford. Here they found a second Napochie village on the bank of river.

The people of both Napochie villages were standing on an island on the other side of an arm of the river. When the Coosas and Spaniards begin crossing, the Napochies fled and crossed the second arm of the same river, but the invading force soon caught them.

The Spanish-Coosa army quickly brought the Napochies to their knees, and they agreed to again become dutiful tributaries of the Coosas. The Spaniards appropriated a large quantity of corn from the Napochies' storehouses, and they returned to Coosa. Well before the time of the raid on the Napochies, Luna and his colonists had abandoned Nanipacana and had fallen back to Polonza. And it was not long after the raid that Sauz and his detachment at Coosa also returned to Polonza. Here the colony disintegrated in disorder and litigation.

The record of the Luna expedition provides some intriguing insights into the Southeast after de Soto's time. Many areas that were densely occupied at the time of the earlier expedition, such as the upper Alabama River and the Coosa River in the area of the Talisi Province, appear to have been reduced in population or even abandoned by the time Luna came. Even the once imposing central area of Coosa had been reduced to unimpressive villages. At the same time, areas that had not had firsthand contact with the de Soto expedition, such as Nanipacana on the middle Alabama River and the Napochie towns on the Tennessee River, appear to have been in better condition. Nanipacana was said to have been a larger town than any of the Coosa towns, but it is possible that it had taken in refugees following the warfare, famine, and probable epidemics of European disease that ensued after the de Soto expedition.

The power of the Napochies had increased in relation to that of Coosa following the latter's experience with de Soto. The Napochies were rebelling from paying tribute to Coosa, and had it not been for the intervention of the Spaniards they eventually might have eclipsed Coosa in power. It is clear that the Southeast seen by the members of the Luna expedition was undergoing rapid change following the de Soto expedition (see chapter 10). These changes would in time alter fundamentally the complexion of the Southeast as the once-powerful chiefdoms collapsed. Such a collapse was no doubt accelerated by the presence of the Luna expedition itself. As with de Soto's expedition, the Luna narratives provide important information on the native societies, but the very presence of the expedition was partially responsible for the ultimate destruction of those same societies.

Marvin T. Smith

10 / Indian Responses to European Contact: The Coosa Example

ccording to the accounts of the de Soto and Luna expeditions, Coosa was one of the most important native provinces encountered in eastern North America. It was a powerful and complex chiefdom society with a paramount chief who ruled lesser chiefs and their subjects. Corn, beans, and squash were grown, and meat was supplied by hunting deer, bear, and small mammals and by fishing.

The chief of Coosa was treated like a god. He was carried around on a litter, probably fed special food, and housed in a special dwelling on a mound constructed by his subjects. He commanded a large army and collected tribute from his subjects. In many ways he was typical of other chiefs in the Southeast, although his political authority probably covered more territory than most, extending over a large portion of the Piedmont and Ridge and Valley regions near the southern end of the Appalachian Mountains. Within Coosa there was also a hierarchy of villages, some towns having greater importance than others. Population size, presence of mounds, and other factors reflect differences in importance.

European contact in the province of Coosa occurred on two occasions during the sixteenth century. Hernando de Soto and his army visited Coosa for over a month during 1540, and the Sauz detachment of 100 men from the Tristán de Luna expedition of 1560 were there for several months. Both expeditions left valuable written records of Coosa, naming several towns, detailing political relationships, and providing other information on the area. Subsequent to these relatively brief contact episodes, no Europeans visited the core of the Coosa Province until the late seventeenth century, although the Juan Pardo expedition of 1568 did enter its northern portion in eastern Tennessee.

The core of the Coosa province is the area from the provincial capital, the Little Egypt archaeological site, near the headwaters of the Coosa River drainage in northwestern Georgia down the Coosa drainage to the area around Childersburg, Alabama, the location of the tributary Talisi province mentioned in the de Soto narratives. According to the explorers' narratives, this area was a meaningful political unit, one that corresponds with the archaeologically known Barnett and Kymulga cultures. Within this area, 23 village sites that have produced European trade materials have been found. Six additional Barnett villages are known, but European artifacts have not yet been found at them.

In order to study cultural changes that occurred in Coosa during the sixteenth and later centuries, we must have an accurate way to date the villages in the study area. Unfortunately, the radiocarbon dating technique is not precise or accurate enough for sites of the time span in question. But temporal control is provided by datable European trade materials found at sites. Both the types of artifacts and the frequency of European goods present were used to place the villages in their correct temporal sequence. For example, certain

In an early eighteenth-century engraving, the chief of Coosa greets de Soto and his army. Such chiefs were at the top of a complex social system, similar to a European monarchy. Their people afforded them differential treatment, and they were dressed and surrounded by accoutrements that symbolized their social importance. Here Coosa, holding a ceremonial mace, is carried on a litter preceded by trumpet blowers. Although some details are erroneous (e.g., the trumpets should probably be Busycon shells), southeastern aboriginal chiefs were treated in this fashion.

The chiefdom of Coosa, more than 200 miles long, encompassed several river drainages and the lands in between in east and northeast Tennessee and northwest Georgia. It was likely held together by political alliances supported with military force rather than by a rigid central government. The impact of epidemics brought by the Spaniards tilted the balance, and the alliances collapsed as the population declined.

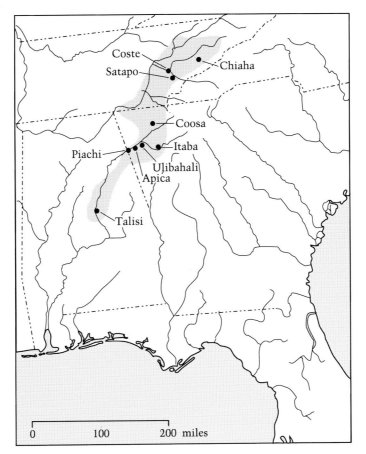

types of glass beads have been excavated in Spanish colonial town sites such as St. Augustine, Florida, or Nueva Cadiz, Venezuela. We know the exact dates that these cities were occupied from the historical records the Spaniards left us. Thus, when we find the same types of glass beads on an Indian site in the interior of the Southeast, we can be reasonably certain that it was occupied at the same time these bead styles were popular in the Spanish towns. Furthermore, there was a steady increase of European artifacts reaching the interior. Therefore, villages that produce an abundance of European artifacts are almost always more recent in time than villages where European artifacts are scarce. Using these trade items and knowledge about them, the Coosa archaeological sites can be divided into a sequence of periods one-third century long beginning with the mid-sixteenth century and continuing through the early eighteenth century. Here we will concentrate on the period 1540–1670, when Spaniards provided the only possible European contact in the area.

Contact with the de Soto expedition in 1540 probably provided the first opportunity for the peoples of Coosa to obtain European artifacts, although it is possible that European goods reached the interior from coastal areas via Indian trade routes anytime subsequent to

1513, when Ponce de León first came to La Florida. The de Soto expedition was motivated primarily by the desire for conquest, and trade was apparently not an important item of business, although gifts to chiefs are mentioned in the accounts of the expedition. We suspect that more trading was carried out than is mentioned in the narratives of the expedition. Glass beads and iron implements are specifically mentioned as gifts, and archaeological finds of swords, a crossbow bolt tip (arrowhead), and other military hardware suggest that the Indians were scavenging European goods.

The Luna expedition included a large number of Mexican Indian farmers and their families as settlers. It is likely that anything and everything was traded by the starving colonists and soldiers to the local Indians for food. Much of the earliest sixteenth-century European goods found on archaeological sites in the interior of the Southeast probably originated with this expedition. Documentary evidence suggests that both de Soto and Luna visited many of the same

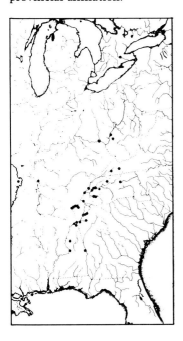

towns in the same locations, and it is doubtful that it will ever be possible to sort out many of the artifacts left by them.

Finally, the second expedition of Juan Pardo (1568) entered a portion of the province of Coosa in eastern Tennessee north of the core area. Although this expedition did not have any direct contact with the study area, it could have been responsible for the European diseases that reached the region through epidemics.

Following the exploratory expeditions of the sixteenth century, no European set foot in Coosa until sometime late in the seventeenth century. European goods clearly continued to reach the interior, as material recovered from sites increased in quantity and variety over time. Glass bead styles changed, brass ornaments were found more frequently, and more natives gained access to European goods. There is evidence that during the sixteenth century European items were wealth objects hoarded by the aboriginal elite. By the early seventeenth century virtually everyone had access to European goods. Such material must have reached the interior through aboriginal trade networks from areas of coastal European settlement. St. Augustine in Florida, Santa Elena in South Carolina, and coastal missions in Georgia were established in the mid-1560s. Interior Florida missions were established beginning in 1606, with additional missions expanding westward to Tallahassee, Florida, by 1633. Surprisingly, perhaps, the quantity of European goods reaching the interior is greater than the quantity found in mission Indian villages, suggesting that the Spaniards traded goods in remote areas in an attempt to cement political alliances and bring Indians into the mission fold. The fur trade was not to become important in the area until after the founding of Charleston in 1670, although some Spanish deerskin trade with southern Georgia is recorded during the 1640s.

Evidence for Demographic Collapse

Population collapse brought about by the introduction of European diseases is one result of European contact. American Indians had no natural immunity to the diseases that had evolved in the Old World, so when these diseases were introduced into the New World mortality rates were high. Childhood diseases to which Europeans had developed natural immunity, such as measles or various kinds of flu, were significant killers in the New World, and others such as smallpox or bubonic plague were even more serious.

Using historical documents, Henry Dobyns in his book *Their Numbers Become Thinned* demonstrated that population decrease was dramatic in coastal areas where contacts with Europeans was frequent. He further suggests that these were pandemics, quickly

Many anthropologists and historians believe that even before the first Spaniards entered Coosa and other interior provinces, epidemics from the Old World may have ravaged North America. Many regionalized epidemics in the sixteenth and seventeenth centuries are mentioned in documents. This engraving reflects Jacques le Moyne's sixteenth-century observations of attempts to cure disease among Timucuan peoples in northeastern Florida. Tobacco leaves were also used in curing: "For the sick, whom they lay face downward, a fire of hot coals is prepared, onto which seeds are thrown. The sick man inhales the smoke through his nose and mouth . . . as a purge expelling the poison from the body and thus curing the disease."

spreading inland. Work by Ann Ramenofsky in several areas, including the Mississippi Valley, suggests that Dobyns is correct: the diseases did spread inland, although a recent study of New England Indians suggests that epidemics did not reach that area until the seventeenth century. New data to test these findings have been assembled, using better techniques to date population reduction more closely. There are several lines of evidence for demographic collapse in the Coosa area, including decreasing numbers of villages, decreasing village size, burial evidence, and population movements.

Within the Coosa core area, the number of villages occupied decreased dramatically during the early historic period. There are eleven mid-sixteenth century villages that can be dated by the presence of diagnostic European artifacts and an additional six that appear to date to the mid-sixteenth century on the basis of aboriginal pottery types, although no European artifacts have been found. Then there is a dramatic decrease: only five late sixteenth-century villages, four early seventeenth-century villages, and three mid-seventeenth-century villages are known.

Decrease in village size is more difficult to demonstrate, since some sites are multicomponent (that is, they were often occupied at several different times in prehistory) and the size of the early historic

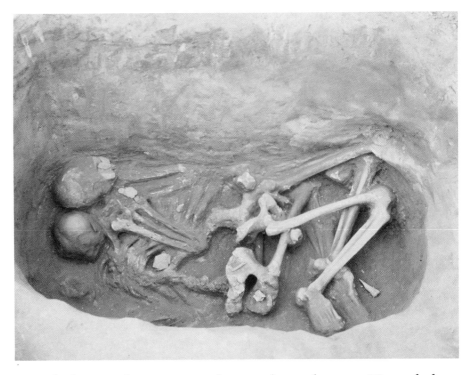

Multiple burials, like these from the King site in northwest Georgia, may have resulted from high mortality rates from epidemics in the early sixteenth century.

period aboriginal component is not always known. Nevertheless, there seems to be a trend in decreasing village size over time. Using size estimates that appear to be reliable, the average village size for the mid-sixteenth century is approximately 41,000 square meters. Only one village of the late sixteenth century has been identified in the northern portion of the study area, where there had formerly been at least ten, but at 72,000 square meters it is one of the largest sites known, if the survey data are accurate. It is possible that surviving villages had temporarily consolidated following the Spanish expeditions of the mid-sixteenth century. Although it is not possible to determine the total village area occupied during each period since data are not available for some sites, it is clear that the more numerous mid-sixteenth-century villages contain many times the area of any subsequent period.

There is also evidence from burial patterns for disease epidemics. Mass burials (more than two individuals) and multiple burials (two individuals) are common occurrences on sites of the early historic period and are known from sites of the mid-sixteenth and early seventeenth centuries. These burials probably represent the victims of European diseases. A French account of double burials in Arkansas makes it clear that such burials resulted from an epidemic. In 1698, St. Cosmé noted, "Not a month elapsed since they had rid themselves of smallpox, which had carried off most of them. In the village are now nothing but graves, in which they were buried two together, and we estimated that not a hundred men were left."

Not all of these multiple burials may be the result of disease epidemics, however. Recent research by Robert Blakely and David Mathews of Georgia State University indicates that many of the multiple burials at the King site—believed to be a village of Coosa—show evidence of wounds, many from European weapons. It is not certain whether these cuts were the result of conflict with Europeans, such as that chronicled during the de Soto expedition, or if they represent wounds from aboriginal warfare after the introduction of metal weapons and tools. It is also clear that not all of the wounds in these multiple burials were a cause of death—some had clearly healed before the individual's death.

Population movements also suggest disease epidemics, since one documented response to disease episodes is to flee the diseased area. The Gentleman of Elvas, a member of the de Soto expedition, reported that inhabitants of the town of Talomeco in present South Carolina fled to other towns following an epidemic. This pattern probably also occurred in Coosa, and we have archaeological evidence pointing to it. In the Weiss Reservoir area of northeastern Alabama, a cluster of archaeological sites suddenly appears in a region that had not previously been occupied. Evidently new villages and people appeared, migrants from another region perhaps fleeing epidemics. After the early seventeenth century, there is continued archaeological evidence of a gradual migration of towns farther downriver toward the south. This movement continued until the eighteenth century.

There is also historical evidence of the movement of towns. Using evidence of town names recorded by Spanish explorers, Charles Hudson and his colleagues have identified several of the archaeological sites in Coosa by name. It is thus possible to relocate these named towns again when European records become available in the early eighteenth century. For example, the main town of Coosa in the sixteenth century, identified as the Little Egypt archaeological site, was located near the headwaters of the Coosa River drainage on the Coosawattee River in Murray County, Georgia. By the early eighteenth century, Coosa is located 130 miles to the southwest at the Childersburg archaeological site. Similarly, the town of Apica described by members of the Luna expedition in 1560 has been identified as the Johnstone Farm site near present Rome, Georgia, but by the early eighteenth century it was located not far from the Childersburg site at the Bead Field site.

The region where these two towns migrated was the center of the chiefdom of Talisi in the sixteenth century, and Talisi was still present in this location during the eighteenth century. It is clear that many Coosa towns had moved south and had merged with the Talisi towns by the late seventeenth or early eighteenth centuries. These

After about A.D. 1000 people of southeastern aboriginal chiefdoms—like the later ones of Apalachee, Coosa, and Cofitachique—constructed large pyramidal earthen mounds as bases for shrines and other buildings. Often the structures were rebuilt and the mound enlarged, resulting in huge earthworks like this one at the Etowah site in northwest Georgia (de Soto's Itaba). With the collapse of Coosa and the other chiefdoms, such mounds were no longer built.

towns became a portion of the Upper Creeks and were an important part of the Creek Confederacy during the eighteenth century.

It is important to note that some towns named in the sixteenth century are not identifiable in the eighteenth century, suggesting that population amalgamation took place. Apparently small towns banded together to attain a larger population. Such population movements and amalgamation were part of the catalysts for the formation of the Creek Confederacy, probably late in the seventeenth century.

The Demise of Chiefdoms

With the catastrophic decline in population, there was a subsequent collapse of aboriginal culture in the Southeast. While many aspects of culture undoubtedly changed, including social organization and the belief system, we will focus on the demise of the chiefly political organization. There was simply insufficient manpower to continue to construct impressive mounds and buildings and to conduct organized warfare of the type carried out in the Southeast before European contact. Furthermore, there were insufficient farmers to produce large agricultural surpluses to support the chiefs, their families, armies, and craft specialists, such as those of Coosa.

Anthropologists Christopher Peebles and Susan Kus have proposed archaeological correlates of ranked societies or chiefdoms, including the presence of monumental architecture, hierarchical settlement patterns, part-time craft specialization, and elaborate burial ritual signifying ascribed status, that is, superior social status conferred on a person simply because of kinship with the chief. Less complex societies have social status achieved only by individual acts, such as heroism in warfare. It is possible to look at the demise of these criteria to help document the political collapse of the southeastern chiefdoms.

Mound building was an important activity among the prehistoric people of the study area. The numerous temple mounds found served as platforms for chiefly residences and mortuary temples. Presence of the mounds serves as testimony to the coercive power of the chiefs to conscript labor for large construction projects. The chiefs had the power to force their subjects to perform such labor and controlled the stored food surpluses to support the workers. Based on evidence of European trade goods associated with mound sites, usually as grave goods in mound burials or in village burials around the mound, it is apparent that substantial mound building in Coosa had ceased by the end of the sixteenth century. No evidence has been found that any mounds were begun or even added to after the sixteenth century, although one mound farther down the Alabama River may have had some additions made in the early seventeenth century.

With the end of mound construction, obvious settlement hierarchies also disappeared. In the sixteenth century, the inner core of the Coosa chiefdom consisted of eight villages along a 20-mile stretch of the Coosawattee River. The Little Egypt site, the capital of Coosa, had three mounds, the Thompson site (probably a secondary administrative center) had one small mound, and six village sites had none.

By the beginning of the seventeenth century no village within the entire study area had a mound, and the four known villages were tightly clustered in a small area. There is no longer an obvious hierarchy of sites according to size or presence or absence of earthworks.

The political elite in Coosa probably supported part-time craft specialization. Such objects as shell gorgets and native copper ornaments apparently were manufactured by specialists who were fed from the chief's granaries. These objects appear in Indian graves no later than the first third of the seventeenth century, and it is entirely possible that none was actually manufactured after the sixteenth century. This sudden end of craft specialties that had been carried out for centuries again suggests political collapse. Chiefs simply no longer had control of enough agricultural surplus to support crafts specialists.

Settlement pattern changes also took place. By the first third of the seventeenth century there was a general trend away from compact, nearly square fortified towns, to long, linear arrangements of occupied area. Apparently towns were no longer palisaded but were more dispersed, again suggesting a lack of strong, centralized leadership.

The disappearance of objects of high status can also be documented by comparing the associations of such artifacts with datable European trade goods. Status markers such as embossed native copper and spatulate stone celts, found in prehistoric elite graves, disappear by the first third of the seventeenth century. These objects had previously served as tangible symbols of elite status, just as a king's scepter functioned in medieval Europe.

The demise of these artifacts signaled the demise of the aboriginal status categories. Chiefly organization gave way to less centralized organization. European goods became increasingly common as burial furniture, and the frequency of grave goods increased dramatically until nearly all burials contained artifacts, usually of European manufacture, by the late seventeenth century.

At the same time, there was another breakdown in the burial ritual of the political elite. Formerly, the elite were buried together in

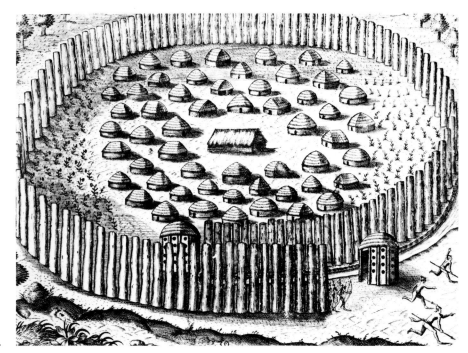

Prehistoric chiefdoms possessed stored food and other wealth as well as territory that had to be protected. Wooden palisades, like this one recorded for coastal Georgia or northeast Florida in the sixteenth century, were built around villages. Some were also protected with a ditched embankment in front of the palisade. Like mounds, palisades required labor and leadership for construction and maintenance, and they too began to disappear as chiefdoms broke apart.

In the eighteenth and early nineteenth centuries, few people realized the demographic catastrophe and the nature of cultural changes that had taken place in La Florida as a result of European contact. Scientists could not believe that native Americans residing in the Southeast, for example, were the descendants of the builders of the large prehistoric mounds, some of which contained magnificent objects. *Facing page*: A painted ceramic urn (of the Weeden Island culture, A.D. 400–600), from the Buck Mound in Fort Walton Beach, Florida, 36 miles east of de Luna's landing camp, is a fine example of the skills of the prehistoric people. A portion of the urn was excavated in 1959 by William E. Lazarus of the Temple Mound Museum, who found the remainder of it in 1966. *Right*: The motif incised on a ceramic beaker from the Moundville site probably represents the skull and long bones of a revered ancestor and is a symbol associated with ancestor cult. Cleaned bones were stored in shrines or mortuary temples built atop pyramidal mounds. The vessel is 4.5 inches tall and is dated A.D. 1200–1500.

a specific locale, such as a burial mound or within their own houses erected atop a mound. As the chiefly system broke down, there was no longer an elite social stratum segregated from the common people in special burial areas. The exact timing of these changes has not been carefully documented, but they seemed to occur by the early seventeenth century.

Acculturation is a type of culture change where one group becomes more like another group during a period of (usually) prolonged contact, most often by a dominant group influencing another, weaker group. It has been argued that although dramatic changes took place in the study area during the early historic period, these changes were not acculturation but deculturation, a loss of cultural elements. In the interior of La Florida there was severe population loss, political collapse, and probably a loss of elements of the belief system. However, with no Europeans present in the interior, there was no opportunity for the natives of the study area to adopt elements of Spanish culture. They had no model to copy. The Indians of the interior Southeast were not becoming hispanicized but were simply losing parts of their own culture. Changes were taking place, but they were not acculturation.

The belief systems of the late prehistoric people of La Florida were intimately connected with social and political organization. A rich array of complex symbols and iconography, often displayed on ceramics, stone, and shell, provided visual representations of these beliefs. Archaeologists and art historians are still trying to grasp their meanings. Images of falcons, serpents, skulls, and hands seem to be associated with cults that, among other things, emphasized kin ties to ancestral shrines and the bones of deceased relatives stored there. Through such ties social status was reaffirmed. Snakes were also associated with agricultural fertility. This slate palette or disc excavated from the Moundville site in central Alabama exhibits a hand-and-eye motif within two entwined horned rattlesnakes; it is 12.5 inches in diameter and is dated A.D. 1200–1500.

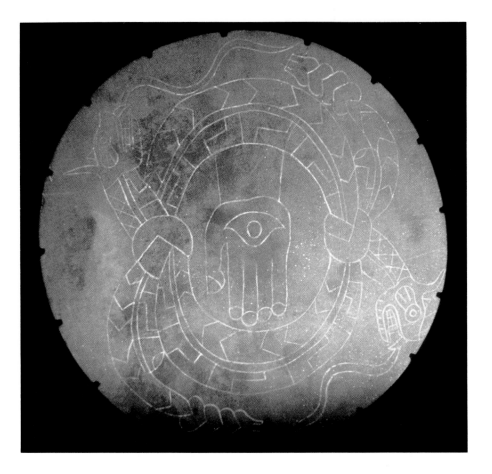

By applying schemes for measuring acculturation in archaeological situations, it can be demonstrated that indeed little acculturation took place. Most new items of European manufacture introduced prior to the late seventeenth century simply acted as substitutes for native categories and represent little real change. Thus glass beads replaced shell beads, brass gorgets replaced shell gorgets, and iron axes replaced stone celts. The Spaniards made it a policy not to trade firearms to the Indians, and this policy seems to have been effectively implemented: only archaeological sites dating to the late seventeenth century, after French and English traders began to appear, produce evidence of firearms. Hunting and warfare patterns were consequently not changed.

The Spaniards also did not trade metal kettles, and the southeastern native ceramic tradition did not decline during the early historic period. By way of contrast, the Dutch and the French in the Northeast had a heavy trade in metal cooking kettles with the local Iroquoian groups. As a result, by the first half of the seventeenth century, the aboriginal ceramic tradition of the Onondaga Iroquois of New York was all but destroyed.

Some new cultivated plants, such as peaches, were introduced into the interior Southeast no later than the early seventeenth cen-

A reconstructed prehistoric shell ornament from the Etowah site, about 5.5 inches in diameter, depicts a human-bird figurine, probably a person dressed in a falcon costume (A.D. 1200–1450). The individual is wearing a bird-beak mask, and the columella of a Busycon shell is suspended from the neck. The falcon impersonator is a symbol associated with chiefs. Chiefs were possibly costumed in this fashion on certain ceremonial occasions. As social and cultural changes took place following European contact, the iconography and crafts associated with the maintenance of chiefdoms also changed as a way of life that had persisted for hundreds of years disappeared.

tury, although no evidence has come from Coosa. But Coosa's inhabitants were horticulturalists prior to contact, and the addition of new crops would seem to have caused little change. Metal working, the medium of native copper, had been practiced prior to contact, so some native-made ornaments of European brass or copper likewise do not reflect any significant level of acculturation.

Dramatic loss of cultural elements took place during the late sixteenth and early seventeenth centuries in the interior of La Florida, but only during the eighteenth century did true acculturation take place. Contact with the de Soto, Luna, and Pardo expeditions resulted in the demise of Coosa as a major aboriginal political unit. Similar changes occurred elsewhere in the Southeast. But it is in Coosa that we have the most dramatic archaeological evidence of the collapse of the chiefdoms that dominated much of the Southeast prior to the sixteenth century.

Eugene Lyon

11 / Pedro Menéndez's Plan for Settling La Florida

The efforts of the several sixteenth-century explorers of North America were based on shared geographical and other knowledge, some fact and some fiction. Each learned from those who had gone before. And the later adventurers inherited the wisdom or folly of their predecessors, whatever their nationalities.

Among the motives that had brought them was the lure of precious metals—the dream of finding another Cuzco or Tenochtitlán. But they also burned with the desire to build proprietary empires, earning the noble titles appurtenant to them. By creating trading and agricultural settlements, they hoped to replicate Castile, France, or England in North America. They sought passage through the continent to the Pacific and the East Indies. The Spaniards also expected to advance the Evangel among native Americans, check the ambitions of rival states, and enlarge their sovereign's domains.

What then were the continental strategies of one of the most important entrepreneurs of the Spanish conquest, the one who made a lasting foundation in North America, Pedro Menéndez de Avilés? How did his motives relate to the Florida peninsula?

By virtue of his *asiento*, or contract, with Philip II, Menéndez was created adelantado and required to explore a Florida of continental

Pedro Menéndez de Avilés, founder of St. Augustine and governor of Florida, in a family portrait. His direct descendant, the Conde de Revilla Gigedo of Avilés, retains the title of governor of Florida.

scope, extending from the present West Florida panhandle around the Florida Keys to Newfoundland. He had to build two or three fortified cities and populate them with settlers and slaves, and he was to spearhead the conversion of the Indians.

Manifestly, Menéndez's eyes had first been directed elsewhere than the peninsula. He had originally planned his chief settlement at the Santa Elena area in present coastal South Carolina, and he expected to control the Grand Banks (where ships from several nations came to fish for cod) in the name of the king.

Somewhere between Newfoundland and the Chesapeake, Menéndez believed he would find a major waterway. This channel, he thought, would lead to another which traversed the continent to a point near the New Spain mines, reaching the South Sea and opening the way to the Pacific islands and the riches of Asia. Since Menéndez had commercial and political connections in the city of Mexico and held ship licenses for the Vera Cruz trade, this waterway was of direct interest to him.

Knowledge of René de Laudonnière's 1564 establishment at Fort Caroline on the River May (St. Johns River) reached Spain at the end of March 1565, after Menéndez's royal contract had been signed. This

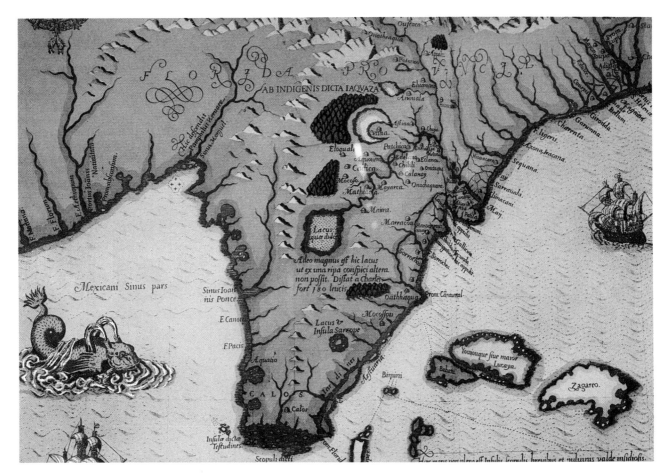

La Florida, based on a map drawn by the Frenchman Jacques le Moyne, who was a part of the colony at Fort Caroline. Locations of many of the place-names are based on hearsay, so the map offers a schematic representation rather than a geographically correct one, though it does contain important information on the names and relative locations of many native groups.

news altered significantly the intentions of Philip II and Menéndez. Not only did the military urgency it generated change the expedition into a royal joint venture through the addition of crown-paid troops; it also redirected Menéndez's efforts away from Santa Elena toward the peninsula of Florida.

As is known, after establishing a settlement at St. Augustine in September 1565, Menéndez rapidly and decisively expelled the French. First he captured Fort Caroline, which he renamed San Mateo. Next he killed the French leader, Jean Ribault, together with many of his followers, on the beaches of Matanzas, south of St. Augustine. Only then could Menéndez begin to explore Florida and proceed with its exploitation. But he still feared that Laudonnière, who had escaped, or some other Frenchman might yet plant a base near enough to the Gulf Stream to endanger the return route of the Spanish fleets.

Pedro Menéndez was first and foremost a seaman. It was always his plan to defend and exploit the land by means of seas and inlets. Therefore, although he sought to establish agricultural and pastoral enterprises, Menéndez realized the need for forest resources for shipbuilding and naval stores. He described his schema in a statement to Philip II: "Fix our frontier lines here, gain the waterway of the Ba-

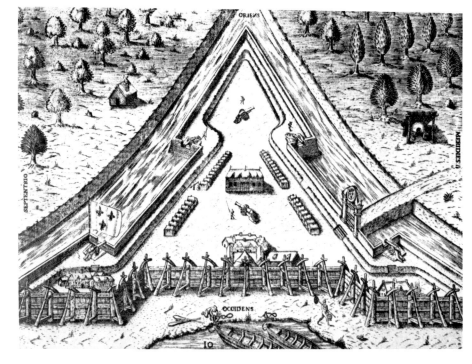

Fort Caroline, established by the French near the mouth of the St. Johns River, was destroyed by Menéndez, effectively ending French attempts to establish a settlement on the Atlantic coast of La Florida.

hamas, and work the mines of New Spain." It was his purpose to anchor and defend his provinces by fortifying ports on their perimeters. In the same way, by means of waterways, he would advance into the trackless continent. He would span the Southeast from the Gulf of Mexico across the rich areas of Coosa to Santa Elena. The adelantado had read the Cañete relation of the de Soto entrada. He knew enough of the failed settlement of Tristán de Luna y Arellano at Pensacola to have heard rumors of the richer inland areas near Coosa and was aware of Ángel de Villafañe's attempt to settle Santa Elena. French prisoners, including a pilot, had told him of the putative continental

The first mass at St. Augustine on 8 September 1565 was celebrated by Father Francisco López de Mendoza Grajales, a member of Menéndez's original colony. This 1875 engraving was commissioned by Bishop Augustín Verot.

St. Augustine, Santa Elena, and the coastal outposts established by Menéndez. Using historical documents and Spanish artifacts, archaeologists have established the general locations of Tocobago (near Safety Harbor), San Antonio (on Mound Key south of Fort Myers), and Tequesta (on the Miami River in downtown Miami). Stanley South of the South Carolina Institute of Anthropology and Archaeology has located and excavated portions of Santa Elena, and Kathleen Deagan and other archaeologists have excavated in St. Augustine. The site of Santa Lucía, for which modern St. Lucie County is named, remains unknown.

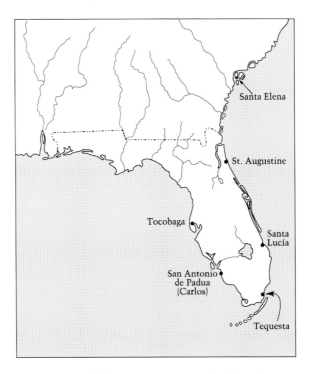

passage and about a system of inland peninsular waterways. At his disposal he also had the services of Gonzalo de Gayón, a pilot with previous experience in Florida waters. From the diverse data he gathered in the course of his initial Florida experience, Menéndez began to evolve his strategy for the mastery of the continent.

When it came, Pedro Menéndez's first peninsular exploration arose more out of necessity than design. He had sent his major vessel, the *San Pelayo*, away from St. Augustine on 10 September 1565 to avoid its possible capture by Jean Ribault's ships. With it went the bulk of still-unloaded goods. After the actions against the French, the Spaniards at St. Augustine quickly ran short of foodstuffs and munitions. It was incumbent upon Menéndez to go to Cuba and seek supplies for his colony.

Menéndez marched down the east coast to Cape Canaveral, while two small craft accompanied him by sea. After dealing at the cape with French survivors who had fortified themselves there, Menéndez continued southward, noting the communication afforded by the protected inland waterway of the Banana and Indian rivers. In the land of the Ais Indians, he proceeded to treat peace with the natives. He left the bulk of his forces in Ais, together with some 50 French prisoners. After Menéndez departed, Fort Santa Lucía was built, probably in the Port Salerno–Jupiter area, called "Jega."

Meanwhile, while sailing in a small craft to Havana, Menéndez realized that a strong inshore countercurrent to the Gulf Stream enabled easy sailing southward along the Florida coast. From Cuba, Menéndez established a supply network for his Florida garrisons. The

The Calusa Indians of southwest Florida, among the first
native groups contacted by
Juan Ponce de León in 1513,
maintained a complex social
and political system, controlling much of South Florida.
Menéndez chose to place a
mission and garrison in
Calos, their main town. This
beautiful wooden panther
(about 6 inches tall) was excavated in the late nineteenth
century by Frank Hamilton
Cushing from a site on
Marco Island south of Calos.

An exquisite woodpecker painted on a wooden tablet, 17 inches long, was also found at the Marco Island site. Cushing's photographer and artist, Wells Sawyer, painted this watercolor of the artifact.

records of this supply are helpful in determining the life of the several posts built in South Florida and along the Gulf coasts.

Menéndez's next voyage took him to southwestern Florida in February 1566. There he was welcomed by Hernando Escalante Fontaneda and other captives of the Calusa Indians. Menéndez planned, and later did establish, a colony near the main village of the Calusa chieftain, Carlos. On this voyage he located a passage for major ships between the Dry Tortugas and Half-Moon Shoal, which would enable vessels to utilize prevailing winds and currents to save precious time on their voyages. This opening, known as the Cuchiaga passage, became vital for the homebound New Spain fleets on their way from Vera Cruz to Havana.

Upon his return to St. Augustine in March 1566, Menéndez's explorations were delayed. He had first to deal with his mutinous soldiery; rebellions and desertions had almost destroyed the colony. Fort Santa Lucía had already been abandoned because of starvation and Indian attacks, amid widespread rumors of cannibalism among the besieged Spaniards. After reasserting his authority at St. Augustine, Menéndez resumed his outreach program. Sailing northward amid the sea islands, he passed through Guale and founded the city of Santa Elena, on present Parris Island, at Eastertide. He sent the Chesapeake Indian, Don Luis de Velasco, to his homeland by an expedition in August 1566. It was also his expectation that the voyagers to the Chesapeake, which he named the Bay of Santa María, and which the Indians called "Jacán," would also uncover the "secret of a river which goes to discharge in the South Sea on the route to China." The expedition, which only reached the Carolina capes, failed in its mission, and returned directly to Spain.

Although Pedro Menéndez had expected eventually to build a South Florida settlement to check possible French moves into that area, events forced his hand when 128 of his mutineers fled San Mateo in a stolen ship, sailing toward the Caribbean. They put into Biscayne Bay for water and left 20 men stranded ashore. Later, when these men were captured and then pardoned, they formed the nucleus of Menéndez's Tequesta colony. Since one of the San Mateo mutineers was named Miguel de Mora, it is likely this man who gave his name to a geographic feature on Spanish maps and *derroteros* for many years, the Bocas de Miguel Mora, the shoal-studded inlet located south of Key Biscayne. When a Spanish fort was built near the mouth of the Miami River, Jesuit Brother Francisco Villareal arrived to establish a mission.

After the mutinies, in the late summer of 1566, Menéndez undertook his own expedition up the St. Johns. He had to attempt to make peace with and among warring Indians in the interior of Florida. Upcountry he sailed in small craft, past Utina and Potano, to the land of Mayaca. There, probably near present Sanford, he found the way blocked by stakes the Indians had planted across the narrowing river. Unable to complete his exploration, Menéndez in the fall of 1566 sent Gonzalo de Gayón to Mayaca via the east coast. Gayón entered the Mosquito inlet (present Ponce de Leon Inlet), established contact with the Indians at Nocoroco and other nearby towns, and ransomed several Frenchmen who had fled from Ribault's forces the year before. These in turn became interpreters for the Spaniards. Gayón could not penetrate to the interior. Unable to pass back out of the inlet due to rough weather, he entered the upper Tomoka River system and made his way back to the area of Matanzas before returning to St. Augustine.

By October 1566, Pedro Menéndez was able to write the king and furnish an appreciation of the wide geographic extent of the provinces of Florida. He told Philip II that he planned to interdict the northern codfishing trade off Newfoundland with a fleet of rapid

R Holata Outina

small craft, levying tribute upon foreigners who intruded upon Spanish jurisdiction to fish there. He went on to describe the Florida peninsula and how he had learned that the upriver St. Johns connected with a great lake, 30 leagues around, where all the land was flat and the water collected.

From this lake, Menéndez believed, navigable rivers flowed into the Gulf at the town of Cacique Carlos and also reached Biscayne Bay. The planting of fort-missions at those exterior points would anchor this inland waterway route. To utilize the waterway, he would ship goods directly from Spain to Florida, transship them from the St. Johns to sailing craft well-protected against Indian attack. The cargoes would be carried to the Gulf exit and be warehoused for shipment to Vera Cruz on Menéndez's galleons, and the swifter, safer passage would save time and money. Because Menéndez possessed ship licenses for that trade, he would personally benefit. The river, which Menéndez first called San Pelayo and which later became the St. Johns, would also be the key to the conquest of the peninsula, serving as the highway into the interior for its pacification and settlement. Pedro Menéndez thus became the earliest proponent of an idea that would recur in the twentieth century as the proposed Cross-Florida Barge Canal.

Now his continental plan could take further shape. Once the Jesuit missions were fully functioning and a *colegio* was built in Havana to educate the sons of the Indian elite, Pedro Menéndez would erect two outposts (fort-missions) spaced along the way to New Spain with settlers and soldiers to develop and protect them. Additional colegios would be established at those outposts. In the first attempt to discover and mark out this route, Menéndez sent Captain Juan Pardo on two entradas from Santa Elena to the Appalachians and beyond. Later, Menéndez applied for another royal conquest contract, this time for Pánuco, which would cement the link between New Spain and Florida and would provide a circumgulf route from Tampico to peninsular Florida.

In the peninsula, Captain Pedro de Andrada made entradas into the Utina and Potano country in 1567. The last of these resulted in an ambush of his forces, in which many Spanish soldiers were killed by the Indians. Andrada's men were only part of casualties suffered in battles and skirmishes with the Timucua, Ais, and other Indian groups. In addition to the fort-mission of San Antonio de Padua near Carlos's village, the Spaniards had left another garrison on the west coast at Tampa Bay, near the Indian town of Tocobaga. Its soldiers were supplied from Havana.

Menéndez decided to make still another effort to search out the cross-peninsular water route from the lower west coast. In early

Facing page: While at Fort Caroline, the French made an expedition up the St. Johns River (traveling to the south). Across the river west of Picolata they anchored and traveled overland 5 leagues to the town of Holata ("chief") Utina, an aboriginal leader who controlled much of the region and who is depicted in this de Bry engraving of 1591. The path they took was a part of the main east-west trail from St. Augustine to Tallahassee (Apalachee) and beyond that would become the Spanish mission trail and later, in 1824, the Bellamy Road, the first federally funded road in the United States.

1567, he sent Hernando de Miranda to explore the area for that purpose. At the same time, he planned to dispatch an expedition from San Mateo upriver on the St. Johns to make contact with those starting inland from the west coast.

In the exploration and supply of Florida, the adelantado's nephew, Pedro Menéndez Marqués, played an important role. This son of Menéndez's brother, Álvar Sánchez, had served the adelantado for many years as a skilled seaman; now his uncle put his abilities to use in the Florida conquest as its chief explorer. Menéndez Marqués also acted as the enforcer when Indians rebelled, bringing order to unruly areas. By 1567, he had been appointed regional governor over the South Florida colonies of Tequesta, Carlos, and Tocobaga.

The adelantado's nephew described his duties:

In 1565–1569, I went by order of Pedro Menéndez de Avilés as his Lieutenant Captain-General of the discovery of the coast of said Florida, to reconnoitre and sound, see and discover the coast, shoals, rivers and ports, bays and coves which are in the said coast of Florida, and in conformity with the contract which His Majesty took, and to search for whatever captives who might be in the possession of Indians, and if there were any enemies fortified in the ports of said coast. And in order to comply, he turned over to me four frigates, two large and two small, with 150 soldiers and sailors of those whom he brought for his account in said conquest of Florida, without counting other small boats which came and went, visiting the forts and going in the coast of Santa Elena, San Mateo and St. Augustine and the other presidios to Havana.

In compliance with which, I have run the length of the coast from the Bay of St. Joseph [in northwest Florida], which is eighty leagues from the River of Pánuco [in Mexico], to Tocobaga [on Tampa Bay] once, and from Tocobaga to Santa Elena and Santa Elena to Tocobaga many times, and from Santa Elena to Jacán and from there to Newfoundland, where the district of the said adelantado ends, once—where I took possession of the land in many Indian towns, calling the caciques Majesty. Since I did not have a cosmographer with me, nor any man who could draw a navigation chart, I did not mark on the charts any more than keeping it in memory, in order that it might be precisely marked and painted; I am giving it by memory by order of Sr. Don Juan de Ovando, President of the Royal Council of the Indies, to Juan de Velasco, Cosmographer and Chronicler of His Majesty and give this certificate at the request of Pedro Menéndez de Avilés.

The Tocobaga and other native peoples around Tampa Bay were closely related and shared many culture traits, including pottery styles. This bottle-shaped pottery vessel was excavated in the 1930s from a mound near the Alafia River that also contained late sixteenth-century glass beads and other European artifacts that may have been distributed when Tampa Bay chiefs assembled at Tocobaga during Menéndez's visit.

Clearly, then, the Reconocimiento of Menéndez Marqués, described in a fragment by Barcía, must have taken place before 1573, even though Barcía dates it to that year. It must have formed the basis for the Florida portion of López de Velasco's work, written down in 1574 but not published until 1894.

Although Philip II had effectively renewed Menéndez's Florida contract in 1568, things by that time were going poorly for the enterprise in peninsular Florida. Eventually, Indian hostility and the sparse response of the native Americans to the missionaries resulted in the loss or closing of the Spanish posts at Santa Lucía, Tequesta, Tocobaga, and Carlos. As dissatisfaction about their Florida experience reached the highest levels of the Jesuit Order in Spain, the missionaries moved to reestablish themselves at Santa Elena.

The abandonment of the South Florida outposts was but a part of a dramatic northward shift within the Florida colony that led to a diminished emphasis on the peninsula. In truth, this shift constituted a reemergence of Pedro Menéndez's original plan for the colonization of Florida. Fort San Mateo, northern anchor of the St. Johns River, was evacuated in 1569, signaling the end of the Menéndez's development scheme for the great river. To replace it, San Pedro was built at Tacatacuru on Cumberland Island, demonstrating the enhanced importance of the sea-island passage to Santa Elena. Straining his resources to the utmost, Pedro Menéndez recruited, paid for, and sent large numbers of settlers to Santa Elena. By 1569, it had become the capital of Spanish Florida, thus affirming the long interest of Europeans in this part of the North American coast.

In 1569–1570, there came a pause in the dynamics of Florida's settlement, brought about by the momentary exhaustion of Menéndez's resources. By stripping the garrisons of men in the summer of 1570, the adelantado denuded the Florida defenses and forced the king's hand. Finally, four major royal councils—state, treasury, Castile, and Indies—met to resolve the crisis in Florida. It was

When ships carrying wealth from the New World back to Spain sank off the Florida coasts, the survivors were often captured and the ships salvaged by native groups such as the Tocobaga and the Calusa. Protecting and recovering the men and cargos was one reason for Spain to desire a permanent presence in Florida. Native artisans used the salvaged metals to fashion ornaments and other objects, like these silver ornaments (*right*) from a site in South Florida. Each has a central perforation through which a thong was attached to a wooden or leather button embossed with gold or another metal. The loose end of the thong could then be used to hold the ornament in place. *Facing page*: The three stylized birds with golden eyes were made by South Florida aboriginal craftsmen using salvaged silver and gold. They may have functioned as hair ornaments.

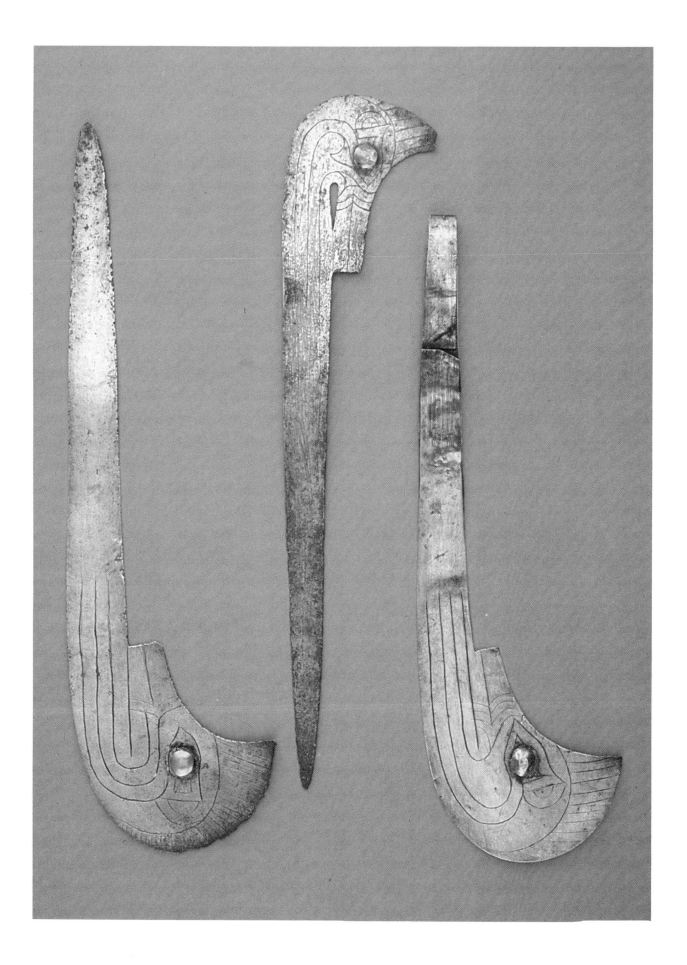

agreed, in November 1570, to establish a regular crown subsidy for the support of the Florida garrisons, which would supplement the private efforts of the adelantado on a regular basis.

With the royal subsidy, a new flowering of the Spanish colony at Santa Elena began. Pedro Menéndez brought his wife, his household, his daughter, and his son-in-law, Don Diego de Velasco. Velasco was appointed to govern Florida from Santa Elena. Based upon the Juan Pardo journeys and the fort-missions that had been established in the areas he explored, Menéndez planned to build his own estate near Guatari, in the Carolina piedmont. It would support the title of marquis, offered to him in his asiento.

But the death of Pedro Menéndez de Avilés in 1574 left his colony in less able hands. The inability of the Spanish to penetrate to richer soils in the interior of the continent reflected the failure of their government to reach an accommodation with the native Americans.

Menéndez's other son-in-law, Hernando de Miranda, was unable to prevent the loss of Santa Elena to Indian attack in 1576. Although Pedro Menéndez Marqués, who followed as governor, proved a vigorous and effective executive, he presided over the dismemberment of Santa Elena in 1587. Ironically, the Spaniards abandoned their northernmost post just as the English settlers under John White landed at Roanoke. The Pánuco contract for Florida gulf coast expansion was allowed to lapse by Pedro Menéndez's heirs, and St. Augustine again, and permanently, became the Spanish capital of Florida.

Long after the death of Pedro Menéndez, however, a few echoes of his policy of geographic outreach still resounded. Governor Gonzalo Méndez Canzo hoped to push Florida's boundaries into modern Georgia, the oft-discussed land of Tama, and westward, but was unable in his brief tenure to carry out his plan. Early in the seventeenth century, expeditions touched at Pohoy below Tampa Bay. In 1680, a later governor expressed renewed concern over the possible linkup of Florida to New Mexico via "Gran Quivira." But no definitive actions were undertaken at the time. Yet Spanish influence over Guale and Apalachee, buttressed by the Franciscan missionary expansion, continued for a time. Seventeenth-century Spanish establishments featured economic development in the Alachua savannah and in Apalachee. Eventually, at the end of the seventeenth century, facing the threat of French activities in the Gulf, the Spaniards resettled Pensacola.

Even though the efforts of Pedro Menéndez de Avilés represented the culmination of a century of effort by crown and conquerors to explore and hold North America, Menéndez never made good even that part of his plan for continental development which featured the exploitation of the Florida peninsula. Gradually forced southward by

English settlements in Virginia, the Carolinas, and Georgia, his Spanish successors saw their territory shrink to the area south of the St. Marys River. Yet the Menéndez years had left a lasting mark upon peninsular Florida, and not only at St. Augustine, the nation's oldest continually occupied city. One instance of this influence occurred in the last decade of the sixteenth century. In Seville, on 30 December 1593, a royal order was issued to Pedro Ambrosio Anderiz, cosmographer of the king, to upgrade the quality of the master navigation chart, the Padrón of the Indies, and create improved astrolabes.

Accordingly, instructions went out to fleet officials and several Indies governors to conduct mapping expeditions. In the instructions, traces that several earlier Florida explorers had left on the map of Florida were evident, together with Indian names. The expeditions were to survey points in "the Martyrs, Cuxiaga, Tortugas, coast of Carlos and Bay of Juan Ponce."

When the governor of Havana returned his report to Ambrosio, he described his expedition's voyage down the east coast of the peninsula. From Cape Canaveral, it had proceeded past Ais to Jega, to Bocas de Miguel de Mora, where an astrolabe shot was taken on the Cayo de los Vizcaínos. Passing old Tequesta, now called the Cabeza de los Martires, the Spaniards sailed along Key Largo, called the Cayo de Doce Leguas, past Matacumbe, and ended at Cuchiaga, where they landed to observe the sun again with their astrolabe. This rutter, or derrotero, listed only a few of the place-names fixed upon the Spanish maps by Pedro Menéndez and his followers during the period 1565–1574, when the Florida peninsula was the subject of their active exploration. Few other traces remained of the Menéndez years, years of outreach, struggle, and vast expenditure of men and monies.

Edward Chaney

Kathleen Deagan

12 / St. Augustine and the La Florida Colony: New Life-styles in a New Land

R ecent research by historians and archaeologists has shown the story of St. Augustine to be as dramatic as that of the first English settlements. The tribulations faced by the settlers of St. Augustine were not greatly different from those that confronted the pioneers at Jamestown and Plymouth. What was distinct, however, was the way in which the Spanish reacted to these hardships. Our expanding knowledge of life at St. Augustine has informed us about more general issues than survival—about the European perception of the New World and the ways in which early settlers responded to the inhabitants and unfamiliar resources of North America.

In the fall of 1565, St. Augustine, Florida, the oldest continuously occupied European community in what is now the mainland United States, was founded by Spain 20 years before England's first, unsuccessful attempt to establish a settlement on Roanoke Island, North Carolina, and more than 40 years before the landing at Jamestown. By the end of the sixteenth century, St. Augustine was a well-established town, while the other European powers had not yet succeeded in their efforts at New World colonization.

Pedro Menéndez de Avilés arrived in Florida on 6 September 1565 with a force of 800 soldiers, sailors, and colonists, including the

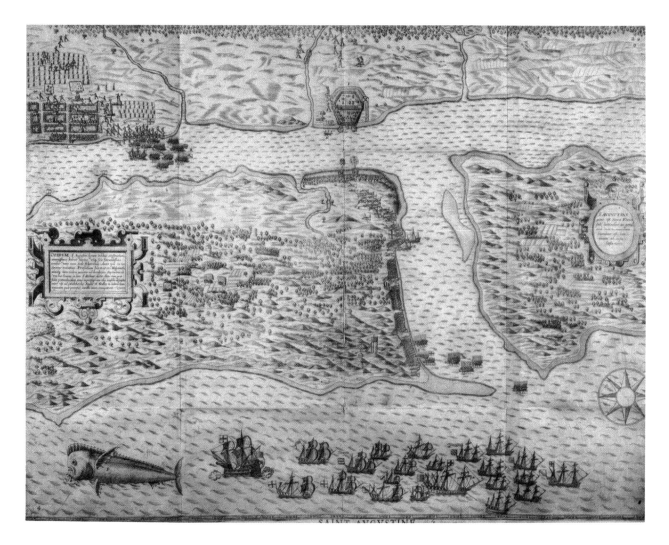

Sir Francis Drake raided and sacked St. Augustine in 1586. His cartographer drew this detailed map of the town, the earliest known. The town, laid out in a grid, is in the upper lefthand portion of the map, and in the upper center is the wooden castillo or fort that was supposed to protect the small settlement.

wives and children of 26 of the men. Philip II of Spain had granted Menéndez permission to found and govern a colony in La Florida, a task that could be completed only after destruction of the French settlement of Fort Caroline, already founded on the Florida coast.

After arriving off Florida's northeast coast, Menéndez initially took refuge in a Timucua Indian town ruled by a chief named Seloy. The Spanish immediately began to fortify the aboriginal village against possible attack by the French from nearby Fort Caroline. They dug a ditch or dry moat around the great house of the chief, and inside of it they erected a defense work made of earth and bundles of sticks.

Original Spanish accounts describing the construction are unclear about the extent of the fortification. It is also uncertain whether all of the Spaniards took up occupation within the Indian town and whether the resident Timucua stayed at their village or moved elsewhere. According to contemporary French accounts from the period, the Spanish occupied at least some of the smaller aboriginal houses of Seloy's town, but it seems likely that they would soon have begun to construct their own, copying an architectural style familiar to them, perhaps adapting Old World traits to the New.

At first Spanish relations with the Timucua were good. The Indians told Menéndez of an overland route to Fort Caroline located to the north near the mouth of the St. Johns River. Following their directions, the Spanish were able to launch a surprise attack on 20 September, destroying the fort and effectively ending the French presence in Florida.

The danger posed by the French to the Spanish at St. Augustine was soon replaced by a threat from the Timucua. Relations between the settlers and the Indians turned sour, and the natives began to set up ambushes when the Spanish left the security of their fortified settlement to search for food. The situation reached a low point on 19 April 1566 when much of the fort was destroyed in a fire blamed on attacking Indians. Menéndez decided to move the settlement to a safer site, the location of which is still debated. It is certain that by 1571, perhaps earlier, St. Augustine was situated in the area it has occupied to the present. To the north of this new settlement, a series of short-lived wooden forts was built to replace the original 1565 fort. The exact locations are also unknown, but they were probably not far from the first fort at Seloy's village.

Investigations have been conducted at a Spanish-Indian archaeological site tentatively identified as the location of Seloy's village and Menéndez's first settlement. It is on the grounds of the Fountain of Youth Park, a tourist attraction situated less than a mile north of Fort San Marcos, the prominent National Park Service monument in St. Augustine. Local tradition places the Spanish landing in this vicinity, and indeed cartographic evidence, such as the 1593 map attributed to de Mestas and the Puente Map of 1769, suggests that the first settlement of St. Augustine was near the Fountain of Youth Park. According to the Spanish, Seloy's village was not visible from the sea but at the same time was situated so ships could be observed entering the St. Augustine harbor. The archaeological site at the Fountain of Youth Park is consistent with this geographical setting, set in a low area hidden by marsh islands yet near high ground to the south and west from which could be seen the entrance to what was then the harbor.

The most persuasive evidence concerning the identity of the site comes from archaeological investigations. Excavations conducted by the University of Florida in the 1950s and by Florida State University in the 1970s revealed that an extensive Timucua Indian village existed on the site at the time of the Spanish arrival in St. Augustine. The archaeological evidence for the village includes the presence of postmolds in a circular pattern (indicative of a round building), of

Bottom: A sixteenth-century Spanish barrel well excavated by Kathleen Deagan and Edward Chaney probably served Menéndez's earliest St. Augustine settlement. *Top*: A rusted barrel hoop was also found. The barrels often rotted, making it necessary to dig the well again and put in new ones.

hearths and cooking pits, of large shell middens where trash was disposed of, and of numerous pieces of aboriginal pottery and other artifacts. In addition, a small section of what appears to be an aboriginal thatched-wall building (or possibly a fence line), consisting of a double row of small, shallow posts placed closely together, has been uncovered. Sixteenth-century Spanish artifacts have also been recovered.

Excavations directed by Kathleen Deagan of the Florida Museum of Natural History in 1985 and 1987 have provided additional evidence for a sixteenth-century Spanish occupation at the Fountain of Youth Park. Perhaps the most dramatic find was a Spanish well. It had been constructed by digging a large hole to a depth below the water table, then stacking in it two white oak barrels held together with iron hoops. Each barrel was about three feet tall without lid or base. Dirt was filled back into the hole around the barrels. Water could then be removed from the well by dipping a bucket down into the stacked barrels. Because the bottom barrel was situated below the water table, and was thus relatively immune to the decomposition caused by microorganisms, it was perfectly preserved (even the bung cork was in place) despite being more than 400 years old.

Numerous Spanish artifacts were found in the well. Before the days of modern garbage collection, any open hole in the ground was an inviting place to dispose of trash. When a well no longer served its original purpose—probably as a result of water contamination that appears to have occurred frequently—it was quickly filled in with refuse for both convenience and safety. For this reason, and because of the fine conditions for preservation in wells, such features are rich sources of artifacts and invaluable resources for archaeologists.

The most common artifact recovered from the well was pottery; nearly 1,400 potsherds were found. A majority of these were Spanish, and the most numerous were from coarse earthenware vessels known as olive jars. Olive jars are ubiquitous in Spanish colonial sites where they served a wide range of utilitarian household functions. Originally used to ship food, oil, and other products, the large amphora-like vessels were recycled for many uses in the New World. A few sherds from finer tableware vessels, such as plates, made from a hand-painted, tin-glazed pottery known as majolica, were recovered as well. Majolica was produced in a variety of distinctive types (defined by the pottery's physical traits and decorative motifs), and each type was manufactured during a known time period. A number of new types were introduced around 1580, but none of these was recovered from the Fountain of Youth Park well, suggesting that it was constructed and abandoned before that date.

Spanish ceramics from early St. Augustine, including majolicas.

Indian pottery sherds were also found in the well. Most of these were manufactured by the resident Timucua Indians. Very few were types produced by more distant tribes who began to appear in St. Augustine later in the sixteenth century and left behind their distinctive pottery. Apparently the Spanish were quick to adopt certain items of aboriginal material culture, such as pottery, because they had difficulty obtaining Spanish-made ware.

Other artifacts include glass trade beads, copper straight pins and lacing tips, water dippers made from conch shells, and various pieces of carved or adzed wood. Small lead shot balls, probably use for hunting birds, were found as well. The shot may have been made at the site.

Other sixteenth-century Spanish features have been discovered. At least two types of building have been revealed. One type is a rectangular structure, approximately 25 by 38 feet, supported by large corner and wall posts driven into the ground. The building was at least partially burnt and later rebuilt. The other is characterized by a number of narrow, linear trenches, which appear to be footing trenches for framed wooden buildings. As yet, not enough of the footings have been uncovered to determine the size of the buildings, but they appear to have been fairly substantial structures. Other features include a possible fence line and various small fire pits and trash pits.

Although only a small portion of the site has been excavated, enough has been revealed to indicate a substantial Spanish occupation in the sixteenth century, one probably associated with the first year of settlement in St. Augustine.

Spanish Missions

Pedro Menéndez had other goals in colonizing Florida besides his economic and military concerns; one was a desire to convert the native inhabitants of the region to Catholicism. The first Catholic mission in North America was founded at St. Augustine in 1565, apparently near the village of Seloy. Known as Nombre de Dios, the mission was not a successful enterprise until the Franciscans took over its operation in the late 1570s or early 1580s, but it remained in existence throughout most of the First Spanish Colonial Period (1565–1763). Many other Spanish-Indian missions were established throughout La Florida during its first century as a Spanish colony. Because of its proximity to St. Augustine, Nombre de Dios served as the flagship of this mission chain.

At the end of the sixteenth century, Nombre de Dios consisted of a sizable Indian village with its own stone chapel (perhaps the only masonry building in Florida at that time) and a resident priest. The other missions of La Florida were also associated with Indian villages, although the smaller missions often lacked resident priests. Missions in less stable parts of the colony were sometimes provided with a small garrison of Spanish troops.

Missions were important to the civil leaders of Florida for reasons other than conversion of the natives. They served as a mechanism

The earliest Spanish mission in La Florida was Nombre de Dios, here shown on a 1595 map. Above the small cluster of buildings is written "Pueblo de Indios Nombre de Dios" (Indian village Nombre de Dios). The mission was located at the north end of St. Augustine near today's chapel of the mission of Nombre de Dios (reconstructed in 1915).

Location of the Florida missions based on information provided by Gabriel Díaz Vara Calderón, bishop of Santiago, Cuba, who visited the colony in 1674–1675. The Tallahassee site of the mission San Luis de Talimali, the main Spanish-Indian settlement in Apalachee, is under study by the Florida Bureau of Archaeological Research and is open to the public.

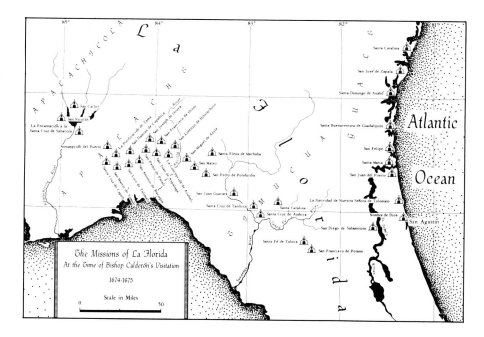

through which the Spanish could strengthen their political and social control over the natives. For example, the Spanish would often try to influence the selection of the chiefs who ruled the various Indian towns and tribal groups. This interference in aboriginal political affairs sometimes proved to be counterproductive, and Indian rebellions would occasionally result.

More important, the missions functioned as distribution points in a network of trade and tribute that led back to St. Augustine. From the beginning, Menéndez had attempted to impose an obligatory tribute system on the natives of La Florida, obtaining corn, animal skins, pottery, and other goods needed by the Spanish. In the late sixteenth century, a scheme of labor tribute was instituted as well. Adult male Indians were sent from their homes to St. Augustine for several months each year to help build fortifications, work in the Spaniards' fields, and provide other services to the colonists. The missions played an instrumental role in organizing this tribute system, which remained in effect until the eighteenth century.

Because the tribute goods were vital for the continued existence of the Spanish colony, certain concessions to the native belief systems were allocated by the missionaries, particularly in the sixteenth century. At certain early missions, such as Santa Catalina in Georgia or Nombre de Dios, some aboriginal practices with prehistoric roots were maintained; they disappeared in later centuries because of their incompatibility with Catholic beliefs. For example, at the early missions, grave goods are often found associated with Christian Indian burials but are more rare in later mission burials. Traditional housing patterns were often continued in the mission villages as well. How-

Left: The governor of Florida had this plan of mission Santa Catalina on Amelia Island drawn and sent to the king of Spain in 1691. The church (*iglesia*), at the lower left, is separated by a plaza from the friary (*convento*) and kitchen (*cocino*) on the right. A second plaza separates the church from quarters for Spanish soldiers. Surrounding the buildings is a moated palisade with ramped bastions. Subsequent documents indicate that the fortifications were never completed, nor, apparently, were the buildings placed in this configuration.

ever, those social practices which were deemed "sinful," such as polygyny and shamanism, were more actively suppressed by Spanish religious and civil leaders.

In the 1930s, a Christian Indian cemetery containing over 100 graves and an associated village, apparently dating to the sixteenth and seventeenth centuries, was discovered at the southwest corner of the Fountain of Youth Park, less than 200 yards from the early Spanish settlement site described. Hundreds of glass beads and other goods were found with the burials. The cemetery and village were probably associated with the mission of Nombre de Dios.

Later St. Augustine

The second phase of the St. Augustine's early history, after it was moved from its original location at Seloy's village, is better understood than the first because a wider range of documentary and archaeological evidence is available. Although it was not a thriving community during the sixteenth century, St. Augustine did stabilize and develop many of the traits that were to characterize it throughout the Spanish colonial era.

In the sixteenth century the town was a male-dominated military garrison, isolated from the rest of the Spanish empire. When Menéndez died in 1574, the colony became a Crown-subsidized dependency

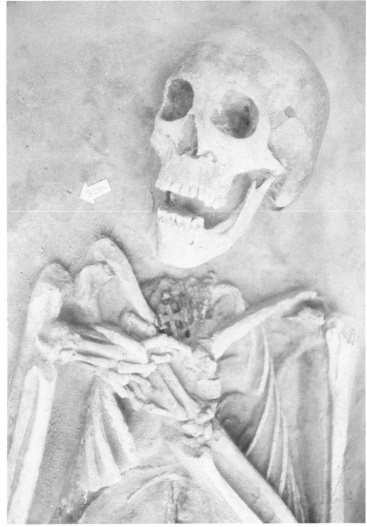

Facing page right: Santa Catalina was established on Amelia Island in 1686 at the site of the earlier mission of Santa María. Raids by English pirates had forced relocation of the mission from its former site on St. Catherines Island, Georgia. Known as the Dorion site, the two Amelia Island missions were discovered as a result of clearing for development. Archaeologist Donna Ruhl excavates the interior of the Santa María church, the western third of which has been eroded away by an adjacent tidal stream. The oyster shell was apparently used to help anchor the eastern wall.

Right: the cemetery for mission Santa Catalina, discovered by Kenneth Hardin of Piper Archaeological Research and excavated in its entirety by Rebecca Saunders of the Florida Museum of Natural History, contained 123 individuals, including adults and children, interred in shallow graves. *Above left and right*: Catholic Guale Indians were buried in shrouds with hands clasped on chest. One person was holding a small metal cross.

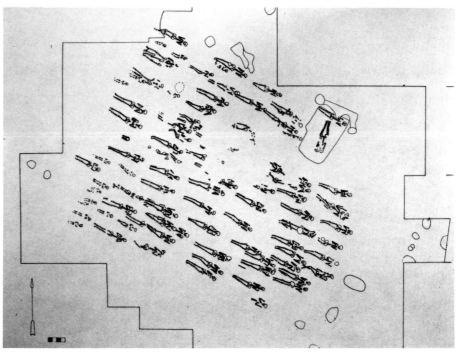

In the northeast corner of the cemetery at Santa Catalina, archaeologists uncovered a large grave containing the remains of more than 50 people. The bones were stacked on top of a single wooden coffin that contained two adult men. Why the bones were buried in this fashion is unknown. Analysis by physical anthropologist Clark Larsen of Northern Illinois University, who helped excavate the cemetery, has not turned up any evidence that these people died as a result of warfare.

because it lacked abundant natural resources or a large native population that could be exploited. La Florida never became self-sufficient, but as a result of the vital role St. Augustine played in the defense of shipping and in the religious conversion of the Indians of the region, the Spanish government was willing to provide the support needed to maintain the colony. The most important aspect of this support was in the form of an annual subsidy of cash and goods, known as the *situado*. The supplies provided by the situado were sent to Florida primarily from Mexico and the islands of the Caribbean. Because inadequacies in the distribution system, combined with official corruption and the threat of shipwreck, made the system an unreliable source of support, poverty and hardship typified life in St. Augustine.

Natural and human-made disasters were also frequent occurrences in sixteenth-century St. Augustine. Floods, fires, and hurricanes racked the town. Epidemics of disease, which hit Florida in 1570, 1586, and 1591, proved to be particularly devastating to the region's native population. For example, the Timucua Indians who lived in northeastern Florida were reduced from a population that probably numbered in the tens of thousands at the time of European contact to about 550 individuals in 1698. Native uprisings, notably that of the Guale Indians along the Georgia coast in 1597, were a threat to the Spanish, especially to the missionaries. Much of St. Augustine itself was destroyed in an Indian attack in 1577. And finally, there was the attack on St. Augustine by the English privateer Francis Drake in 1586, in which the entire town was sacked and burned and its inhabitants forced to flee into the surrounding country. But the town was able to recover from each of these destructive episodes.

Since the 1970s, a number of archaeological excavations have been conducted on sixteenth-century Spanish sites in St. Augustine proper. These investigations have revealed much about daily life in the town, information not apparent from historical evidence alone. For example, the excavations by Kathleen Deagan have confirmed that St. Augustine was a "planned" community, laid out in a regular pattern. The location of streets, public buildings and areas, and individual lots all conformed to the specifications of a town planning ordinance promulgated by the Spanish government in 1563. Residential lots were indicated by the presence of barrel walls, and these also followed a standard pattern. Every sixteenth-century well uncovered in St. Augustine has been located 12–15 yards in from a street edge and at intervals of 12–15 yards along the street. This too is a function of the planning ordinance, as the standard Spanish house lot was approximately 12 yards wide.

The buildings themselves were made of wood. Brick and stone

Modern St. Augustine lies atop its past. Florida Museum of Natural History archaeologist Kathleen Deagan directed this excavation of the Franciscan convento of the Immaculate Conception (headquarters for mission efforts in La Florida), digging down through utility lines and water pipes. The convento, first built of wood in 1588, was destroyed and rebuilt on the same spot several times, the last time of coquina shell blocks. From 1783 to the present, the site functioned as barracks for Spanish soldiers, a jail, an orphanage, a military reservation, and, most recently, the headquarters of the Florida Department of Military Affairs and State Arsenal.

were almost never used in sixteenth-century Florida, although a local shellstone, known as coquina, was discovered by the Spanish in 1580 and came to distinguish later St. Augustine architecture.

Some of the structures in the sixteenth-century town were built from posts placed in the ground. Small, thin sticks were woven around and between these posts, in a technique know as "wattling." The wattle was then covered with a thick layer of clay daub, forming the walls of the building. Wall surfaces were usually smoothed and covered with whitewash.

This Old World method of wall construction, however, was apparently not much used in the earliest years of St. Augustine. Little daub has been found at the Fountain of Youth Park site, suggesting that the Spanish buildings there were made with board or thatch walls. A drawing of St. Augustine made in 1593 shows buildings with what appear to be vertical board walls. It may be that this architectural style was the most common type of construction by that time. Roofs of sixteenth-century buildings in St. Augustine were steeply pitched and typically made with thatch.

Artifacts from St. Augustine dating to the second phase of the town's settlement are similar to those from the earlier Fountain of Youth Park site. Pottery is the most common artifact, and olive jars and other utilitarian earthenware are again by far the most abundant kinds. However, the fine tablewares—mostly majolicas of Spanish or Mexican origin—are twice as common in later St. Augustine than at the park site, and there is a greater variety. This difference may reflect St. Augustine's maturation from a pioneer settlement into a stable community, as well as its increased integration into the Spanish empire after the situado was begun. Nevertheless, the relative scarcity of nonceramic artifacts from St. Augustine, particularly those items that might indicate luxury or wealth, suggests that Florida was still an impoverished backwater throughout the sixteenth century.

Over half of the pottery found in the later sixteenth-century town is of aboriginal manufacture. Much of it is sooted or was found in contexts that indicate use in food preparation and cooking. About half of this aboriginal pottery was produced by the Timucua Indians who lived in the region around St. Augustine; the other half was of nonlocal manufacture, mostly types associated with the Guale Indians of the Georgia coast. This distribution contrasts with the earlier park site, where nonlocal Indian ceramics were rare. No doubt the Spanish expansion throughout La Florida during the course of the late sixteenth century, with the accompanying increase in trade and the development of a tribute system, accounts for the differing amounts of nonlocal Indian ceramics between the early and later sites. Imported aboriginal pottery was simply not available during St. Augustine's early years. The trend toward increased use of imported Indian wares continued throughout the Spanish colonial period, and by the eighteenth century more than three-quarters of the aboriginal pottery in St. Augustine was nonlocal, although the drastic decline in the Timucua population during that time is no doubt partly responsible for this occurrence.

The reliance on aboriginal ceramics by the Spanish population of St. Augustine points to an important aspect of social life in the community. When St. Augustine was first settled, few Spanish-born women moved to the town. Spanish men who lived there often took Indian women as wives. The offspring of such marriages were known as *mestizos*. By 1580, more than 25 percent of the households in St. Augustine may have had a female Indian member. This integration of native women into Spanish households produced certain changes in the lifeways of the town. Not unexpectedly, most of these changes centered around female activities, such as food preparation and child care. (Male activities tended to follow the traditional Iberian pattern largely because there was little integration of Indian men into Spanish society.) Indian women brought to St. Augustine those practices that were most familiar to them in these spheres of activity, and they in turn passed them on to their mestizo daughters. Thus, the Indian women not only used their own ceramics to process and store food;

they also made meals using many native foods, prepared in traditional fashion.

In Spain, sheep and cattle were the primary animal food sources, providing both meat and dairy products. Poultry was also an important dietary component; pigs, goats, and other domestic animals were less frequently eaten. Wild game was usually reserved for the upper classes, but deep-water fish were commonly available. Legumes and cereal grains, such as wheat and barley, were also a major part of the typical Iberian diet, as were a wide variety of fruits and vegetables.

But this dietary regime was not transferred intact to La Florida. Research by Drs. Elizabeth Reitz and Margaret Scarry has shown that in St. Augustine constraints imposed by the distinct environmental conditions of the region caused drastic changes in the Spaniards' diet, changes no doubt expedited by the presence of Indian women in St. Augustine households. Sheep were not able to adapt well to life in Florida, so mutton was supplemented by pork, which, along with beef, became the primary domesticated meat. However, wild fauna, particularly deer and estuarine fishes, became the most important source of animal protein.

Major plant foods of Spain were also largely replaced in Florida by indigenous crops, such as maize, beans, and squash, although Old World fruits and vegetables that could survive in Florida were raised as well. Native techniques for cultivating these indigenous crops, and for the acquisition of game and fish, were also adopted by the Spanish.

St. Augustine's Spanish past, including foodways, is brought to life through living exhibits.

In general, the Spanish diet in sixteenth-century St. Augustine quickly took on a distinct flavor, one greatly affected by aboriginal subsistence practices. Of course, aboriginal foodways were also modified by contact with Europeans. Old World fruits and vegetables, as well as domesticated livestock such as chickens and pigs, were raised by the native peoples. In addition, the introduction of European farm implements, such as metal hoes, combined with the increased sedentism imposed on the Indians by the mission system, allowed for the adoption of more intensive farming practices.

Because a number of later sixteenth-century sites have been excavated in St. Augustine, we can glean some idea of the distinctions in social and economic status during that period. Such differences are based on subtle variations in the types of artifacts recovered from each site, judged on the basis of analogy to artifacts recovered from eighteenth-century contexts in St. Augustine. The status of the occupants of the eighteenth-century houses could be determined through historical records, thus providing a model that could be tested archaeologically.

As with the eighteenth-century sites, the clearest indicator of status in the sixteenth century appears to be the ratio of imported (and therefore costly) majolica ceramic wares to inexpensive aboriginal ceramics. Those sites with the highest percentage of majolica have the lowest amount of aboriginal pottery and thus are thought to represent high status residences. In contrast, those sites with little majolica have the highest percentage of Indian ceramics and probably represent low status households. The number of types of imported pottery also varies with the percentage of majolica, so that sites with the most majolica have the greatest variety of imported wares. Yet another indicator of status is the number of nonceramic kitchen items (glassware and utensils) found on a house lot. As expected, high status households have the greatest percentage of these items.

Several themes emerge from the history and archaeology of sixteenth-century St. Augustine. Perhaps the most significant is the nature and degree of the adaptations the Spanish were forced to make when confronted by the conditions in the New World. Most notable were the modifications in Iberian diet and food patterns that resulted from constraints imposed by Florida's environment. Interaction with the aboriginal peoples of Florida, particularly the women, produced changes in Spanish social patterns as well.

Certain aspects of Spanish culture changed only a little, such as the development of a town plan based on an Iberian model or the use of majolica and other European goods to reflect status. The integration of all these elements—Old World and New, Indian and Spanish—ultimately produced a distinctive *criollo* culture. Criollos

The Castillo de San Marcos, built of coquina block in the late seventeenth century, dominates modern St. Augustine as it must have dominated Spanish St. Augustine in the past. Today a national landmark open to the public, it is a dramatic symbol of our nation's Hispanic heritage.

were men and women of Spanish descent (and, usually, in St. Augustine, Indian as well) who were born in the New World and were considered second-class citizens, inferior to the *peninsulares* of Old World birth. However, in St. Augustine, criollos constituted the largest segment of the population, and their way of life came to dominate the nonnative culture of Florida. The criollo culture was apparently conservative: those aspects of it seen to be developing in the sixteenth century were little modified in the eighteenth century.

Native cultures were also greatly changed by the Spanish presence in La Florida, with a sort of aboriginal criollo society developing around the missions. The imposition of Christianity and tribute labor brought vast changes to the Indians' social, political, and religious systems, but some prehistoric elements of native culture—the organization of villages, the methods by which status distinctions were manifested, and some aspects of traditional subsistence patterns—were maintained at the missions. But the final effect of European contact upon the native peoples of La Florida was their extinction, a result of both disease and overwhelming social disruption.

The story of sixteenth-century St. Augustine is of significance to U.S. history. No longer should the Spanish enterprise in Florida be viewed as a side note of no relevance in the development of an Anglo-American nation. The Spanish presence in the Southeast affected the way in which the English colonies were settled and evolved. Tribulations and hardships faced by the Spanish in La Florida were similar to those confronting the colonists to the north, and it is not unreasonable to assume that the English learned some lessons from the Spanish experience. And even if there was no direct Spanish influence on the English colonies, an understanding of the ways in which the Spanish adapted to life in North America should lead to a better understanding of the English settlers' reactions to their surroundings.

Susan Milbrath

13 / Old World Meets New: Views across the Atlantic

The voyages of Christopher Columbus transformed the Atlantic Ocean from a mysterious abyss into a pathway to the wealth of the New World. Columbus gave trinkets to natives in the Bahamas and Caribbean, and he carried gold, artifacts, plants, and captive natives back to Europe, beginning an exchange of epic proportions. The ensuing traffic of people, plants, animals, raw materials, and art is well known. Not so well documented is the more enigmatic part of the Columbian exchange—the effect these early encounters had on the human imagination.

Letters, chronicles, works of fiction, and visual arts in the sixteenth century indicate that the discovery of the New World engaged the popular imagination, as images of the encounter spread rapidly via the newly developed printing press. Some of what was printed was more fantasy than fact. Artists did not accompany the earliest voyages, and many visual images of the New World during the first half of the sixteenth century reinforced existing myths or created new ones. Written descriptions also distorted, and often the Europeans saw what they wanted or expected to see.

The Asian Connection

At the time of the earliest European voyages to the New World, monstrous creatures were thought to inhabit regions of Asia. Columbus owned and annotated an account of Marco Polo's travels, illustrated with images of such races. In his widely published letter describing the first voyage, Columbus said that he had heard that people living to the west of Juana (Cuba) were born with tails but that he had not seen any human monstrosities. Nevertheless, at the time of his first voyage, he was convinced that there were dog-faced men, such as are illustrated in *The Voyages and Travels of Sir John Mandeville*. In this narrative, first published in French in 1356, Mandeville claimed to have traversed more than half of the earth's latitude.

Mandeville's account of monstrous races became increasingly popular after the discovery of the New World. In 1530 it was reprinted three times, and many believed that Columbus's discoveries confirmed Mandeville's claims. Although Columbus found no human monstrosities, his description of the man-eating Caribs did seem to confirm the existence of the anthropophagy described by Mandeville.

The connection between cannibalism and human monstrosities is made clear in Frie's *Uslegung der Carta Marina* (1525), which illustrates dog-headed monsters performing cannibal activities on an island discovered by Columbus. They are shown butchering and eating people, while human body parts hang from rafters of their house, recalling illustrations of cannibalism in accounts relating to Vespucci's

This painting of monstrous races of Asia was used to illustrate a fourteenth-century edition of Marco Polo's *Travels*.

Statue of a Moor dressed like a Timucuan Indian from Florida. Fanciful images connecting the New World and Asia persisted long after the earliest European exploratory expeditions.

voyages. As late as 1623, in his book *Aggivnta alla qvarta parte*, published in Venice, Alessandro Vecchio depicts dog-faced cannibals purported to live on an island discovered by Columbus.

Imagery of the New World in the early sixteenth century also placed native Americans in Asia. In 1513 Emperor Maximilian I, with an apparent lack of modesty, commissioned a series of 109 miniature drawings depicting the *Triumph of Maximilian I* over the races of the world. Woodcuts of these drawings published in 1526 show Brazilian Indians in scenes of the "People of Calicut."

In the realm of decorative arts, the Asian connection lived on in fanciful ornaments. Helmut Nickel of the Metropolitan Museum of Art notes that a feathered headdress and jewelry modeled after sixteenth-century images of Timucuan (Florida) Indians grace an eighteenth-century statue of a Moor, now in the Grünes Gewölbe collection. And figures of Timucuan and Algonquian Indians appear in a Chinese landscape represented in an early eighteenth-century lacquered cabinet now in the Walters Art Gallery in Baltimore.

Myths of monstrous races in the New World also persisted in visual imagery. Some of the tales of monstrous races were the result of direct information from the native Americans, such as Raleigh's account of headless Indians from Euyana who had mouths in the middle of their breasts, illustrated by Hulsius in *Die funfte Schiffart* (1599). As late as 1754, Lafitau pictures similar headless beings among the races of North American Indians in *Moeurs des Sauvages Ameriquains.*

America was exotic, and in the absence of direct observation artists let their imaginations run wild. Long after the early explorers, fanciful images connecting America and Asia persisted in decorative arts and other art forms.

The Earliest Images of Native Americans

Since artists did not accompany the earliest voyages, visual images were based on European preconceptions and literary descriptions by the explorers. The earliest European description of the New World is found in Columbus's letter written upon returning from his first voyage in 1493, printed in Barcelona without illustrations in April 1493 and published subsequently in many editions.

An edition of Columbus's letter in the collection of the New York Public Library may show the first illustration of the Americas. This

Columbus meeting the Taíno on Hispaniola in a woodcut published in Giuliano Dati's edition of Columbus's 1493 letter. King Ferdinand, on his throne, is in the left foreground. The engraver used information in the letter to portray native dress.

This 1493 woodcut depicting Christopher Columbus landing on the island of Hispaniola (*Insula hyspana*) was used to illustrate a Latin version of his letter, probably printed in Basel. The ship is inaccurately portrayed as a Mediterranean galley, and descriptions of the Taíno Indians he encountered are only loosely based on his information in the letter.

edition lacks a date and place of publication, but it probably was printed in Basel in 1493. The flags of Aragon and León identify Columbus's sailing vessel, inaccurately rendered with the oars characteristic of Mediterranean ships. Some of the natives wear beards, even though the text says they lack facial hair. The scene in the Basel edition has been identified as both Guanahani (San Salvador) and Hispaniola, now known as Haiti and the Dominican Republic. The latter identification seems more likely since the title of the print is *Insula hyspana*, which is a Latin translation of "Island of Española."

Most subsequent editions of Columbus's letter had woodcut prints based on descriptive information in the letter. These woodcuts are a good clue to the types of images that the discovery evoked in the European imagination. A Rome edition published in June 1493 depicts King Ferdinand enthroned in the foreground while Columbus lands at an island in the background. This woodcut seems to be a more accurate illustration than the Basel edition. The three ships are rendered as ocean-sailing caravels rather than Mediterranean ships. The women have their genitals covered with leaves, in accord with a passage in the letter describing the women of Hispaniola. The Rome edition depicts all the natives running away, unlike the Basel edition which shows some people trading.

Some details seem to be drawn from the tradition of fifteenth-century woodcuts. The thatched rectangular structures pictured in the Rome woodcut are not mentioned in the letter. They seem to be modeled after the type of structure found in late fifteenth-century European woodcuts representing early human history. These subtle references suggest that the artist, without having seen anything of the New World, cast the natives in the role of primitive people living prior to the development of European civilization.

In October 1493, Dati published a pamphlet that included an Italian poem, a translation of Columbus's letter, and a new image of Columbus landing, entitled "La lettra dell isole che ha trovato nuovamente il Re di Spagna." Rendered in the style of illustrations in early Renaissance romances, this Florentine woodcut is appropriate to Dati's poem, which is written in the form of a chivalric epic. Like the 1493 Rome edition, the woodcut has two thatched structures, three ships, a tall palm tree, and fleeing natives, including women with leaf belts covering their genitals and men with beards that are long and patriarchal. The major differences are the border treatment, details of the boat, the vegetation, and the placement of the king's throne in the foreground. A related scene appears in a 1495 Florentine edition, but here the artist added an inaccurate detail by dressing both men and women in leaf belts. It seems that as time passed, artists relied less on Columbus's descriptions, and more on visual images supplied in previous publications of the letter, sometimes introducing new details not related to descriptions in the letter.

The next important eyewitness account is Vespucci's letter to Lorenzo di Pier Francesco de'Medici written in 1500, which describes his first voyage to South America in 1499. Traveling with the Spanish captain Alonso de Ojedo (Hojeda), Vespucci encountered cannibals and discovered the Amazon and Pará rivers. Subsequent letters to de'Medici describe his second voyage, under the Portuguese flag. All of the extant Vespucci letters to de'Medici remained unpublished in the sixteenth century, but in his *Amerigo Vespucci: Pilot Major* (1966), Frederick Pohl notes that the letters circulated after de'Medici's death in 1503 provided information for two spurious accounts: *Mundus novus* (1502–1504) and *Lettera delle isole novamente trovate* (1505–1506). Scholars sympathetic with Vespucci attribute these accounts to publishers eager to capitalize on the new discoveries, while others suggest Vespucci himself invented two added voyages to make the claim that he was first to see the South American continent and forestall Columbus's legitimate claim to the discovery of a mainland on his third voyage in 1498.

Cannibalism, mentioned in both the Columbus and Vespucci accounts, was first illustrated in a woodcut published in a Nuremberg edition, entitled *Von der neugefunde Region* (1505), probably printed

by Johann Froschauer of Augsburg. The "encounter" is evoked by European ships in the background. A seated woman with a leaf belt suckles a child, and standing males wear headdresses, skirts, armbands, and legbands made of feathers. The poses seem naturalistic, and the total effect is more realistic than illustrations of Vespucci's accounts.

The German caption says the illustration shows the people and the islands discovered by the Christian king of Portugal or by his subjects, without mentioning Vespucci by name. It states that the men and women wear feathers covering their private parts and precious stones inset in perforations in their faces and chests, as illustrated in the woodcut. The text mentions their cannibalism, saying they hang body parts to smoke, a detail also depicted in the woodcut.

The caption seems to embellish an account found in a letter from Vespucci to Lorenzo de Pier Francesco de'Medici, written from Lisbon in 1502, describing his voyage for Portugal along the coast of South America in 1501–1502. Vespucci says the natives pierce their lips and cheeks and set the perforations with ornaments of stone and bone, whereas the woodcut and caption indicate the stones are inset in the cheeks and chest. The caption says that they lack government and live to be 150 years old. According to Vespucci's letter, the people are long-lived; he estimated that one old man had reached the age of 132. The letter says that they live without laws, according to nature, with each man being his own master. Cannibalism is mentioned, but the letter does not describe cooking human flesh. Vespucci does not describe the feathered costumes worn by the males in the woodcut. The female apparel seems to be based on leaf belts worn by women in illustrations of Columbus's letter. Depictions of

These woodcuts are from the 1509 Strassburg edition of *La Lettera* attributed to Amerigo Vespucci. *Left*: Tupinamba Indians, showing cannibalism and other scenes from daily life. *Right*: The murder of one of Vespucci's men, here facing a group of Tupinamba women depicted in the style of European representations of the "Three Graces." The mariner was cut up and roasted, according to Vespucci's text.

male garb seem to be accurate, in accord with Tupinamba costuming recorded by Dürer in 1515, who drew native costumes or captive Brazilian Indians brought to court.

Vespucci's letter to Pier Soderini, a spurious account variously entitled *La Lettra, Lettera delle isole novamente trovate*, or *Four Voyages*, elaborates on Vespucci's description of his second voyage. It was originally published between 1504 and 1506 in Florence. The earliest illustrations of this account appear in a 1506 Magdeburg edition, which depicts the Indians looking like Adam and Eve, covering their nakedness in shame—even though the text indicates the natives were shamelessly naked. Here the artist apparently evokes a link between the terrestrial paradise and the New World mentioned in the accounts of Vespucci and Columbus.

A 1509 German translation of *Four Voyages*, published in Strassburg, is the first edition to depict specific narrative incidents purportedly described by Vespucci, including cannibal activities, trade, and hostile attacks. In one scene, the Europeans hand out items that may be metal plates and bells, like those described as trade goods in the second voyage of *Four Voyages*. Another woodcut illustrates a woman nursing a baby, a man urinating, and a cannibal woman cutting up a body. These are all scenes described in Vespucci's account, but the round and hexagonal houses depicted in the background are pure invention. The nude female suckling a baby may relate to medieval images of wild folk, particularly *The penance of Saint John Chrysostom* engraved by Dürer around 1497.

A third illustration depicts the murder of a mariner described by Vespucci. The illustration follows details in the text, showing an unsuspecting sailor about to be knocked out by a woman coming up from behind. The sailor faces three seductive woman, who resemble the three nude women in Lucas Cranach's woodcut *The Judgement of Paris* (1508), and the three graces in Botticelli's painting *Primavera* (1477). Although the Strassburg artist clearly modeled the scene on Vespucci's account, Vespucci does not specifically mention three women and the artist subtly suggests a link with the classical themes, casting the New World in the realm of the "golden age" of classical antiquity.

Mundus novus describes Vespucci's third voyage to South America, but the information actually is based on his second and final voyage to the New World in 1501–1502. Illustrations in the earliest version of *Mundus novus* appear to be unrelated to the text. In subsequent editions the imagery is linked to the text but often reflects European concepts rather than ethnographic reality. In effect, the artistic image was filtered through a literary mesh that was partially a product of the European imagination.

The sixth Latin edition of *Mundus novus* was published in Strassburg in 1505 with the subtitle "De ora antartica." Like the woodcuts accompanying Columbus's letter, the emphasis is on the European landing and the reactions of the natives. The title page depicts three European caravels and two small boats that may be native canoes.

Two 1505 woodcuts show *(top)* nude South American natives and *(bottom)* Amerigo Vespucci's boats arriving in the New World. The scenes are from the title page of *Be ora antartica,* a work attributed to Vespucci.

South American natives visualized like Adam and Eve in a 1505 edition of Vespucci's *De nouo mundo.*

In a separate scene above, several nude people gesture their surprise on seeing the Europeans. The nude figures in *Mundus novus* seem hastily rendered, like those illustrated in Columbus's letters, but, rather than depicting a herd of fleeing people, they are distinguished as separate individuals, adding a touch of humanity.

A 1505 Latin edition of Vespucci's letter published in Rostock shows a nude male and female standing in graceful classical poses. Vespucci's descriptions of the attractive physique typical of native women may have inspired the image of a voluptuous female with long curly hair, but the stronger source of inspiration seems to be European images of the early Renaissance.

The muscular bearded male and sensuous female with long curly hair resemble sixteenth-century German woodcuts representing Adam and Eve, such as Lucas Cranach's 1509 woodcut printed in Dresden. And the female, a *contrapposto* figure wrapped in knee-length hair holding a hand up to her breasts, seems reminiscent of Botticelli's *Birth of Venus* (1480). This painting was influenced by Neoplatonism, a movement that infused classical imagery with Christian meaning. Except for the lack of body hair, the long-tressed Rostock nude also resembles females in medieval scenes of wild folk of the forest living beyond the bounds of civilization as illustrated in Timothy Husband's *The Wild Man* (1980). The Rostock woodcut evokes imagery of Venus, Eve, and the "wild women" living apart from civilized society. These concepts are not as different as they would seem, for all reflect the idea of an earlier stage in history. There is little ethnographic detail in the Rostock image, except for the nudity and the bow and arrow carried by the male, an appropriate weapon based on Vespucci's descriptions, but the actual form of the bow may be drawn from fifteenth-century European woodcuts showing similar bows.

Although images accompanying Vespucci's letter are often inaccurate and the published letters themselves may be forgeries, they are a primary source for our understanding of European perceptions of the New World during the first decade of the sixteenth century. Vespucci's accounts were more widely circulated than Columbus's letter, and while Columbus claimed only to have found a new route to Asia, Vespucci's account of discovering a "new world" was more exciting to the European imagination. By 1505 there were 14 Latin editions of *Mundus novus*, and by 1515, 30 editions had been printed in modern languages. The letters attributed to Vespucci and Columbus published in the sixteenth century mention both nudity and cannibalism, but only accounts attributed to Vespucci illustrate cannibalism. These early illustrations show that the Europeans had a fascination with traits that were considered primitive or outside the bounds of civilization.

In the first book ever published about Peru, Christobal de Mena's *La conquista del Peru* (Seville, 1534), the Incas are depicted carrying bows and wearing leaf belts and swaddled loincloths, unlike the text

Pizarro and a Spanish priest meet the Inca ruler Atahualpa (woodcut published in Seville in 1534). Native dress of the Peruvian Indians is drawn from other European images of Caribbean Indians, probably from early editions of Columbus's letter, rather than the text that accompanied the woodcut.

which says the men were dressed in livery (tunics) under which they hid clubs. Their leaf belts were probably copied from illustrations in editions of the letters of Columbus. An Inca ruler on a palanquin with an umbrella may be drawn from woodcuts of Asian potentates, like the *King of Cochin China* (1508) by Lucas Cranach the Elder. Mena also shows people holding bows and arrows, as in the Cranach image, a trait totally inappropriate to the text, which specifies that the natives carried clubs.

Early visual images of native Americans have little ethnographic value. Most of the images draw largely on descriptions by Columbus and Vespucci, sometimes linked with concepts of the golden age of antiquity, the Garden of Eden, or the medieval tradition of the "wild man"—all references to an early stage in human development. A turning point toward more accurate images of the New World occurred when artists began to accompany expeditions and render scenes from life. Here the variations in presentation reflect differences in artistic skill and attitude toward the subject, rather than fantasies or inventions based on written descriptions that were themselves often the result of preconceptions and fantasies.

Early Illustrations of Native Americans from Life

Albrecht Dürer may have been the first artist to draw a New World native from life. Illustrating a Book of Hours for Emperor Maximilian I in 1515, he rendered an ink drawing of a Tupinamba man with great accuracy, including a feather scepter like those known from ethnographic collections of the Mundurucu Indians of Brazil. There is, however, a touch of idealization in the graceful pose of the figure and his gentle face.

According to William C. Sturtevant in Chiapelli's *First Images of America* (1976), both Dürer and Burgkmair, creators of the woodcuts for the "Peoples of Calicut" in the *Triumph of Maximilian I*, probably used Tupinamba models or costumes. Tupinamba costuming became standard for images of Amerindians, and even the Aztecs were so depicted on the title page of a 1523 Latin edition of the second letter from Cortés.

Gonzalo Fernández de Oviedo y Valdés is credited with the first-known illustrations done by a traveler to the New World. These crude renderings are an important but inadequately studied source of ethnographic information. His drawings of Hispaniola, Central America, Peru, and Patagonia (dating between 1526 and 1557) depict a variety of subjects, including housing, weapons, canoes, fire drilling, and gold-panning. Of more than 20 drawings, only 3 were published in 1526 in his *Sumario*; 7 more were published as part of the first

Hans Staden, an untrained artist, was one of the first Europeans to depict native Americans from life. This woodcut, printed in 1557 in an account of his captivity among the Tupinamba, shows a prisoner being prepared for sacrifice.

19 books of his *Historia General y Natural de las Indies* printed in 1535. Subsequently his image of a Patagonian camp was published posthumously in Book XX in 1557, but all the other drawings remained unpublished until the nineteenth century. His simple illustrations do not reveal his sentiments; it is only in the text that we become aware of his negative attitude toward Amerindians.

The first illustrations of Mexican natives drawn from life are the watercolors by Christoph Weiditz done when the court of Charles V was in Toledo or Barcelona in 1529. Scenes include accurate representations of a *patoilli* game, a man juggling a log with his foot, and a ball game played by two men. He also illustrated six standing figures with costumes appropriate to their different ranks and roles. It is unlikely these images had a strong impact, since they remained unpublished; nevertheless, they represent an important development toward more accurate ethnographic representations, and they probably were seen by other artists.

In 1553, Pedro Cieza de León published his *Primera parte de la crónica del Peru* with 42 woodcuts of Peruvian Indians, but only 12 were of different scenes and only two of those seem based on any ethnographic reality. Cieza de León's sympathetic view of the Incas was reinforced by their benevolent appearance in the woodcuts.

In 1557, Hans Staden published a German account illustrated with woodcuts depicting his adventures as a captive among the Tupinamba Indians of Brazil in 1553–1554. A translation of the title, *Description of a Country of Wild Naked, Cruel, Man-eating People in the New World*, reveals his attitude toward his captors. Nevertheless, the illustrations are important ethnographic documents depicting details of Tupinamba life, such as village plans, agriculture, longhouses, cooking, fishing, warfare, and cannibalism. The wood-cuts were done from Staden's drawings or under his supervision. The natives in group scenes are nude, but there is considerable detail in the activities shown and some scenes focus on individual figures to illustrate costuming and weapons.

Staden's chronicle reached a much larger audience in 1592 when the Flemish engraver Theodore de Bry published it, reworking the primitive woodcuts into elegant engravings. De Bry maintained the emphasis on cannibalism and nudity, but he added many costumes and landscape details. He misinterpreted body paint as hair, introducing a subtle link to established European images of the "wild man," a legendary being living beyond the bounds of civilization—the sixteenth-century equivalent of Bigfoot.

In 1565, Girolamo Benzoni published an illustrated Italian account, *La Historia de mondo nuovo*, which described his extensive travels in America between 1541 and 1556. Benzoni's field sketches were of great ethnographic value and served as models for eighteen woodcuts depicting a variety of subjects, including scenes of fire drilling, Incas worshipping the sun, natives of Hispaniola committing suicide to avoid capture by the Spanish, and Indians of Darien forcing the Spaniards to swallow molten gold and roasting and eating their flesh.

Between 1594 and 1596, de Bry published Benzoni's work in three volumes as part of his compendium on America. De Bry's treatment takes great liberties with Benzoni's images, incorporating many European elements, and inventing scenes not illustrated in Benzoni's original work. The overall effect was to romanticize the imagery and remove it from ethnographic reality. De Bry also invented illustrations to support Benzoni's description of the cruel European treatment of the Indians. He depicted a number of gruesome scenes not illustrated by Benzoni, including Spaniards throwing natives to the dogs and de Soto torturing the Indians to find out where they acquired gold, adding fuel to a growing controversy about Spanish attitudes toward native Americans.

Published images of the far north were rare during the sixteenth century. The most notable are a set of illustrations based on two voyages by Martin Frobisher under the English flag to the southern Baffin Islands in 1576–1577. These first appeared as woodcuts in a 1577 French translation of Dionyse Settle's *A True Report of the Laste Voyage into the West and Northwest Regions*. The artist on this voyage may have been the Englishman John White. One of White's surviving paintings, a scene of English sailors in a skirmish with the Eskimos, probably represents the battle off Bloody Point in Frobisher's expedition. A modified version of this painting appears as the wood-

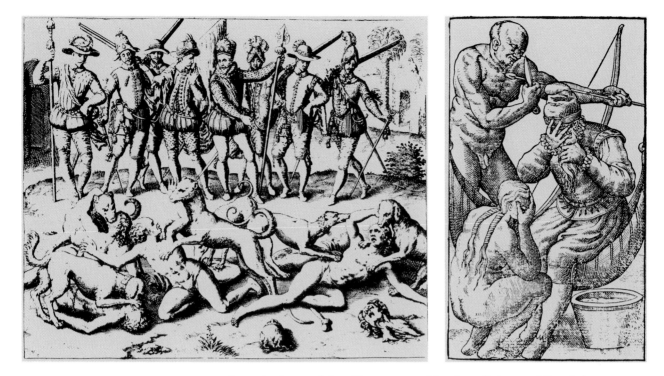

Left: Theodore de Bry and his family engraved hundreds of images which were used to illustrate books about the New World. This engraving, published in 1596, accompanied an account by Girolamo Benzoni of Spaniards throwing native peoples to the dogs. Illustrations and accounts such as these help to spread the "Black Legend" of Spanish atrocities in the New World. *Right*: A Frenchman and a Tupinamba woman engaged in the weeping greeting, depicted by Jean de Léry in his 1578 book.

cut frontispiece of the German and Latin editions of Settle's account published in 1580.

In 1557, André Thevêt published *La singularitez de la France antarctique*, which was illustrated with 24 woodcuts. Since Thevêt spent only a few months in Brazil in 1555–1556, much of his book is based on hearsay and imagination. He includes a number of illustrations of things he could not have seen firsthand, such as Plains bison and Amazon women warding off attacks by men landing in canoes. Even though the illustrations of the Tupinamba (attributed to the French Mannerist painter Jean Cousin the Younger) were not done from life, they apparently depict activities of Brazilian Indians with fair accuracy, indicating the artist had reliable guidance in their execution.

Thevêt's *La Cosmographie Universelle*, published in Paris in 1575, is also illustrated with woodcuts by Jean Cousin the Younger. Some of the woodcuts published in Thevêt's earlier volume were reworked, and he included some new Tupinamba views and portraits. One scene inside a hut depicts him visiting a mourning woman while a Tupinamba boy lifts the hem of Thevêt's garment with curiosity. Such scenes went far toward humanizing the natives in European eyes, countering the negative tone of the text.

In 1578, Jean de Léry published a French account of his travels to Brazil, *Histoire d'un voyage fait en la terre du Brésil*, illustrated with elegant woodcuts of Brazilian Indians. He borrowed some of Thevêt's images and included new scenes showing personal ornaments, hammocks, dancers with rattles, and mourners. He copied

Timucuan chief Athore showing René de Laudonnière how Timucuans worship a stone column erected by the French in 1562. The painting by Jacques le Moyne is the only one of his paintings of America known to survive.

the famous Tupinamba weeping greeting from Thevêt but improved on the image. His natives were muscular individuals posed in the heroic postures that were fashionable in European art of the epoch. Romanticized images effectively convinced the viewer of the grace and beauty of the Tupinamba.

The tendency of trained artists to borrow from the work of other established artists was as common in the sixteenth century as it is today. Jean de Lery's artist was influenced by Jean Cousin the Younger, who in turn drew on a number of different sources for his inspiration. In addition to Hans Staden and several other unidentified sources, he was inspired by the work of Jacques le Moyne.

Jacques le Moyne de Morgues, a Frenchman who sailed with Laudonnière's expedition in 1564, was the first trained artist to cross the Atlantic specifically to paint scenes of America. Unfortunately, all but one of his original works depicting the New World have disappeared. Many surviving paintings of European plants and animals by le Moyne attest to his artistry. His plant studies are especially skillful, and they suggest that le Moyne was fully trained in the late Gothic and Early Renaissance traditions. The single surviving painting of the New World and the engravings of works now lost suggest he held the Indians in high esteem.

Le Moyne accompanied the French expeditions to Florida in 1564–1565. His Florida images are known primarily from engravings in *Brevis narratio* (1591), published by Theodore de Bry as part of a fourteen-volume compendium on America begun in 1590. The engraved inscriptions on the plates were probably not written by le Moyne, since de Bry acquired the le Moyne paintings after the artist's death in 1588. The inscriptions borrow whole passages from Laudonnière's account of the Florida Indians published in Paris in 1586 and in London in 1587. Le Moyne's narrative text, however, seems to be his own; and since he quotes Laudonnière's text, it must have been written by le Moyne during 1587 or early 1588, just prior to his death.

Le Moyne's only surviving painting of the Timucuan Indians is now in the New York Public Library. It depicts the 1564 encounter between Laudonnière and a Timucuan chief and was probably painted between 1565 and 1587. A later date is likely, given the style of armor pictured at the far right of the painting. The fact that le Moyne used armor of the latest style indicates he probably did the paintings in a studio using European props. In the offering scene, he inappropriately used European models for the native quiver and pack baskets instead of Timucuan Indian artifacts. The small-handled bowls in the scene, however, seem to be accurately rendered, resembling Timucuan examples known from archaeological collections.

Comparing the surviving painting with de Bry's 1591 engraving of the same subject indicates that the engraver followed le Moyne closely, making only such minor changes as the form of body tattooing. The legend on the engraving says that King Athore took Laudonnière to see his people worshiping a French monument (which had been set up two years earlier by Ribault to commemorate the French expedition on the St. Johns River in 1562). Athore, the inscription reports, was exceedingly tall and handsome, traits that are captured in both painting and engraving, albeit the skin color of the Indian in the painting is too light. The Frenchmen by contrast appear exceedingly small and dandified.

The majority of le Moyne's Timucuan images probably were done from memory rather than from life. Le Moyne's hasty departure from Florida in 1565, fleeing a Spanish assault on Fort Caroline, suggests his field sketches were left behind. He may have spent the return voyage reconstructing his record of Florida. It is generally assumed that he created the final paintings after he came to England and began working under the patronage of Sir Walter Raleigh.

There are inaccurate elements in the de Bry engravings of le Moyne's images that may be due to use of inappropriate props in the original paintings, faulty memory on le Moyne's part, or modifications introduced by de Bry. Most notable are the depictions of a nautilus shell not native to Florida, probably either *Nautilus pompilius*, found in the Central Pacific to Indian oceans, or *Nautilus scrobiculatus*, which ranges westward from the Solomon Islands. Other inaccurate details include European hoes in a Timucuan farming scene rather than the native fishbone hoes described in the caption. Nevertheless, according to Sturtevant in Paul Hulton's *Work of Jacques le Moyne de Morgues* (1977), de Bry's images show many ethnographic details that appear to be the result of le Moyne's direct observation, especially small bowls with handles, bird-leg ear ornaments, oval metal pendants, and long-stemmed tobacco pipes.

As Sturtevant notes, the earliest pictorial treatment of North American Indians is based on South American precedents—which he terms the "Tupinambization" of the North American Indian. It seems likely that de Bry used illustrations of the Tupinamba in Staden and Thevêt for some details in the Florida images, such as the mourning pose seen in Thevêt. The headdresses and clubs in de Bry's engraving of the scenes of Florida natives look suspiciously like those in Staden's account, which de Bry was preparing for publication at the time he published le Moyne's work. One of the plates is illustrated with images that recall the severed bodies in Staden's depictions of Tupinamba cannibalism.

Even though de Bry had purchased the le Moyne paintings by 1588, he used John White's images of Carolina-Virginia Algonquian Indians when he published his first volume of the series on America in 1590. De Bry was under pressure from Richard Hakluyt and Sir

Timucuan Indians of Florida mourning a dead chief, who has been buried in a mound. The shell on top of the mound is inaccurately portrayed as a nautilus shell that is not native to Florida. It is not clear whether these inaccuracies in the 1591 de Bry engraving were also in the original, now lost, by Jacques le Moyne.

Walter Raleigh to publicize the struggling English colony at Roanoke Island. White was hired by Raleigh to accompany an expedition that founded the first English colony in the New World. Using Roanoke as a base, White explored the area and sketched native life between 1584 and 1586.

White probably produced the final paintings upon his return to England in 1587. His paintings provide a highly accurate ethnographic record, considered to be the most interesting and important sixteenth-century illustrations of North American Indians. He presented an attractive picture of the natives of Virginia (which also incorporated North Carolina at that time).

In 1590, de Bry published 23 engravings of White's paintings along with Thomas Harriot's *Brief and true report of the new found land of Virginia,* which had been published two years earlier. In de Bry's edition, Hariot wrote captions for White's paintings after White had returned to the ill-fated colony of Roanoke. White's image of ancient Europeans (the Picts) published in this volume resemble his paintings of the Indians of Virginia and a tattooed Timucuan man and woman inspired by le Moyne. White visualized the New World natives as representatives of an early stage of development like the ancient inhabitants of Britain. His sympathetic treatment suggests he thought of the Amerindian as noble savage rather than rude barbarian. When de Bry engraved White's images of ancient Britons and Picts in his first volume, Hariot's caption stated that the inhabitants of ancient Britain had been in past times as savage as those of Virginia.

Comparison of White's paintings with the engravings in the first volume of de Bry's compendium, *America,* reveals that either de Bry embellished the works or White sold de Bry a modified set of paintings which is now lost. In a scene of the town of Secota, de Bry added a sunflower garden, a tobacco garden, a squash garden, fish prepared for a banquet, and a deer foraging among the trees. And in an image of a religious dance around a circle of columnar idols, de Bry omitted or changed some of the objects held by the dancers. What is especially notable is the transformation of the Indians into elegant classical figures. In general, White's original paintings seem less detailed than de Bry's engravings. Nevertheless, de Bry was more faithful to the original paintings by White and le Moyne than to the work of artists represented in later volumes of *America,* such as the woodcuts originally published by Staden and Benzoni. Neither Staden nor Benzoni was a trained artist, and the temptation to improve on their primitive ethnographic images may have been overwhelming.

De Bry's monumental series of 14 volumes, published between 1590 and 1634, includes more than 35 accounts by explorers and

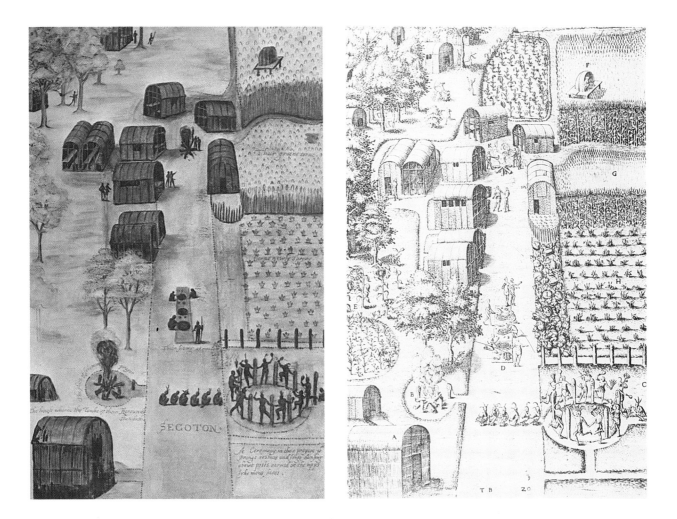

Left: John White's painting of a native village and gardens in Virginia (actually today in North Carolina). *Right*: De Bry's 1590 engraving based on White's painting of a native village and gardens introduces elements not in the original, including tobacco plants and a sunflower garden.

more than 250 illustrations based on woodcuts, drawings, and paintings by a variety of artists. De Bry sometimes even invented images to illustrate the texts. His work, with the numerous scenes of confrontation between Spaniards and natives, and his elegant, heroic Amerindian figures, helped to spread tales of Spanish atrocities known as the "Black Legend."

There was as much fantasy as fact in the sixteenth-century imagery of the New World. In his comprehensive exhibit catalogue *The European Vision of America* (1976), Hugh Honour points out that European visual images of the Americas were created largely by artists who never went there. The works of the sixteenth century often reflected European dreams of a terrestrial paradise, a golden age, or fantasies about Europe's own primitive past. This trend was counterbalanced by a few European artists, like Jean Cousin the Younger, who worked directly with the explorers upon their return from the Americas, and artists like Dürer and Weiditz, who created their images by drawing directly from native artifacts or captive natives brought to the Old World. By far the most reliable images were those produced by individuals who actually traveled to the New World.

Some were clearly unskilled, like Benzoni and Staden; others were trained artists, such as le Moyne and White. The accuracy of these ethnographic images was diminished in reworking by de Bry, and his classicizing image of the noble savage left the more lasting impression due to the wide circulation of de Bry's monumental series on America.

Allegories Depicting America

An enigmatic woodcut of a chained woman carrying an oxen's yoke may be the earliest allegorical image depicting a native American. The illustration is from a lace pattern book published in Paris in 1530 by the Florentine artist Francesco Pellegrino (François Pellegrin). He was one of the first artists of the French School of Fontainebleau (1528–1571), creators of the murals and tapestries in the palace at Fontainebleau that included native American themes.

The woodcut reflects influence from a drawing in the British Museum entitled "The Young Prisoner," attributed to the school of Andrea Mantegna. A closer link is seen with the allegory of servitude by Adamo "Ghisi" Scultori, but this work postdates Pellegrino's woodcut. All three works depict a female wearing a yoke and a ball and chain. The yoke is characteristic of early allegorical images depicting servitude, patience, or obedience, as seen in Cesare Ripa's *Iconologia* (1603), but the ball and chain are not represented in any of Ripa's allegories and the British Museum image clearly links it to imagery of a prisoner.

The engraving by Scultori identifies the person wearing a ball and chain as servant. The image has an inscription in Latin at the bottom saying, "The servant is happier in accordance with his patience." In the Pelligrino woodcut the female holds a banner proclaiming "exitus acta probat," which translates as "the final result sets the seal of approval on what has been done," an early version of our saying "the ends justify the means." This phrase remains enigmatic in the context of an image of imprisonment or servitude, especially since the banner makes it appear that the figure states the phrase. The concepts of a prisoner and a servant may be combined if the image represents a slave, and the inscribed banner might justify the practice of slavery.

None of the parallel or prototype images shows vegetation, but the Pelligrino scene depicts unusual vegetation, reminiscent of New World plants, in the foreground. Another element without parallel in the related images is the woman's nimbus and her nude body, revealed under a transparent sleeveless tunic. The nudity suggests links with New World imagery, and although there are a few nude figures among Ripa's allegories, none is shown wearing a yoke. The only allegorical figures with a nimbus in Ripa are entitled "Gratia di Dio" (the Grace of God) and "Punitione" (Punitive Justice). The nimbus in Pelligrino's 1530 image may indicate that the servant girl is deified.

The nudity, sleeveless tunic, and vegetation all suggest a New World setting for the slave girl. The image might signal the beginning of the sympathetic view of native Americans that characterized France in the latter part of the sixteenth century, reflected in the paintings of Jacques le Moyne and the writings of Ribault, le Challeux, de Léry, and Montaigne.

The second half of the sixteenth century revealed an increasing tendency to romanticize the Amerindians, seen especially in the works by de Bry and the genre of allegorical images of the Americas. From 1570 through the early nineteenth century, personified images of the four continents appeared in a wide variety of media, including theatrical pageants, relief sculptures, fresco decoration, engravings, and small-scale decorative arts. These allegorical representations synthesized imagery of the New World developed earlier in the century.

The four continents were first personified as four empresses in a transient *tableau vivant* at a festival in Antwerp in 1564. The earliest known set of allegorical prints depicting the four continents, dating to 1575, shows America (the New World) as a nude woman with bow and arrow, accompanied by an animal that may be a llama. This print

Francisco Pellegrino's 1530 allegorical engraving may represent an enslaved native American woman. It was originally published as the frontispiece in a book of lace patterns.

Detail of a ceiling fresco by Ludovico Buti (1588) in the Uffizi Palace Armory depicting an allegorical image of America with a native ruler carried on a litter.

by Etienne Delaune, now in the collection of the New York Historical Society, may have derived from a project for mural decoration at the French palace Fontainebleu.

America was usually represented as a bare-breasted woman with a feathered headdress, accompanied by symbols of wealth and New World animals such as llamas, parrots, armadillos, or alligators. The other three continents (all Old World) were represented fully clothed with emblematic animals: the horse for Europe, the lion for Africa, the camel for Asia. The four continents joined a roster of already familiar quadripartite subjects, such as the four seasons and the four elements.

Mural images of the continents also appeared in the frescos of the Uffizi Palace armory painted by Ludovico Buti in 1588. The armory ceiling depicts an allegorical image of America with a native ruler carried on a litter by Indians wearing feathered headdresses. By the seventeenth century, images of Indians with feather skirts and headdresses were ubiquitous in the great Baroque palaces.

A late sixteenth-century German lead plaque, in the collection of the Metropolitan Museum of Art, shows America represented as

Visscher's seventeenth-century allegorical engraving depicts America as a female riding an oversized armadillo. In the background the Europeans wage war against the aborigines, while cannibals roast human flesh.

a bare-breasted female with bow and arrow, surrounded by monkeys, a parrot, pearls, vessels of precious metal, and a sack of gold nuggets. Instead of the New World armadillo, here the artist confuses the continents and substitutes another armor-skinned animal, the rhinoceros. A monstrous creature on the left may be intended to represent an opossum.

Martin de Vos created a bare-breasted America riding an oversized armadillo for decorations of the Triumphal Arch erected in Geneva in 1594. An engraving of this image was widely circulated, inspiring a number of subsequent images, including Visscher's seventeenth-century engraving of America seated on a giant armadillo viewing a battle between Europeans and Indians. The figure of America is heroic, conveying a certain grace, but the background portrays a scene of the natives cutting up and roasting human flesh. The engraved inscription synthesizes negative European attitudes about the Amerindians: "America is by far the strangest continent; Here people live like lawless savages. . . . The inhabitants of this land take each others' lives. . . . Like mindless and innocent animals, they destroy each other, then roast the flesh as their usual fare."

Cannibalism in the New World loomed large in the European imagination, especially after publication of Hans Staden's book on the Tupinamba in the second half of the sixteenth century. A number of allegorical images evoked this violent aspect of the Amerindian, first depicted in a 1505 woodcut illustrating a text derived from Vespucci's account. An allegorical scene of Vespucci discovering the New World, illustrated by Stradanus in 1589, and now in the collection of the Metropolitan Museum of Art, depicts America as a nude female in a hammock surrounded by New World animals, with cannibals roasting human flesh in the background. An image by Philippe Galle, engraved between 1579 and 1600 (in the New York Historical Society collection), shows America as a nude female carrying a trophy head, stepping nimbly over severed body parts. Even though allegorical images were by nature romanticized, the vision of the noble savage was often countered by references to cannibalism in personifications of America.

Hugh Honour illustrates a 1595 ink drawing by Paola Farinati depicting a male Amerindian turning away from human flesh roasting

A late sixteenth-century German lead plaque represents an allegorical image of America, shown as a bare-breasted female with bow and arrow and surrounded by gold, pearls, and New World animals (except for the obviously misplaced rhinoceros).

on a spit, pivoting toward a figure of Christ on a cross. The drawing was a study for the fresco lunettes of the four continents painted by Farinati at the Villa Stegano at Mezane, near Verona. The fresco adds a crowd of cannibals surrounding the spit as the Christianized Indian turns away, conveying the message that Christianity is the salvation of a savage race.

In the seventeenth century, the allusion to cannibalism became a standard reference, and the alligator began to replace the armadillo as the archetypal American animal. In 1603, when Cesare Ripa published *Iconologia*, used as a source for imagery by many artists, he depicted America as a bare-breasted female, bow and arrow in hand, trampling a severed human head. Her companion was an alligator, which embodied what America was in the European view—both strange and savage. It remained the most popular archetypal animal in allegorical images of America through the eighteenth century.

Personifications of America sometimes consciously blended aspects of Old and New World imagery in order to elaborate a theme. A sixteenth-century Spanish gold and enamel pendant, now in the collection of the British Museum, depicts America in her classic garb, bare-breasted with a feathered headdress, but she rides a hippocampus, a mythical horse-fish combination, evoking an image of Neptune. Here an Old World sea creature become a symbol of the Atlantic crossing to the New World.

Precious Metals and the American Connection

Sixteenth-century European jewelry may be one realm where the New World had a profound influence on the visual arts of the Old World. A quote from Dürer's diary of 27 August 1520 describes his reaction to the objects of gold and silver brought from the Aztec capital to Europe: "All the days of my life I have seen nothing that has gladdened my heart so much as these things, for I saw amongst them wonderful works of art, and I marveled at the subtle genius of men in foreign lands." Artists working in metal were similarly inspired. Jeweled animal pendants replaced the geometric forms popular in the fifteenth century as a flood of Precolumbian animal images in imported goldwork inspired Spanish jewelers of the sixteenth century.

The influx of gold, silver, and pearls led to a greater excess in display in European mannerist jewelry, although Spain maintained a more austere style, emphasizing naturalistic animal forms often inspired by Precolumbian jewelry. In addition to the New World images and materials in European jewelry, Amerindian metalworkers began making Christian religious jewelry for the Spanish market. Thus artists and art works from the New World did have an immediate impact on the Old World in the sphere of metalwork. New World influence on other European visual arts in the sixteenth century, however, seems restricted to images specifically representing the Americans, and even here the imagery was fit into a romanticized European mold. Nevertheless, the enormous influx of wealth from the New World eventually inspired seventeenth-century artists working in the Baroque style to ornament their work with gold and silver. Thus, the New World affected European visual arts slowly and subtly, hidden in the media rather than the iconography.

European Images of Amerindians

We have a relatively small corpus of visual images depicting the Caribbean and the Americas in the sixteenth century. The earliest are by artists who had never traveled to the New World. In their effort to illustrate written accounts, sometimes they drew on established imagery of primitive peoples living outside the bounds of civilization, such as the wild man, who had somehow reverted to a primitive state. Nudity, described in the earliest accounts, suggested the Amerindians were related to the wild man of medieval lore, but the New World natives usually were depicted without body hair, in contrast to representations of European people living in a wild state. A more direct influence on the earliest imagery of the New World seems to be medieval representations of remote epochs in human history. Artists incorporated subtle references to the Garden of Eden or classical antiquity. References to the golden age before the development of civilization are sometimes indistinguishable from images of mankind before the fall from grace, when people still lived as one with nature. Nudity was fascinating to artists and the public, but it was appropriate only in representations of epochs in the distant past, before the trappings of civilization. The discovery of the New World provided another avenue for artists to explore this popular theme.

Cannibalism aroused public interest long before the discovery of the New World. Tales and illustrations of man-eating races appear in John Mandeville's best selling travelogue describing remote areas of Asia. When Vespucci's accounts seemed to confirm the existence of these monstrous beings, artists were quick to exploit the theme in visual imagery. Scenes depicting cannibalism in the first half of the sixteenth century all seem linked to his accounts.

When explorers to the New World, such as Staden and Oviedo, tried their hand at depicting the Amerindian, the results were often crude. Nevertheless, these images are a good source of ethnographic information, and they have direct quality lacking in the classicizing images of the Amerindian done by trained artists.

The tendency of sixteenth-century artists depicting the New World to follow the norms of the time, favoring classical or heroic poses, influences our impression of the images as somehow related to the concept of the noble savage. Since it was the established style of representation in that epoch, the sixteenth-century observer may not have been similarly swayed. Nevertheless, images that did not fall into this classicizing style, such as Staden's crude depictions of nude cannibals, probably had an especially startling impact. Shortly after publication of his account of the Tupinamba of Brazil in 1557, a number of allegorical images of the Americas depicted cannibalism, and this theme remained a standard reference in the seventeenth-century allegories of America.

Many sixteenth-century works depicting native Americans reflect European fantasies of a lost or primitive world. Relatively few images can be said to be accurate portrayals done by trained artists working in the New World. The paintings by John White and Jacques le Moyne are exceptions rather than the norm. These works reached the public in a somewhat modified form in the engravings by Theodore de Bry. Because de Bry's works received wide circulation, it is his vision of the New World that best represents the public perception of the Americas at the close of the sixteenth century. His earliest engravings, based on illustrations by White, le Moyne, and Staden, seem to be more accurate than subsequent representations published in the series. When de Bry illustrated Benzoni's account in 1594–1596, many of the engravings were invented images based on written descriptions, once again coming around full circle to what had been the trend at the beginning of the century, when the first images of the Americas captured the European imagination.

Selected References

Alexander, Michael, ed.

    1976   *Discovering the New World, Based on the Works of Theodore de Bry.* New York: Harper and Row, Publishers.

Badger, R. Reid, and Lawrence A. Clayton, eds.

    1985   *Alabama and the Borderlands from Prehistory to Statehood.* Tuscaloosa: University of Alabama Press.

Bennett, Charles E., trans.

    1975   *Three Voyages: René Laudonnière.* Gainesville: University Presses of Florida

Blakley, Robert L., ed.

    1988   *The King Site: Continuity and Contact in Sixteenth-Century Georgia.* Athens: University of Georgia Press.

Bourne, Edward G., ed.

    1922   *Narratives of the Career of Hernando de Soto.* 2 vols. New York: Allerton Book Co.

Casas, Bartolomé de las

    1974   *The Devastation of the Indies, a Brief Account.* Translated by Hera Briffault. New York: Seabury Books.

Covey, Cyclone, trans. and ed.

    1986   *Cabeza de Vaca's Adventures in the Unknown Interior of America.* Albuquerque: University of New Mexico Press.

Crosby, Alfred W.

    1973   *The Columbian Exchange: Biological and Cultural Consequences of 1492.* Westport, CT: Greenwood Press.

Cumming, W. P.; R. A. Skelton; and D. B. Quinn

    1972   *The Discovery of North America.* New York: American Heritage Press.

Davis, T. Frederick

    1935   History of Juan Ponce de León's Voyages to Florida. *Florida Historical Quarterly* 14:1–70

Deagan, Kathleen A.

    1983   *Spanish St. Augustine: The Archaeology of a Colonial Creole Community.* New York: Academic Press.

1987 *Artifacts of the Spanish Colonies of Florida and the Caribbean, 1500–1800.* Vol. 1: *Ceramics, Glassware, and Beads.* Washington: Smithsonian Institution Press.

DePratter, Chester B.; Charles Hudson; and Marvin T. Smith
1983 The Route of Juan Pardo's Explorations in the Interior Southeast. *Florida Historical Quarterly* 62:125–158.

Dunn, Oliver, and James E. Kelley, Jr., trans.
1988 *The Diario of Christopher Columbus's First Voyage to America, 1492–1493.* Norman: University of Oklahoma Press.

Elliot, J.H.
1966 *Imperial Spain, 1469–1716.* New York: Mentor Books.

Fuson, Robert H., trans.
1987 *The Log of Christopher Columbus.* Camden, ME: International Marine Publishing Company.

Gibson, Charles
1966 *Spain in America.* New York: Harper Colophon Books.

Hann, John H.
1987 *Apalachee: The Land between the Rivers.* Gainesville: University of Florida Press/Florida Museum of Natural History.

Haring, C.H.
1963 *The Spanish Empire in America.* New York: Harcourt Brace Jovanovich, Inc.

Henige, David
1986 The Context, Content, and Credibility of La Florida del Ynca. *The Americas* 43:1–23.

Hodge, Frederick W., and Theodore H. Lewis
1984 *Spanish Explorers in the Southern United States, 1528–1543.* Austin: Texas State Historical Association.

Hudson, Charles
1976 *The Southeastern Indians.* Knoxville: University of Tennessee Press.
1988 A Spanish-Coosa Alliance in Sixteenth-Century Georgia. *Georgia Historical Quarterly* 72:599–626.
n.d. *The Juan Pardo Expedition: Spanish Explorers and the Indians of the Carolinas and Tennessee, 1566–1568.* Washington: Smithsonian Institution Press. Forthcoming.

Hudson, Charles; Marvin Smith; David Hally; Richard Polhemus; and Chester DePratter
1985 Coosa: A Chiefdom in the Sixteenth-Century Southeastern United States. *American Antiquity* 50:723–737.

Hulton, Paul H.
1977 *The Work of Jacques le Moyne de Morgues: A French Huguenot Artist in France, Florida, and England.* 2 vols. London: British Museum Publications.

Lorant, Stefan
1946 *The New World: The First Pictures of America.* New York: Duell, Sloan & Pearce.

Lyon, Eugene
1976 *The Enterprise of Florida: Pedro Menéndez de Avilés and the Spanish Conquest of 1565–1568.* Gainesville: University of Florida Press.

Milanich, Jerald T., and Samuel Proctor, eds.
1978 *Tacachale: Essays on the Indians of Florida and Southeastern Georgia during the Historic Period.* Gainesville: Unversity of Florida Press/Florida Museum of Natural History.

Morison, Samuel Eliot

    1974   *The European Discovery of America: The Southern Voyages, A.D. 1492–1616.* New York: Oxford University Press.

    1983   *Admiral of the Ocean Sea: A Life of Christopher Columbus.* Boston: Northeastern University Press.

Priestley, Herbert Ingram, trans. and ed.

    1981   *Tristán de Luna, Conquistador of the Old South: A Study of Spanish Imperial Strategy.* Philadelphia: Porcupine Press.

Quinn, David B., ed.

    1971   *North American Discovery, ca. 1000–1612.* Columbia: University of South Carolina Press.

    1977   *North America from Earliest Discovery to First Settlements: The Norse Voyages to 1612.* New York: Harper and Row.

    1979   *New American World: A Documentary History of North America to 1612.* 5 vols. New York: Arno Press.

Sauer, Carl O.

    1966   *The Early Spanish Main.* Berkeley: University of California Press.

    1971   *Sixteenth-Century North America: The Land and the Peoples as Seen by the Europeans.* Berkeley: University of California Press.

Smith, Marvin T.

    1987   *Archaeology of Aboriginal Culture Change in the Interior Southeast: Depopulation during the Early Historic Period.* Gainesville: University of Florida Press/Florida Museum of Natural History.

Smith, Marvin T., and Mary Elizabeth Good

    1982   *Early Sixteenth-Century Glass Beads in the Spanish Colonial Trade.* Greenwood, MS: Cottonlandia Museum Publications.

Solís de Merás, Gonzalo

    1964   *Pedro Menéndez de Avilés, Adelantado, Governor and Captain-General of Florida.* Gainesville: University of Florida Press.

South, Stanley; Russell K. Skowronek; and Richard E. Johnson

    1988   *Spanish Artifacts from Santa Elena.* Anthropological Studies 7. Columbia: South Carolina Institute of Archaeology and Anthropology, University of South Carolina.

Swanton, John R., ed.

    1985   *Final Report of the United States de Soto Expedition Commission.* Washington: Smithsonian Institution Press.

Varner, John G., and Jeannette J. Varner

    1983   *Dogs of the Conquest.* Norman: University of Oklahoma Press.

Vega, Garcilaso de la

    1951   *The Florida of the Inca.* Translated and edited by John G. Varner and Jeannette J. Varner. Austin: University of Texas Press.

Weddle, Robert S.

    1985   *Spanish Sea: The Gulf of Mexico in North American Discovery, 1500–1685.* College Station: Texas A&M University Press.

Weber, David J., ed.

    1979   *New Spains's Far Northern Frontier: Essays on Spain in the American West, 1540–1821.* Albuquerque: University of New Mexico Press.

Index

Illustration Credits (by page number)

2, courtesy Trustees of the British Museum; 4, J.T. Milanich, Florida Museum of Natural History (FMNH); 5, Royal Chapel, Grenada, by Felipe Vignarny (1522); 6, from Hartmann Schedel, *Liben chroniarium ad inicia mundi*, 1493; 8, engraving by de Bry in Girolamo Benzoni, *Americae pars quarta . . . historia . . . Occidental India* (Part IV of *Historia Americae sive Novi Orbis*), 1594; 10, de Bry, *Americae* (IV), 1594; 11, Bibliòteca Estensa, Modena; 12, Martin Waldeseemüller, *Universalis Cosmographia*, 1507; 13, Antonio de Herrera [y Tordesillas], *Historia general de los hechos de los castellanos . . .*, 1730; 14, Alfredo Chiavero, *Lienzo de Tlaxcala*, 1892; 15, Archivo General de Indias, Sevilla; 16, courtesy John Carter Brown Library, Brown University; 17 left, Álvar Núñez Cabeza de Vaca, *Relación de los naufragios y commentarios*, 1542 (New York Public Library); 17 right, woodcut by Huaman Pomo de Ayala; 19, *Hamburgische Festschrift fur Erinnerung an die Entdeckung Amerika's*, 1892; 21, drawn by Heidi Perry; 22, Sebastian Münster, *Cosmographia*, 1544; 24, engraving by de Bry in Jacques le

Moyne de Morgues, *Brevis narratio eorum quae in Florida Americae* (Part II of *Historia Americae sive Novi Orbis*), 1591; 25, Kathleen Deagan, FMNH; 26, P.K. Yonge Library of Florida History, University of Florida (UF); 28, Juan de Escalante de Mendoza, *Itinerario de navegacion de los mares y tierras occidentales*, 1575 (reprinted, Instituto de Historia y Cultura Naval, Madrid, 1983); 29, drawn by Heidi Perry; 30, portrait by Ridolfo Bigordi, courtesy Museo Civico Navale, Pegli; 31, Alonzo de Chaves, *Quatri partitu en cosmografia practica, y por otro nombre llamado espejo de navegantes*, ca. 1530 (reprinted, Paulino Castañeda, Mariano Cuesta, and Pilar Hernández, eds. Instituto de Historia y Cultura Naval, Madrid, 1983); 32, Pierre d' Ailly, *Imago Mundi*, 1480 (Biblioteca Colombina, Seville); 34, engraving by de Bry in Girolamo Benzoni, *Americae pars quarta . . . historia . . . Occidental India* (Part IV of *Historia Americae sive Novi Orbis*), 1594; 35, Palazzo Municipale, Genoa; 36, engraving by Wolf Kilian, 1621, in Honorius Philoponus, *Nova typis transacta navigatio*, 1621; 38, painting by Alejo Fernandez, courtesy Reales

Alcazares, Seville; 39 left, wood engraving by Tobias Stimmer, in Paulus Jovius, *Elogia virorum bellica virtute illustrium*, 1575 (Basel); 39 center, engraving by de Bry in Girolamo Benzoni, *Americae pars quarta . . . historia . . . Occidental India* (Part V of *Historia Americae sive Novi Orbis*), 1595; 39 right, engraving by Aliprando Capriolo, *Cento Capitani Illustri*, 1596 (British Museum); 42, painting by Michael Falck, FMNH; 43, Duke of Alba Collection, Palacio de Lira; 44, Columbus's letter, Basel edition of 1493, Rare Books and Manuscripts Division, New York Public Library, Astor, Lenox and Tilden Foundations; 45, drawn by Heidi Perry; 47, 48, Kathleen Deagan, FMNH; 50, 52, James Quine, St. Augustine; 56, de Bry in Benzoni, *Americae* (IV), 1594; 60–61, 63, Stan Blomeley FMNH; 67, drawn by Heidi Perry based on a map provided by the authors; 68, Morales map (Bologna copy,1516), Biblioteca Universitaria, Bologna; 71, Stan Blomeley, FMNH; 72, University of Florida Information Services; 73, Raymond Willis, U.S. Forestry Service; 75, James Quine, St. Augustine; 76, from Maurice Williams, "Sub-surface Patterning at Puerto Real: A 16th-Century Town on Haiti's North Coast," *Journal of Field Archaeology* 13 (1986); 78 top, *Retratos de los Españoles Ilustres con un epitome de sus vidas*, 1791 (Library of Congress copy); 78 bottom, *The Saturday Evening Post*, July 9, 1949; 79, Marvin T. Smith, University of Georgia; 80, J.T. Milanich, FMNH; 81, drawn by Heidi Perry, based on John R. Swanton, *Final Report of the de Soto Expedition Commission*, 1939, and information provided by the authors; 83, drawn by Heidi Perry from Chester D. DePratter, Charles M. Hudson, and Marvin T. Smith, "The Route of Juan Pardo's Explorations in the Interior Southeast, 1566–1568," *Florida Historical Quarterly* (October 1983); 84, Chaves, *Espejo de navegantes*, ca. 1530; 85 (top), J.T. Milanich, FMNH; 85 (bottom), *Ballou's Pictorial Drawing-Room Companion*, 1855; 87, The Hernando de Soto Expedition Encounters Chief Tascaluza . . . in *De Gedenkwaardie Voyagie van don Ferdinand de Soto . . .* , 1706, courtesy of the W. S. Hoole Special Collections Library, University of Alabama; 88, Johnson Fry and Co., New York, 1888 (from an original picture by Powell); 92, 93, Robert L. Blakely, Georgia State University; 94, Archivo General de Indias; 95, Jeronimo de Chaves (undated, but known to have been made by 1582 when it was published by Abraham Ortelius in his *Theatrum Orbis Terrarum*); 96, 97, Marvin T. Smith, University of Georgia; 100, drawn by Heidi Perry; 102, David H. Dye, Memphis State University (MSU); 104, Robert Allen; 105, 106, Jeffrey M. Mitchem, FMNH; 107, top, David H. Dye, MSU; 107, middle, Jeffrey M. Mitchem, FMNH; 107, bottom, Bunny Stafford, UF; 108, Stan Blomeley, FMNH; 109, Dale Hutchinson, University of Illinois; 111, drawn by Heidi Perry; 112, K.C. Smith, Florida Bureau of Archaeological Research; 113–17, Roy Lett, Florida Bureau of Archaeological Research; 121, drawn by Heidi Perry; 122–23, courtesy Trustees of the British Museum; 125, *Das Trachtenbuch des Christoph Weiditz (von seinen resisen nach Spanien, 1529, und den Niederlanden, 1531–32)*; 127, drawn by Heidi Perry; 130, 131,

courtesy Read Stowe, Archaeology Laboratory, University of South Alabama, photograph by David H. Dye, MSU; 132, engraving by de Bry in Benzoni, *Americae*, V, 1595; 133, courtesy James B. Langford and the Coosawhattee Foundation, drawing by Julie Barnes Smith and Jodie Lewis; 136, Chief Coosa Welcomes the de Soto Expedition . . . in *De Gedenkwaardie Voyagie van don Ferdinand de Soto . . .* , 1706, courtesy of the W. S. Hoole Special Collections Library, University of Alabama; 137, drawn by Heidi Perry based on Charles Hudson, Marvin Smith, David Hally, Richard Polhemus, and Chester DePratter, "Coosa: A Chiefdom in the Sixteenth-Century Southeastern United States," *American Antiquity* 50 (1985); 138, Michael McKelvey, courtesy Laboratory of Anthropology, University of Georgia, map drawn by Julie Barnes Smith, courtesy David J. Hally, Marvin T. Smith, and James B. Langford, Jr.; 140, de Bry in le Moyne, *Brevis narratio*, 1591; 141, Marvin T. Smith, University of Georgia; 143, J.T. Milanich, FMNH; 145, de Bry in le Moyne, *Brevis narratio*, 1591; 146, courtesy Temple Mound Museum, Fort Walton Beach; 147, 148, courtesy Mound State Monument, Alabama; 149, courtesy Etowah Museum, Etowah Mounds Archaeological Area, Georgia; 151, courtesy the Conde de Revilla Gigedo (Avilés, Spain) and the University of Florida Press; 152, 153 top, de Bry in le Moyne, *Brevis narratio*, 1591; 153 bottom, engraving commissioned by Bishop Augustin Verot (1875), courtesy University of Florida Press; 154, drawn by Heidi Perry; 155, 156, Smithsonian Institution; 158, de Bry in le Moyne, *Brevis narratio*, 1591; 161, Stan Blomeley, FMNH; 162, Roy Craven, UF; 163, David H. Dye, MSU, courtesy South Florida Museum and Bishop Planatarium; 167, Boazio map, courtesy John Carter Brown Library, Brown University; 169, Edward Chaney, FMNH; 171, James Quine, St. Augustine; 172, Archivo General de Indias, Sevilla; 173, Michael V. Gannon, *The Cross in the Sand*, 1965, courtesy University of Florida Press; 174 left, P.K. Yonge Library of Florida

History, UF; 174 right, J.T. Milanich, FMNH; 175, Rebecca Saunders, FMNH; 176, J.T. Milanich, FMNH; 178, 180, Kathleen Deagan, FMNH; 182, James Quine, St. Augustine; 184, Marco Polo, *Travels* (Bibliothèque Nationale, Paris); 185, Staatliche Kunstsammlungen Grunes Gewölde (Dresden) in Helmut Nickel, "The Graphic Sources for the Moor with the Emerald Cluster," *Metropolitan Museum Journal* 15 (1981); 186, Rare Books and Manuscripts Division, New York Public Library, Astor, Lennox and Tilden Foundations; 187, British Library, London; 189, Bayerische Staatbibliothek, Munich; 190, British Library, London; 191, Library of Congress, Rare Book Division, Washington, D.C.; 192, *De nouo mundo*, 1505 (Rostock edition); 193, *The Conquest of Peru [as Recorded by a Member of the Pizarro Expedition]* (*KB 1534), Rare Books and Manuscript Division, New York Public Library, Astor, Lenox and Tilden Foundations; 195, Hans Staden, *The True History of his Captivity . . .* , 1557; 197 left, de Bry engraving in Girolamo Benzoni, *Americae pars quarta . . . historia . . . Occidental India* (Part VI of *Historia Americae sive Novi Orbis*), 1596; 197 right, Jean de Léry, *Histoire d'un Voyage Fait en la Terre du Bresil*, 1578; 198, Print Collection (Bequest of James Hazen Hyde), Miriam and Ira D. Wallach Division of Arts, Prints and Photographs, New York Public Library, Astor, Lenox and Tilden Foundations; 200, de Bry, *Brevis narratio*, 1591; 202 left, courtesy Trustees of the British Museum; 202 right, de Bry engraving in Thomas Harriot, *A brief and true report of the new found land of Virginia* (Part I of *Historia Americae sive Novi Orbis*), 1590 (Frankfurt reprint of 1588 edition); 204, *La Fleur de la Scienc3e de Pourtraicture*, 1530 (Paris); 205, from William C. Sturtevant, "First Visual Images of Native America," in *First Images of America: The Impact of the New World on the Old*, vol. 1, edited by F. Chiapelli, 1976; 206, Metropolitan Museum of Art, all rights reserved; 207, James Hazen Hyde Collection, New York Historical Society.